WOMEN ENTREPRENEURS, THEIR VENTURES, AND THE VENTURE CAPITAL INDUSTRY
AN ANNOTATED BIBLIOGRAPHY

Annotated and edited by:
Elizabeth J. Gatewood
Nancy M. Carter
Candida G. Brush
Patricia G. Greene
Myra M. Hart

The knowledge dissemination of the Diana Project and the publication of the annotated bibliography is made in collaboration with ESBRI – Entrepreneurship and Small Business Research Institute – with the support from:

Report 2003:1, ESBRI, Stockholm, 2003

ESBRI – Entrepreneurship and Small Business Research Institute – is an independent research institute located in Stockholm, Sweden.

ESBRI's overall purpose is to increase the knowledge about entrepreneurship and small business.

ESBRI's objectives are to:
- conduct research on entrepreneurship and small and medium sized enterprises,
- initiate and develop high quality undergraduate and graduate education/training and
- actively participate in the public debate and the dissemination of research results to both the research community and a wider audience.

ESBRI was founded by Mr. Leif Lundblad, a successful Swedish inventor and entrepreneur. In addition Föreningssparbanken (Swedbank), Industrifonden (Swedish Industrial Development Fund), Företagareförbundet Företagarforum (The Swedish Association of Free Entrepreneurs) and Öhrlings PricewaterhouseCoopers support ESBRI with general financial support.

The cover has been designed by
Johan Brunzell, Sandler Mergel AB.

Report 2003:1
ISSN: 1403-0195
ISBN: 91-973286-3-4

Stockholm, 2003.
3.000 copies (first printing)
Prinfo Avesta Offset

For more information or to order copies:
E-mail: info@esbri.se
www.esbri.se

Acknowledgements

The creation of this annotated bibliography has been possible through the funding from several sources.

Major support for the Diana Project has been provided by the Ewing Marion Kauffman Foundation.

Support for the production and printing of this report has been provided by: the Confederation of Swedish Enterprise (Svenskt Näringsliv), the Swedish Agency for Innovation Systems (VINNOVA), the Swedish Business Development Agency (NUTEK) and the Swedish Institute for Growth Policy Studies (ITPS).

The authors are most grateful to Atieno Adala and Siti Syahwali for their committed and diligent assistance with preparation of this annotated bibliography.

Table of Contents

PART 1

OVERVIEW AND ANALYSIS

This annotated bibliography seeks to summarize an extensive review of women's entrepreneurship, growth, and financing from top entrepreneurship journals, thereby providing an overview of the context within which women seek venture capital. Earlier reviews focused on articulating the venture capital investment process and the relationships between the three key agents: investors, venture capital firms, and entrepreneurial ventures.[1] However, none of these reviews included the roles of women, either as participants in the VC industry or as entrepreneurial founder/leaders. Similarly, earlier reviews of women's entrepreneurship were limited to a particular theme or are now outdated.[2]

This literature review produced an annotated bibliography of nearly 300 articles. The model produced as a result of this review provides a more specific examination of key variables for equity providers and equity seekers: human, social, and financial capital; cognitions and goals; and strategic choice. In addition, it recognizes the facilitators and structural barriers associated with equity capital acquisition and entrepreneurship.

The bibliography was created with five objectives in mind:

- ♦ To develop a summary of the literature that would provide a base line understanding of the state of research about women's entrepreneurship, business growth, and access to financing;
- ♦ To identify gaps in current research that might be addressed in future studies;
- ♦ To catalyze new research on women's entrepreneurship, business growth, and financing, linking to previous research and suggesting the potential for cross-national collaboration;
- ♦ To refine a model on women's access to equity financing that can guide propositions and hypotheses; and
- ♦ To create a "living document" that can be updated and expanded as research progresses.

Rigorous research provides a powerful base for influencing systems. Information and knowledge derived from solid data can have irrefutable affects on changing attitudes, opinions, and practices. Our hope is that the bibliography will stimulate investigation and discovery to support and advance the growth and development of women-owned businesses.

THEMES, THEORIES AND A PRELIMINARY MODEL

The appearance of Netscape, Amazon.com, and Yahoo on computer and investor radar screens in the mid-1990s marked the beginning of the Internet boom. Thousands of web-based businesses were launched over the next five years, as the promise of enormous payoffs created a gold-rush mentality. These high-growth new ventures had voracious appetites for capital as they raced at "internet speed" to "get big fast." Investors and venture capitalists joined in the competition, pouring billions of dollars into e-commerce and web-related businesses between 1995 and 2000. The National Venture Capital Association reported that in 1995, the U.S. venture capital industry invested $5.7 billion in 1,265 enterprises. By 2000, the amount invested had climbed to more than $102.3 billion, invested in 5,608 deals.[3] This record-breaking $100 billion investment represented more than 187% increase in dollars and a 33% increase from 1999 in the number of firms funded. On average, venture-funded firms received approximately $18.2 million to fuel venture growth in 2000.

This explosive growth of equity investment was not limited to the United States. Zacharakis, Neck, Bygrave, and Cox (2001)[4] determined that in 2000, "the total amount of classic venture capital invested by domestic firms in 24 GEM countries where such data was available was $123.9 billion, or 0.50 percent of the total GDP of those countries. Of the $123.9 billion, $100.6 billion (81 percent) was invested in the United States and $23.3 billion (19 percent) was invested in the other 23 nations," largely because the average amount invested per firm is much higher in the U.S. than in other countries. Informal "angel" investors were estimated as responsible for $195.8 billion investment in growing businesses, 66% of which was invested in the U.S. During that same period, the British Venture Capital Association reported 1999 investments of £7.8 billion in 1,358 companies.[5] Likewise, in 1997 the venture capital funds raised in mainland Europe amounted to 1.5 times more than the amount raised in 1997.[6] In 1996, €9.6 billion was invested by equity providers. The investments skyrocketed to €25 billion in 1999 and nearly €35 billion in 2000.[7] Similarly, the number of venture capital firms rose from 300 in 1997 to 750 in 2000.[8]

Following the dramatic growth of the worldwide venture capital industry and investments, Spring, 2000 brought the crash of the dot com market in the U.S. This event significantly slowed both the raising and the investment of venture capital, but did not stop it. Venture capital investments in the U.S. for 2001 were reported as $42.9 billion, representing 4,932 investments at an average investment of $11.7 million per company.[9] Similar trends were evident for Europe, where investment declined to €24 billion in 2001.[10]

Although U.S. venture capital investments increased more than ten-fold during the five year period from 1995 to 2000, few women-led ventures participated in the boom. In fact, women entrepreneurs historically have received only a very small percentage of total funding. Greene, Brush, Hart, and Saparito (2001) tracked venture capital equity investments between 1953 and 1998 and found that by 1998 women-led ventures had received only about 4.1% of all venture capital investments (see Exhibit 1).

In 1999, this number reached 5%.[11] The comparatively small percentage of funding received by women-led firms compared to those led by men is significant, but the disparity between women-led businesses' share of equity funding and their contributions to the U.S. economy is even more striking.

EXHIBIT 1

Equity Investment Trends in Women Led Ventures 1970-1998

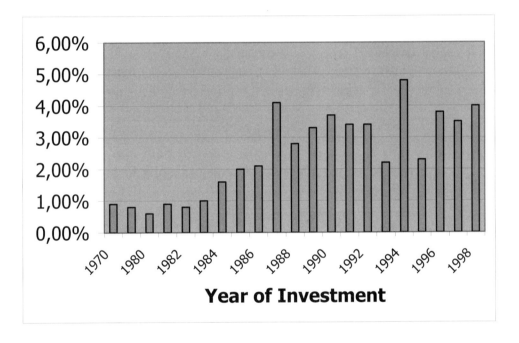

Source:Brush, C. G., Carter, N. M., Gatewood, E. J., Greene, P. G., & Hart, M. (2001). An investigation of women-led firms and venture capital investment: Report to the United States Small Business Administration, Office of Advocacy, and the National Women's Business Council, Washington, D.C., Table 3.

In 1999, women-owned businesses in the U.S. totaled 9.1 million (38% of all firms), employed 27.5 million workers, and generated nearly $3.6 trillion in sales.[12, 13] Women entrepreneurs did make substantial gains in access to business debt in the 1990s and established strong records of reinvestment of business earnings, but they did not share in the enormous growth in investment of equity capital. Their exclusion from the world of venture capital/private equity deals raises a critical question: "Why do women-led businesses in the U.S. receive a low share of venture capital and private equity investments?" Without the financial resources provided by equity investment, women's participation in business innovation, executive career development, and wealth creation may be seriously limited. If unable to access private equity capital, women may not be able to grow their businesses aggressively and participate fully in the new economy.

The apparent gender gap in venture capital investment was the catalyst for "The Diana Project."[14] This multi-year research program was designed to investigate growth models and the supply and demand for equity capital for women-led businesses. The research utilizes multiple methods and data sets, including in-person interviews, archival data, and surveys.

We began the project by developing a working theoretical model from previous literature reviews by Fried and Hisrich (1988), Timmons and Sapienza (1992), and Timmons and Bygrave (1997) that would help us understand the gap revealed when "mapping" the investments in women-led ventures between 1970 and 1998. Frameworks developed in these early reviews focused on articulating the venture capital investment process and establishing relationships between the three key agents: investors, venture capital firms, and entrepreneurial ventures.

EXHIBIT 2

Factors Affecting Women's Access to Equity Capital

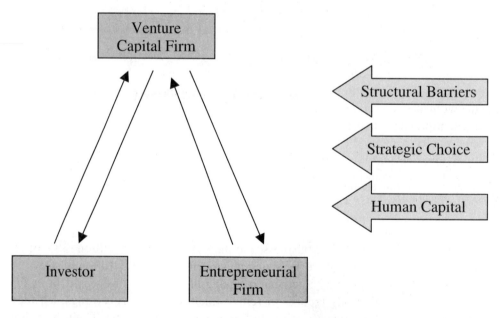

Source: Greene, P. G., Brush, C. G., Hart, M. M., & Saparito, P. (2001). Patterns of venture capital funding: Is gender a factor? *Venture Capital, 3* (1), 63-83.

The "investor" depicted in the model (see Exhibit 2) represents the original suppliers of capital (e.g., individuals, foundations, public and private pension funds, and corporations) who invest in venture capital funds in order to participate in the financial rewards associated with successful entrepreneurial ventures. The "venture capital firm" (VCs) represents the deal-makers who bring the capital suppliers and capital users together. (The venture capitalists are often investors as well.) The VC firms vary in size, industry, geographic preference, and preference for stage of investment, but all participate in some form of deal origination, screening, evaluation, negotiation and structuring processes, and post-investment activities. Their contributions to the entrepreneurial firms often include strategic and operational assistance as well as financial investment. The "entrepreneurial firm" seeks not only financial capital, but also value-added management expertise and network connections. When choosing venture capital investors, entrepreneurs evaluate the intangible contributions of their investors, as well as the financial terms of the deal.[15] When the process works well, entrepreneurial firms flourish, venture capitalists reap both financial and reputational rewards, and investors receive above-average rates of return.

Our initial model also incorporated the influence of three major theoretical factors that we proposed as explanations for the limited investment in women-led ventures: strategic choice, human and social capital, and structural barriers (Exhibit 2). To test the construct validity of the model, we undertook an extensive review of the extant literature on women's entrepreneurship and the equity investment process.

METHODOLOGY

The review was conducted in two phases: first, a representative review of articles about venture capital that provided an understanding of the context within which women seek growth financing, and second, a comprehensive review of articles about women's entrepreneurship. We sought articles on the venture capital investment process, investors, venture capital firms, and the entrepreneurial ventures seeking equity capital. We also sought articles about women entrepreneurs or their ventures, articles that compared women and men entrepreneurs and their ventures, and articles that included sex or gender as an analytical variable relevant to the research constructs.

All issues of "primary" entrepreneurship journals were searched from their founding date through 2001. Journals reviewed included: *Entrepreneurship Theory & Practice, Journal of Business Venturing, Journal of Small Business Management, Entrepreneurship and Regional Development, Journal of Developmental Entrepreneurship, International Small Business Journal, and Small Business Economics.* In addition, *Journal of Business Ethics* was searched because of past publications about women. The review also included the refereed proceedings from the annual Babson College/Kauffman Foundation Entrepreneurship Research Conference, *Frontiers of Entrepreneurship Research.* Finally, we employed a "snowballing" technique, reviewing bibliographies and frequent citations to identify other articles of interest not included in the above journals. The earliest publication date for articles of interest was 1975.

Our procedure for the review was careful and iterative. Each identified article was read first by a research assistant and briefly abstracted. Each article was then read by one of the five Diana researchers, who converted the abstract into a complete annotation. The researcher coordinating the Diana project then reviewed the annotations and made a final decision on their inclusion in the bibliography. Finally, the entire document was copy-edited for consistent presentation. For each article, the annotation describes the research question, proposed theory, setting, and results. We identified the nature of the study, data, and sample, and listed the research variables.[16]

SEARCH SUMMARY

The search yielded 298 articles for inclusion in the bibliography. Of these, 125 (42%) had venture capital as a primary focus and 173 (58%) addressed topics related to entrepreneurship/female entrepreneurship and gender differences. A chart showing the distribution of the articles by journal is shown in Exhibit 3. Although we found a substantial body of research on venture capital, including a literature review,[17] as noted earlier, our search of venture capital articles was representative, not comprehensive. Our purpose in reviewing the articles related to venture capital was to define the context within which women-led ventures seek equity investments.

EXHIBIT 3

Total Annotations by Journal

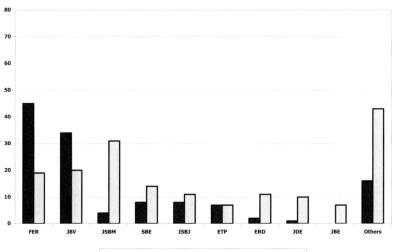

FER	Frontiers of Entrepreneurship Research
JBV	Journal of Business Venturing
JSBM	Journal of Small Business Management
SBE	Small Business Economics
ISBJ	International Small Business Journal
ETP	Entrepreneurship Theory & Practice
ERD	Entrepreneurship & Regional Development
JDE	Journal of Developmental Entrepreneurship
JBE	Journal of Business Ethics

The pattern illustrated in Exhibit 3 reflects clear differences across the publications. *Frontiers of Entrepreneurship Research* published more than twice as many articles related to venture capital as it did articles related to female entrepreneurship or gender differences. *Journal of Business Venturing* exhibited a similar pattern. Conversely, *Journal of Small Business Management, Entrepreneurship & Regional Development, and Journal of Developmental Entrepreneurship* published substantially more articles related to female entrepreneurship. To what extent these differences can be attributed to editorial preferences or the submission pattern is unclear. The search of *Journal of Business Ethics* yielded no articles on venture capital.

EXHIBIT 4

Article Publication Trends Across Time*

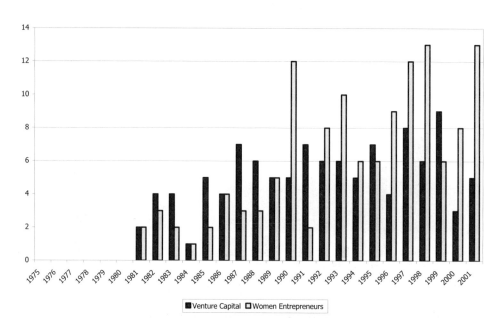

*Excludes journals identified through "snow-ball" technique.

Exhibit 4 displays a comparison of the venture capital and female entrepreneurship articles across time. Only articles published in the journals that were searched comprehensively are displayed. Those identified through the snowball technique are excluded. The number of articles on venture capital published during the 1980s substantially outpaced those reporting female entrepreneurship or gender differences. In the early 1990s, this trend was reversed, and by 2000, the number related to female entrepreneurship was two to three times as many as those reporting on venture capital. This pattern may correspond with the emergence of a new specialty journal *Venture Capital an International Journal* in the mid 1990s. Venture capital researchers may have seen the new journal as a more appropriate outlet for their manuscripts. This may explain why although the number of articles focusing on women entrepreneurship during this time period increased substantially, the number focusing on venture capital plateaued. We suspect that the parallel increase in venture capital articles was diffused when the new specialty journal was added to the list of publication possibilities. No journal dedicated to female entrepreneurship has emerged that would parallel the special interest venture capital journal.

Despite the substantial increase in the number of articles related to female entrepreneurship and to venture capital (especially considering the emergence of the new specialty journal) we did not find a single study on women-led ventures and venture capital or women in the venture capital industry, other than the one written by the *Diana* researchers.[18]

EXHIBIT 5

Methodologies Used to Study Female Entrepreneurship and Venture Capital*

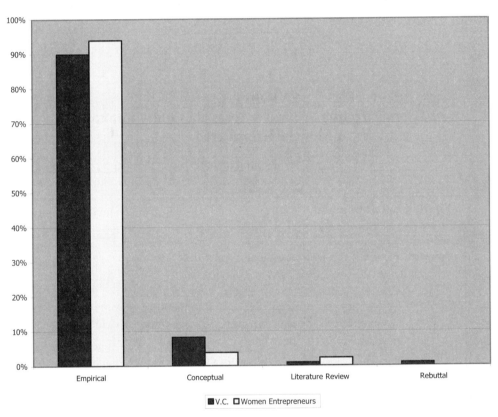

*Excludes journals identified through "snow-ball" technique.

Further examination of the annotations from the journals that were searched comprehensively reveals insights about methodologies used to study venture capital and female entrepreneurship. Exhibit 5 illustrates that 90 percent or more of the studies within each topic were empirical, although a greater percentage of the female entrepreneurship studies were empirical as compared to those in the venture capital category. Conversely, the number of venture capital articles that were conceptual in nature was more than twice the number focusing on women entrepreneurship. A very small percentage of articles in each category were dedicated to literature reviews.

REFINING THE MODEL

The comprehensive literature review led us to refine our theoretical model to better represent the venture capital industry, or the "supply" side of the equity investment equation, and to better articulate the factors that affect the experiences of women owners of growth firms on the demand side of the equation (see Exhibit 6). We identified five theoretical constructs that appear to influence the investment process: human capital, social capital, financial capital, personal cognitions and/or goals, and strategic choice. We believe these constructs have the potential for influencing actions of both the venture capitalist and the women entrepreneurs. In the following sections, we map the literature review to the refined model to illustrate the construct validity of the model.

EXHIBIT 6
Factors Affecting Women's Access to Equity Capital:
A Model Reconsidered

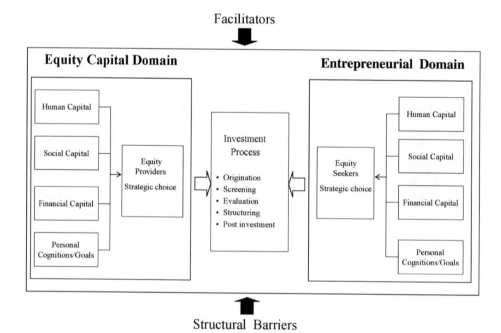

Equity Capital Domain

The equity capital domain depicted in Exhibit 6 encompasses the equity providers (individuals such as venture capitalists or angels) who invest in the entrepreneurial firms (capital users) and the foundations, institutions, public and private pension funds, as well as individuals, partnerships, or corporations who provide the financial capital to the equity providers.

Equity Providers- Research topics identified in the literature review describe the overall equity capital domain, which includes 1) history and trends (for example, size, stage, industry of investment) in venture capital investment;[19] 2) the various types of venture capital firms;[20] 3) the distribution of venture capital firms or investment by geographic region or country;[21] 4) the various sources of venture capital;[22] 5) the size of equity markets;[23] and 6) rates of return in the industry.[24] Finally, two articles looked at the future of the industry. Robinson (1987) predicted the future direction of the venture capital industry using key assumptions about venture capitalists, while Stevenson, Muzyka, and Timmons (1986) used a simulation model for the same purpose.

In addition to articles on formal venture capital, there were also articles focused on informal equity providers. Harrison and Mason (1990) reported that informal equity capital (angel investments) provided more funding annually than did the formal venture capital industry. Neiswander (1985) and Wetzel (1987) focused on the background, investment interests, and capabilities of this important source of capital.

As a result of the literature review, we refined the role of the intermediary in the investment process, in other words, the equity provider who is involved with the "deal," to include in our model the following three elements: human, social, and financial capital; the individual's cognitions and goals; and the strategic choices that result.

Human Capital: The human capital of venture capitalists--their knowledge and experience--is popularly recognized as one of the most important resources provided to portfolio companies. Busenitz and Fiet (1999) investigated the effect of venture capitalists' human capital (knowledge) on venture performance, while Shepherd, Zacharakis, and Baron (1998) studied job experience and its effect on the reliability, consensus, and predictive ability in the venture decision-making process.

Social Capital: Social capital of the venture capitalists has popularly been recognized as crucial to the success of deal origination, screening, evaluation, and post-investment activities, as well as, financial deal-sharing. Fiet (1996) reported that the frequency of consultation with types of network contacts (friends, business associates, and other venture capital firms) varied between venture capital firms and angel investors. Bygrave (1987, 1988) investigated the influence of the innovativeness, technology, stage of investment, and industries of the portfolio companies on the networking of investments by venture capital companies. A number of other researchers[25] examined the effects of risk and information asymmetry on the degree and use of informal or formal networks.

Financial Capital: Less research has explored the financial capital resources of equity providers (self-funded and raised from others). One notable study by Fried and Hisrich (1988) explored the venture capital process from the perspective of the institutional investors of venture capital firms. This research investigated the institutional investors' reasons for making investments, the criteria

15

for selecting among the various venture capital firms, and the pre- and post-investment process.

Cognitions and Goals: Research about venture capitalists' cognitions is of increasing interest. One of the earliest studies[26] used verbal protocols to investigate the sequence of thoughts in the decision process of a venture capitalist. Another study explored the consistency among venture capitalists in identifying the various stages in the development of new ventures. Hisrich and Janocowitz (1990) explored the unique intuitions that venture capitalist use in framing investment constructs. Some research[27] analyzed the actual decision-making of venture capitalists to determine the accuracy of their decisions with respect to their espoused decision policies or as predictors of outcome, while another research study[28] demonstrated that venture capitalists were biased by over-confidence. Shepherd (1999) also compared the consistency of venture capitalists' decision criteria to the criteria suggested by the strategy literature. We did not identify any studies of venture capitalists' personal goals.

Strategic Choice: Numerous articles focused on the strategic choices of venture capitalists and angels, particularly in the 1980s and early 1990s. These researchers examined stages of investment;[29] industry or geographic scope;[30] number and size of investments and fund size;[31] investment in smaller firms;[32] exit strategies;[33] required rates of return;[34] and syndication of investments.[35]

Entrepreneurial Domain

On the other side of the investment process equation, the demand side, we find the equity capital seekers (entrepreneurs and entrepreneurial firms). Although a substantial amount of research is applicable to this side of the model, we found only one article that dealt specifically with characteristics of women entrepreneurs or their firms and their access to equity capital. Consequently, we use the extant research to provide insights about these constructs that later can be used to formulate theoretical propositions about the phenomenon.

<u>Equity Seekers</u>: Manigart & Van Hyfte (1999) compared the survival rate, growth, profitability, and cash flow generation of VC-backed versus non-VC backed companies. A few articles[36] described the characteristics of venture-backed companies, for example, product/service or market (Dubini, 1989) or industry segment and life cycle stage of the industry. Only one article in the venture capital literature addressed the sex of the entrepreneur and its relationship to venture capital. Greene, Brush, Hart, and Saparito (2001) tracked venture capital investment in women-led firms as a percentage of total investments from 1953 to 1998.

In the entrepreneurship literature on women, many studies described the characteristics of women entrepreneurs, for example, their success rate and growth[37] or the race, age, marital status, hours worked, and education of self-employed women (Devine, 1994). Other studies compared men and women entrepreneurs or the self-employed on a number of characteristics, such as the problems they experience[38]; their survival and success rate;[39] their sales volume and business or personal

16

income;[40] location;[41] turnover rates and numbers of hours worked;[42] startup activities;[43] growth rates;[44] and company characteristics related to legal form;[45] age;[46] size.[47] Some studies have focused on the individual's education;[48] past and current employment status;[49] industry or professional experience;[50] marital or family status;[51] spouse's employment history;[52] personal wealth;[53] and race or ethnicity.[54] One literature review[55] summarized the differences between men and women entrepreneurs. This study concluded that women and men business owners are similar on basic demographic characteristics, problems, and business characteristics but differ on human capital, goals, and performance

Human Capital: Several articles focused on the relationship between various aspects of entrepreneurial human capital and venture financing: industry experience;[56] education;[57] functional experience;[58] and, for entrepreneurial teams, prior experience working together[59]. Other researchers[60] examined the experience level of management and directors of venture-capital-backed companies that had initial public offerings. However, the results of research on the importance of experience as critical for successful fund raising were mixed. Robbie and Wright's (1997) study of serial entrepreneurs indicated that prior experience did not predict performance on subsequent start-ups. Furthermore, they found that venture capitalists were more likely to use serial entrepreneurs as consultants, rather than as sources of management talent for subsequent ventures. Some research[61] examined the effect of the entrepreneur's experience on the choice to use venture financing. Other articles[62] examined the relationship between experience and firm or personal performance.

In the woman entrepreneurship literature, many articles focused specifically on human capital capabilities. Some researchers[63] examined the educational and operational experiences of women entrepreneurs. Others[64] provided comparative studies of the differences in experience for men and women entrepreneurs. Holmquist & Sundin (1990) compared choices and performances of well-educated women entrepreneurs to those of less-educated women.

Social Capital: Social capital of the entrepreneur is considered a variable of interest in both the venture capital and the woman entrepreneurship literatures. In the venture capital literature, Sargent and Young (1991) found that social and business relationships of the entrepreneur provided information and resources that shaped expectations for the new venture and venture financing. The impact of social capital was important not only at the earliest stages of the venturing but also as it carried through to exit strategy. Stuart, Hoang, and Hybels (1999) found that firms with prominent strategic alliance partners and equity investors went to IPO faster and achieved greater valuations than firms without this social capital.

In the woman entrepreneurship literature, research addressed the importance of social networks, questioning whether women participated fully in the appropriate networks.[65] Differences were found in the gender of network members for men and women entrepreneurs. Men did not have women in their networks, while women had primarily women in theirs.[66] Other research investigated differences in the way men

17

and women entrepreneurs used their networks: men relied heavily on men as their primary contacts, while women also primarily relied on men as their prime contacts.[67] Women were more likely to rely on their immediate network,[68] using other women as sources of information and for social and instrumental support.[69] Rozier (1998) found that men and women physical therapists who started businesses used women as their role models and men as mentors. Renzulli, Aldrich, and Moods (2000) showed that being female or having females in their networks did not affect startup outcomes for entrepreneurs, but Rosa and Hamilton (1994) showed that some differences existed in co-ownership patterns.

Financial Capital: Entrepreneurial firms frequently experience a funding gap when financing growth,[70] and minorities are especially hard hit.[71] Personal savings were found to be the most common source of funding for small businesses; venture capital was used infrequently to fill the "gap."[72] Freear, Sohl, & Wetzel (1995) reported on entrepreneurial perceptions of angel versus venture capital equity providers.

In the woman entrepreneurship literature, some studies compared financing strategies (amount and type of financing) for women and men. Women were found to be more likely to operate on a shoestring. They typically used less capital in starting their businesses;[73] less debt capital in running their businesses;[74] and fewer non-depository financial services[75] than did their male counterparts. Some studies[76] found that sex of the respondent did not affect the use of equity versus debt in funding a business; however, Chaganti, DeCarolis and Deeds (1996) noted that women preferred internal financing for their businesses. Carter, Williams, & Reynolds (1997) reported that women were no less likely than men to have access to credit from banks and suppliers. In fact, McKechnie, Ennew, & Read (1998) found that women secured larger loans than men---but were charged higher interest. Storey (1993) found that the availability of debt capital was more related to the use of personal savings and legal status of the business than to personal characteristics of the entrepreneur (sex, education, or experience). One interesting finding was that women who used bank financing outperformed women who did not.[77]

Entrepreneurial Cognitions and Goals: In the woman entrepreneurship literature, research on reasons why women choose entrepreneurship fell into two streams: push motivations and pull motivations. Studies[78] about push motivations found that factors such as economic necessity, job security, or job discrimination motivated venture start-up. Investigations of pull motivations found eight categories of explanations for women's entrepreneurship: desire for 1) balance in work and personal responsibilities;[79] 2) challenge and achievement;[80] 3) independence and autonomy;[81] 4) job satisfaction or personal fulfillment;[82] 5) equality and recognition;[83] 6) control;[84] 7) profit goals;[85] and 8) various relationships and roles.[86] Other research about women's entrepreneurial cognitions included studies of their risk propensity[87] and attitudes toward innovation and change.[88]

Studies comparing women and men entrepreneurial cognitions were not consistent in their conclusions. Some researchers[89] found no basis for orientation differences between men and women entrepreneurs. Other scholars[90] found that men rated need for achievement higher than women did, while others[91] found that women rated it higher. Hyrsky (1999) found that women rated entrepreneurial concepts higher than men in a sample of adults from Sweden, Norway, Australia, and Canada. Some studies showed women entrepreneurs were more risk adverse,[92] while others found no gender differences in risk propensity.[93] Stanworth and Stanworth (1997) and Brodie and Stanworth (1998) compared men and women on their reluctance (pushed) to enter self-employment.

Several articles examined differences in cognitive styles of women entrepreneurs, comparing age, education, style, typology, and industry choice. This stream of research included comparisons of women in various conditions: with dependents and without;[94] well educated versus less well educated;[95] younger versus older;[96] in traditional versus traditional industries;[97] in male dominated industries versus other industries;[98] and opportunistic versus craftsman types.[99]

Strategic Choice: Entrepreneurs make strategic choices that affect their ability to finance their businesses with equity capital. Six important strategic choices were discussed in the venture capital literature: 1) industry type;[100] 2) product-market segment;[101] 3) location;[102] 4) innovative or imitative strategy;[103] 5) competitive positioning;[104] and 6) growth rate.[105] Westhead & Cowling (1995) specifically examined technology-based companies, their growth, and their choices related to customer base, financial base, technology, and management functions, as well as background and work experience of the founder.

Many of the strategic choices that women make affect the viability and success of their ventures. According to the literature, women-owned businesses had lower sales volume,[106] income[107] and growth rates[108] than those owned by men. These results (lower sales, income, and growth) may be function of their growth intentions or a result of the types of businesses they choose to start. For example, women-owned businesses are under represented in manufacturing sectors and over represented in service sectors[109], and are labor intensive.[110] DuReitz & Henrekson (2000) found that women-owned firms underperformed men-owned firms only if the growth intentions of women were inferior to those of men. Their analysis found that women-owned firms were smaller in sales but not in profitability, employment, or sales orders.

Another possible explanation[111] is that women's lack of access to capital or their preference for debt versus equity capital restrains the size and growth of their businesses and may actually necessitate starting certain types of businesses that don't require equity financing but also don't hold as high a growth potential. For example, Hisrich & O'Brien (1982) reported that women in non-traditional businesses reported a lack of availability of external financing. Two articles[112] focused on micro-enterprises, or life-style businesses. We found only one article[113] that specifically addressed women entrepreneurs with high-growth businesses, despite Cliff's (1998) finding that women entrepreneurs were just as likely as men to report a desire to grow their businesses (although more likely to set a maximum size limit). Baines &

Wheelock (1998) found that husband/wife partnerships had lower growth aspirations than owners with business partners other than a spouse.

Investment Process

The investment process linking equity providers and equity seekers is depicted as a multi-step process,[114] beginning with the deal search or origination and ending with some form of exit. Similar to previous literature reviews,[115] we identified research on the following processes: *deal search/origination, screening, evaluation, structuring the deal,* and *post-investment activities.* Some studies detailed the criteria that venture capitalists use in the search and evaluation process,[116] while others described the specific aspects of a criterion such as human capital.[117] Rosman and O'Neill (1993) compared venture capitalists' criteria to other financial suppliers. Other articles explored characteristics of venture capitalists preferred by entrepreneurs[118] or examined the relationship from a principal-agent perspective.[119]

Several articles addressed the structuring of deals. The specific foci included choice of financial instruments,[120] negotiation issues, and perception of fairness.[121] Brophy, Aminsen, & Bontrager (1982) used Monte Carlo modeling to determine the implied pricing of venture capital funding.

Research on post-investment activities[122] dealt with the time spent by venture capitalists and/or the nature of the venture capitalists' involvement after funding, including follow-on funding. Moesel, Fiet, Busenitz, and Barney (1996) looked at risk perception and its effect on second round funding, while Sapienza and Korsgaard (1995) investigated the impact of information flow on the investor-investee relationship. Three studies[123] examined the venture capitalists' value-added contribution from the entrepreneur's viewpoint.

Contextual Influence

The equity capital and entrepreneurial domains are embedded in a larger macro environment. Two aspects of that environment appear to affect women's access to equity capital: facilitators and structural barriers.

Facilitators include agencies, organizations, or factors that encourage or enhance the funding relationship between equity capital providers and equity capital seekers. Research on facilitation[124] primarily dealt with various programs or institutions and their effect on the availability of venture capital. Other non-institutional facilitators[125] included tax regime, economic conditions, and stock market trends. One article[126] examined the relationship between geographic location and macroeconomic trends and speed to IPO---speed to IPO is considered to affect the flow of funds to entrepreneurial ventures.

A related body of research[127] addresses programs that assist women in establishing businesses. However, these articles more often focused on lifestyle business entrepreneurs. Some research[128] examined whether women and men differed in the services required from small business assistance programs.

In contrast to facilitators, structural barriers act to preclude women's access to equity capital. Kolvereid, Shane, and Westhead (1993) reported that women perceive the start-up environment as more hostile and difficult than men do. A number of articles detailed the obstacles women face in starting or growing their businesses. Obstacles included 1) attitudes, perceptions (self and others'), and socialization of women;[129] 2) child, dependent, and household care;[130] 3) access to capital;[131] 4) education and training[132]; and 5) CEO or Board experience.[133]

Brophy (1989) wrote that women face significant difficulties in financing their businesses because of the attitudes held by male-dominated institutions; and Bygrave (1992) described the venture capital industry as a closed network that is geographically concentrated, and tightly interconnected. Despite these claims, we identified no studies that focused on the structural barriers women face in securing equity financing for their businesses, although a body of literature[134] focuses on the difficulties or perceived difficulties women face in accessing bank financing.

1/12/03- CB CONCLUSION

Entrepreneurship is recognized as the engine of growth in economies world wide. Over the past 10 years women-owned businesses grew dramatically in number, revenues and employment. Their participation in all aspects of venture creation and growth has attracted significant attention. But, as we note, there is a disparity in the funding provided to women entrepreneurs, as well as in the academic research.

We conclude that the majority of research, regardless of research stream or theoretical framework, approached venture capital studies from the perspective of the venture capitalist, or the venture capital industry, which is the supply side of the industry. Less often did research examine the demand side, or the approaches taken by firms *seeking* venture capital. Earlier industry overviews explicitly pointed out that future research opportunities existed in studying public policy, industry competitiveness and venture capital firm operations and strategies (Timmons & Bygrave, 1997; Sapienza & Timmons, 1992), and called for examination of the factors influencing variations in the ability of some populations of firms to obtain venture capital.

This annotated bibliography provides a starting point for exploring the demand side of the equation for women entrepreneurs. We identified constructs that influence the pursuit and acquisition of capital. There is still significant work to be done. Except for our own work, none of the articles we reviewed indicated that women-owned businesses were included in the samples of ventures seeking equity funding, and no studies of venture capital decision-making or venture capital firms indicated whether or not women venture capitalists were participants. Even the research on financing strategies and access to debt for women-owned businesses was sparse and inconclusive. Hence, the academic literature showed a significant "gap" in our understanding of the ways women finance their businesses and women's participation in the venture capital industry, further justifying the need for this bibliography. It is our hope this document will provide a framework that will guide and inspire new research, and that other scholars will add to it as time moves forward.

CITED SOURCES NOT INCLUDED IN THE ANNOTATIONS

Bowen, D. D. & Hisrich, R. D. (1986). The female entrepreneur: A career development perspective. *Academy of Management Review, 11* (2), 292-407.

Brush, C.G. & Edelman, L.F. (2000). Women entrepreneurs: Opportunities for database research. In Katz, J. A. (Ed.), Advances in Entrepreneurship Firm Emergence and Growth: Databases in SME Research (445-484). Greenwich, CT: JAI Press.

Fineberg, S. (1998) Venture capital financing reaches another high. *Venture Capital Journal,* (Jul 1), 1.

Starr, J. & Yudkin, M. (1996). *Women entrepreneurs: A review of current research.* Wellesley, MA: Wellesley Center for Research on Women.

Timmons, J. & Bygrave, W. 1997, Venture capital: Reflections and projections. In D.L. Sexton and R. Smilor (Eds.) *Entrepreneurship 2000*, 29-47. Chicago, IL: Upstart Publishing.

Timmons, J. & Sapienza, H. 1992. Venture Capital: The Decade Ahead. in Sexton, D.L. & Kasarda, J. *The State of the Art of Entrepreneurship*, 402-437. Boston: PWS Kent .

ENDNOTES

[1] Timmons & Bygrave, 1997; Mason & Harrison, 1999.

[2] Brush, 1992; Starr & Yudkin, 1996; Brush & Edelman, 2000; Bowen & Hisrich, 1986.

[3] nvca.org, 10-07-02.

[4] Zacharakis, A. L., Neck. H.M., Bygrave, W. D., & Cox, L. (2001). *Global Entrepreneurship Monitor: National Entrepreneurship Assessment, United States of America.* Kansas City, Missouri: Kauffman Center for Entrepreneurial leadership at the Ewing Marion Kauffman Foundation.

[5] BVCA, 2000.

[6] Fineberg, 1998; Mason & Harrison, 1999.

[7] evca.com/admin/attachments, 10/13/02.

[8] evca.com/admin/attachments, 10/12/02.

[9] www.nvca.org, 10-07-02.

[10] evca.cvom/admin/attachments, 10/13/02.

[11] Venture One, 2000.

[12] National Foundation for Women Business Owners, 1998.

[13] Figures recently released by the U.S. Census report lower numbers for 1997 because of the adoption of new qualifying criteria. To be considered "women-owned" under the new definition requires 51% ownership, $1,000 minimum annual revenues (up from the previous criterion of $500), and that the business be privately held. The new criteria exclude many high growth ventures that are publicly held and at the upper end of the revenue continuum. The change in definition results in depressing the reported contribution of women-owned businesses. Whichever data is used, the growth and contribution of women-owned business is indisputable.

[14] The Diana Project is funded by the Kauffman Center for Entrepreneurial Leadership, the US Small Business Administration, ESBRI (Sweden) and the National Women's Business Council, principal investigators represent Indiana University, Boston University, St. Thomas University, University of Missouri-Kansas City and Harvard Business School.

[15] Timmons & Bygrave, 1997; Mason & Harrison, 1999.

[16] We note that the abstracts are based on our collective interpretation of each article and study. We invite the authors to let us know of any inaccuracies or errors in the article summaries.

[17] Fried & Hisrich, 1988. Subsequent literature reviews by Timmons & Sapienza, 1992; and Timmons & Bygrave, 1997 were reviewed for background information, but not included in the annotations since they were not published in the targeted academic journals).

[18] Greene, Brush, Hart, & Saparito, 2001. Several additional articles on female entrepreneurs access to equity capital by *Diana* researchers are forthcoming (see *Diana Project Overview* for a complete listing).

[19] Brophy, 1981; Timmons, Fast, & Bygrave, 1983; Hambrecht, 1984; Swartz, 1991; Camp & Sexton, 1992; Timmons & Sapienza, 1992; Wright & Robbie, 1998.

[20] Siegel, Siegel & MacMillan, 1988.

[21] Florida & Kenney, 1988; Harrison & Mason, 1991; Manigart, Joos, & De Vos, 1992; Reitan & Sorheim, 1999.

[22] Maier & Walker, 1987.

[23] Mason & Harrison, 2000.

[24] Bygrave, Fast, Khoylian, Vincent & Yue, 1988; Mason & Harrison, 1997; Mason & Harrison, 1999.

[25] Fiet, 1995; Norton & Tenenbaum, 1993; Sapienza & De Clerq, 2000.

[26] Sandberg, Schweiger, & Hofer, 1988.

[27] Khan, 1987; Zacharakis & Meyer, 1998; Shepherd, 1999.

[28] Zacharakis & Shepherd; 2001.

[29] Wetzel, 1981; Robinson; 1987; Elango, Fried, Hisrich, & Polonchek, 1995; Mason & Harrison, 1997; Amit, Brander, & Zott, 1998.

[30] Wetzel, 1983; Robinson, 1987; Gupta & Sapienza, 1992; Norton & Tenenbaum, 1993; Bowden, 1994; Elango, Fried, Hisrich, & Polonchek, 1995; Mason & Harrison, 1997; DeClerq, Kumpulainen, Makela, & Goulet, 1999; Flynn, 2001.

[31] Gupta & Sapienza, 1992; Bowden, 1994; Mason & Harrison, 1997.

[32] Maier & Walker, 1987.

[33] Wetzel, 1983; Elango, Fried, Hisrich, & Polonchek, 1995; Mason & Harrison, 1997; Amit, Brander, & Zott, 1998.

[34] Wetzel, 1983; Bowden, 1984.

[35] Lockett & Wright, 1999.

[36] Bygrave, Johnstone, Lewis, & Ulmann, 1998.

[37] Hisrich & Brush, 1987.

[38] Honig-Haftel & Martin, 1986; Rosa, Carter, & Hamilton, 1996.

[39] Kalleberg & Leicht, 1991.

[40] Blanchflower & Meyer, 1992; Loscocco, Robinson, Hall, & Allen, 1991; Rosa, Carter, & Hamilton, 1996; Boden & Nucci, 1997; Bruce, 1999; Lin, Picot, & Compton, 2000; Holtz-Eaken, Rosen, & Weathers, 2000; Spilling & Berg, 2000.

[41] Evans & Leighton, 1989; Blanchflower & Meyer, 1992; Boden & Nucci, 1997; Lin, Picot, & Compton, 2000; Spilling & Berg, 2000, Cowling & Taylor, 2001.

[42] Spilling & Berg, 2000.

[43] Carter, Williams, & Reynolds, 1997.

[44] Kangasharju, 2000.

[45] Evans & Leighton, 1989.

[46] Evans & Leighton, 1989; Blanchflower & Meyer, 1992; Boden & Nucci, 1997; Carter, Williams, & Reynolds, 1997; Bruce, 1999; Lin, Picot, & Compton, 2000; Spilling & Berg, 2000; Cowling, Taylor, 2001

[47] Rosa, Carter, & Hamilton, 1996.

[48] Evans & Leighton, 1989; Blanchflower & Meyer, 1992; Boden & Nucci, 1997; Bruce, 1999; Cowling & Taylor, 2001.

[49] Evans & Leighton, 1989; Blanchflower & Meyer, 1992; Lin, Picot, & Compton, 2000; Cowling & Taylor, 2001.

[50] Blanchflower & Meyer, 1992; Boden & Nucci, 1997; Carter, Williams, & Reynolds, 1997; Lin, Picot, & Compton, 2000; Spilling & Berg, 2000; Cowling & Taylor, 2001.

[51] Boden & Nucci, 1997; Carter, Williams, & Reynolds, 1997; Lin, Picot, & Compton, 2000; Spilling & Berg, 2000; Cowling & Taylor, 2001.

[52] Bruce, 1999; Lin, Picot, & Compton, 2000.

[53] Cowling & Taylor, 2001.

[54] Carter, Williams, & Reynolds, 1997; Bruce, 1999; Holtz-Eaken, Rosen, & Weathers, 2000.

[55] Brush, 1992.

[56] Roure & Maidique, 1986; Shefczyk & Gerpott, 2001.

[57] Shefczyk & Gerpott, 2001.

[58] Shefczyk & Gerpott, 2001.

[59] Roure & Maidique, 1986.

[60] Bygrave, Johnstone, Lewis, & Ullman, 1998: Bygrave, Johnstone, Matchett, & Rodell, 1999; Cyr, Johnson, & Welbourne, 2000.

[61] Amit, Glosten, & Mueller, 1990; Amit & Mueller, 1990; Chaganti, DeCarolis, & Deeds, 1996.

[62] Cuba, Decenzo, & Anish, 1983; Brush & Hisrich, 1991; Kallenberg & Leicht, 1991; Loscocco, Robinson, Hall, & Allen, 1991; Dolinsky, Caputo, Pasumarty, & Quazi, 1993;

Fischer, Reuber, & Dyke, 1993; Chaganti & Parasuraman, 1996; Carter, Williams, & Reynolds, 1997; Schiller & Crewson, 1997; Alsos & Ljunggren, 1998; Boden & Nucci, 2000.
[63] Hisrich & Brush, 1983; Hisrich & Brush, 1984; Hisrich & Brush, 1985.
[64] Birley, Moss, & Saunders, 1986; Stevenson, 1986; Hisrich & Brush, 1987; Brush, 1992; Barrett, 1995; Clain, 2000.
[65] Aldrich, 1989.
[66] Aldrich, Reese, Dubini, & Woodward, 1989.
[67] Cromie & Birley, 1992.
[68] Chan & Foster, 2001.
[69] Cromie & Birley, 1992.
[70] Wetzel, 1987.
[71] Hughes, 1997.
[72] Dunkelberg & Cooper, 1983; Manigart & Struyf, 1997.
[73] Carter & Rosa, 1998; Verheul & Thurik, 2001.
[74] Scherr, Sugrue, & Ward, 1993; Carter & Rosa, 1998); less trade credit (Cole & Wolken, 1995; Carter & Rosa, 1998.
[75] Cole & Wolken, 1995.
[76] Chaganti, DeCarolis and Deeds, 1996; Verheul & Thurik, 2001.
[77] Haynes & Helms, 2000.
[78] Schwartz, 1976; Buttner & Moore, 1997; Sullivan, Halbrendt, Wang, & Scannell, 1997.
[79] Collerette & Aubry, 1990; Lee-Gosselin & Grise, 1990; Buttner & Moore, 1997; Caputo & Dolinsky, 1998; Fasci & Valdez, 1998; Boden, 1999; Cooper Maysami & Goby, 1999.
[80] Schwartz, 1976; Hisrich & Brush, 1985; Scott, 1986; Neider, 1987; Bellu, 1993; Romano, 1994; Chaganti & Parasuraman, 1996; Shaver, Gartner, Gatewood, & Vos, 1996; Buttner & Moore, 1997.
[81] Schwartz, 1976; Scott, 1986; Neider, 1987; Sexton & Bowman, 1990; Shane, Kolvereid, & Westhead, 1991; Ljunggren & Kolvereid, 1996; Buttner & Moore, 1997; Cooper Maysami & Goby, 1999.
[82] Schwartz, 1976; Hisrich & Brush, 1985; Scott, 1986; Romano, 1994.
[83] Shane, Kolvereid, & Westhead, 1991; Fagenson, 1993.
[84] Neider, 1987; Romano, 1994.
[85] MacNabb, McCoy, Weinrich, & Northover, 1993; Chaganti & Parasuraman, 1996.
[86] Shane, Kolvereid, & Westhead, 1991; Romano, 1994.
[87] Masters & Meier, 1988; Collerette & Aubry, 1990; Sexton & Bowman, 1990; Bellu, 1993; MacNabb, McCoy, Weinrich,& Northover, 1993; Cliff, 1998.
[88] Sexton & Bowman, 1990; Shaver, Gartner, Gatewood, & Vos, 1996; Zepalska, 1997; Gundry & Welsch, 2001.
[89] Chell & Baines, 1998.
[90] Shaver, Gartner, Gatewood, & Voss, 1996.
[91] Hisrich & Brush, 1985; Bellu, 1993; Chaganti & Parasuraman, 1996.
[92] Collerette & Aubry, 1990; Cliff, 1998.
[93] Masters & Meier, 1988.
[94] Finnerty & Krzystofik, 1985.
[95] Holmquist & Sundin, 1990.
[96] Kaplan, 1988.
[97] Anna, Chandler, Jansen, & Mero, 2000.
[98] Olson & Currie, 1992.
[99] Smith, McCain, & Warren, 1982.
[100] Hustedde & Pulver, 1992.
[101] Roure & Maidique, 1986; Rosa, Carter, & Hamilton, 1996; Singh, Reynolds, & Muhammad, 2001.
[102] Hustedde & Pulver, 1992.

[103] Hellman & Puri, 2000.

[104] Hellman & Puri, 2000.

[105] Wetzel & Wilson, 1985; Kangasharju, 2000.

[106] Loscocco, Robinson, Hall, & Allen, 1991; Loscocco & Robinson, 1991; Chaganti & Parasuraman, 1996; Ehlers & Main, 1998.

[107] Loscocco, Robinson, Hall, & Allen, 1991; Loscocco & Robinson, 1991.

[108] Chaganti & Parasuraman, 1996.

[109] DuReitz & Henrekson, 2000.

[110] Birley, Moss, & Saunders, 1987; Ehlers & Main, 1998.

[111] Hisrich & O'Brien, 1981; Chaganti, DeCarolis, & Deeds, 1996; Carter & Allen, 1997.

[112] Birley, Moss, & Saunders, 1987; Ehlers & Main, 1998.

[113] Gundry & Welsch, 2001.

[114] Tyebjee & Bruno, 1984; Norton, 1995.

[115] Bygrave, 1992; Timmons & Bygrave, 1997.

[116] Bruno & Tyebjee, 1983; Bruno & Tyebjee, 1985; MacMillan, Siegel,& Narasimha, 1985; MacMillan & Narasimha, 1986; MacMillan, Zeman, & Narasimha, 1987; Knight, 1994; Boocock & Woods, 1997; Mason & Harrison, 1996; Ray & Turpin, 1993.

[117] Smart, 1998.

[118] Ehrlich, DeNoble, Moore & Weaver, 1994; Smith, 1999.

[119] Reed, 1996.

[120] Norton & Tenenbaum, 1993; Upton & Petty, 2000.

[121] Busenitz, Moesal, Fiet, & Barney, 1997; Landstroem, Manigart, Mason, & Sapienza, 1998.

[122] MacMillan, Kulow, & Khoylian, 1989; Flynn, 1991; Sapienza, 1992; Murray,1992; Elango, Fried, Hisrich, & Polonchek, 1995; Benaglia, Giudici, & Paleari, 1999.

[123] Frederiksen, Klofsten, Landstrom, Olofsson, & Wahlbin, 1990; Rosenstein, Bruno, Bygrave, & Taylor, 1990; Benaglia, Giudici, & Poliari, 1999.

[124] Schell, 1982; Timmons, 1982; Wetzel, 1982, 1983; Harrison & Mason, 1990; Mason & Harrison, 1995a, 1995b; Smith, 2001.

[125] Mason & Harrison, 2000.

[126] Shepherd & Zacharakis, 2001.

[127] Burr & Strickland, 1992; Price & Monroe, 1992; Weinstein, 1992; Ahwireng-Obeng, 1993; Andre, 1995; Servon, 1996; Nilsson, 1997; Walker & Joyner, 1999; Bliss & Garratt, 2001; Cook, Belliveau, & VonSeggern, 2001; Dumas, 2001.

[128] Chrisman, Carsrud, DeCastro, & Heron, 1990.

[129] Watkins & Watkins, 1983; Longstreth, Stafford, & Mauldin, 1987; Birley, 1989; Miskin, 1990; Scherer, Brodzinski, &Wiebe, 1990; Shragg, Yacuk, & Glass, 1992; Holliday & Letherby, 1993; Loscocco & White, 1993; Matthews & Moser, 1996; Baker, Aldrich, & Liou, 1997; Brush, 1997; Gunnerud, 1997; Marlow, 1997; Baines & Wheelock, 1998; Mirchandani, 1999.

[130] Stoner & Hartman, 1990; Green & Cohen, 1995; Parasuraman, Purohit, Godshalk, & Beutell, 1996; Brush, 1997; Ufuk & Ozgen, 2001.

[131] Pellegrino & Reece, 1982; Brush, 1997.

[132] Pellegrino & Reece, 1982; Brush, 1997.

[133] Daily, Certo, & Dalton, 1999; Spilling & Berg, 2000.

[134] Buttner & Rosen, 1988, 1989; Riding & Swift, 1990; Buttner, 1992, 1993; Fay & Williams, 1993; Read, 1994; Fabowale & Orser, 1995; McKechnie, Ennew, & Read, 1998; Haines, Orser, & Riding, 1999; Haines & Haines, 1999; Cole, 2000.

PART 2

Annotations Women Entrepreneurs

Ahwireng-Obeng, F. (1993). Gender, entrepreneurship and socioeconomic reparation in South Africa. *Review of Black Political Economy, 22* (2), 151-165.

This article discusses gender, entrepreneurship and socioeconomic reparation in South Africa. Entrepreneurial development is increasingly recognized as a functional means of tackling South Africa's socioeconomic challenges of slow growth rate, rapidly increasing unemployment, and racially inequitable distribution of income. However, current policies and programs ignore the potential input of women. Using archival macro-economic financial statistics to show current income distribution in South Africa, it is argued that women are displaced in the economic mainstream. Building on Cooper's (1981) framework that identifies "antecedent influences" to venture creation (incubator organization and environmental influences), gender differences are explored in each category. For instance, most women are mothers and self-employment can be a more flexible alternative for managing multiple roles. Three public policy program approaches for stimulating women's self-employment are offered: a focused program, a women's component of mainstream programs, or a program of mainstream integration. Because women in South Africa still face institutional discrimination, the author argues in favor of a mainstream assistance program with the caveat that implementation must be attentive to gender through social networking and adequate promotion of women.

Nature of the study: Empirical
Nature of the data: Archival
Nature of the sample: NA
Variables: Antecedent, influences, environmental influences, incubator organization, gender, family status

Aldrich, H. (1989). Networking among women entrepreneurs. In O. Hagan, C. Rivchun, & D. Sexton (Eds), *Women-owned businesses* (pp. 103-132). New York: Praeger.

This article is based on the premise that entrepreneurs are embedded in a social context that influences their ability to establish connections to resources and niches in opportunity structures. Central to this are social networks. A review of previous research shows that women entrepreneurs are embedded in different personal and social networks than men are, with far-reaching consequences for their rates of business formation, survival, and growth. After explaining general properties of social networks (ties, density, reachability), the author explores the characteristics of women's networks across three spheres: work, family, and organized social life. Evidence suggests that divisions and barriers within spheres significantly limit the reach and diversity of women's networks. Women may view social relationships in a significantly different way than men do, placing more emphasis on responsibilities and obligations. Men tend to see situations in terms of what they may gain from it and are willing to subordinate affective considerations to ones of effectiveness. Prescriptions are suggested for women as a means to improve planning and monitoring of network activities. For example, they should break the "old boys" network by deliberately invading male turf whenever possible. The "new girls" network will create strong ties and promote social support. However, with less than one in three businesses owned by women and financial centers of power controlled by men, reliance solely on sex-segregated separate networks is a handicap to women.

Nature of the study: Conceptual
Nature of the data: NA
Nature of the sample: NA
Variables: Work, family, organized social life, networking ties, density, reachability

Aldrich, H., Reese, P. R., Dubini, P., Rosen, B., & Woodward, B. (1989). Women on the verge of a breakthrough?: Networking among entrepreneurs in the United States and Italy. In R. H. Brockhaus, Sr., N. C. Churchill, J. A. Katz, B. A. Kirchhoff, K. H. Vesper, & W. E. Wetzel, Jr. (Eds.), *Frontiers of entrepreneurial research* (pp. 560-574). Boston, MA: Babson College.

The literature on work, marriage and the family, and organized social life implies that women are embedded in different personal networks than men, with potential consequences for their rates of business formation, survival, and growth. On the premise that sex roles would be more pronounced in some cultures than in others, this study compared aspects of personal networks of 264 potential and active entrepreneurs in the Research Triangle Area, North Carolina, and 59 in Milan, Italy, by gender. Instead of substantial differences in the networks of men and women, the authors were surprised by the degree of similarity they discovered within and between the countries. Networking activity (size and time spent in networking) and network density were very similar across countries. Multivariate analyses show that sex did not predict significant differences in network activity in either the U.S. or Italy. However, the sex composition of networks differs dramatically by sex in both countries. Men have almost no women in their personal networks, whereas women's personal networks contain mostly men. In some respects, the gap between the male and female worlds appears to have closed substantially, but the personal networks of women in both countries still include few women.

Nature of the study:	Empirical
Nature of the data:	Mail survey
Nature of the sample:	230 entrepreneurial association members from North Carolina, 59 entrepreneurs from Milan, Italy
Variables:	Owner characteristics, networking activity, business characteristics, industry sector

Alsos, G. A., & Ljunggren, E. (1998). Does the business start-up process differ by gender? A longitudinal study of nascent entrepreneurs. In P. D. Reynolds, W. D. Bygrave, S. Manigart, C. M. Mason, G. D. Meyer, N.M. Carter, & K. G. Shaver (Eds.), *Frontiers of entrepreneurial research* (pp. 137-151). Boston, MA: Babson College.

In Scandinavia several policy programs are directed towards increasing the number of women entrepreneurs. They are based on the assumption that women have particular problems in the business start-up process, leading to a lower probability of nascent women entrepreneurs actually starting a business. This study builds on previous work by Carter, Gartner, and Reynolds (1996) investigating whether there are gender differences among nascent entrepreneurs in start-up sequences. Data was collected from 149 nascent entrepreneurs from Norway who were interviewed by phone three times over two years. Statistical tests analyzed the extent to which men and women who attempted to start a business actually succeeded in doing so. Findings show some gender differences in the start-up process, but these differences do not lead to lower start-up probabilities for women. Females are less likely than males to write a business plan, and when they do, they postpone it until relatively late in the start-up process. One reason may be that the women in the study were less educated and therefore less familiar with business plans. Overall, this study shows more similarities than differences between Norwegian male and female nascent entrepreneurs. Therefore, the authors suggest that separate and focused programs targeted towards women may not be the most effective means of stimulating female entrepreneurship.

Nature of the study:	Empirical
Nature of the data:	Phone interviews
Nature of the sample:	149 randomly selected nascent entrepreneurs from Norway
Variables:	Personal characteristics, industry of venture, start-up business activities; planning, financing, interaction with the environment

Andre, R. (1992). A national profile of women's participation in networks of small business leaders. *Journal of Small Business Management, 30* (1), 66-73.

This study examines women's power and participation in economic development organizations (EDO), given the premise that EDOs influence economic development in the U.S. The author posits that 1) women would be more likely to represent smaller than larger businesses, 2) participation of men and women would be similar across regions, and 3) women would be more prominent in areas where opportunities are greatest. The sample included major private sector EDOs in 45 states and 13 major cities identified as the most influential EDOs in these areas. The results indicated that the average number of women in EDOs was nine per state, compared with 65 men per state. Women's participation ranges from 4.5% to 19.6% for the nine regions examined. Nationally, of all small business EDO members, 13.5% are women. The results show that women participated in the EDOs of their states and cities and that their role in EDOs in some ways reflected the patterns of their participation elsewhere in the business community. Women were likely to represent small rather than large businesses, to be active at local rather than state levels, and to achieve network membership in particular regions of the country, namely the West, the Southwest, and the Northeast.

Nature of the study: Empirical
Nature of the data: Archival
Nature of the sample: 5,432 men- and women-led businesses
Variables: Personal demographics, industry sector, geographic location, company size

Andre, R. (1995). Diversity in executive networks: A national study of women's representation in private sector economic development. *Journal of Managerial Issues, 7* (3), 306-322.

This study describes women's participation in the major private sector economic development organizations (EDOs) in the United States--those federations of business leaders which seek to improve the overall business climate in their domains. It presents a conceptual framework for understanding the impact of gender on the business community's agenda for economic development, identifying factors which predict women's involvement in EDOs. A sample of 5,432 men- and women-led companies was compared by size, industry, and region. Results show representation patterns similar to the gender composition of communities and evidence that women's integration into EDOs is slow. However, there is little evidence of barriers to women's inclusion. Regional representation varied, as did women's participation in larger companies. Men were more likely to represent larger companies and to serve at the state level. The analysis showed that company size, industry, region, and locale were significant factors in women's EDO representation, and that gender should be taken into account in the study of power elites and inter-organizational networks. Finally, it is suggested that the elite group of women who belong to EDOs should reflect upon their unique perspectives and influence upon the economic development agenda.

Nature of the study: Empirical
Nature of the data: Archival
Nature of the sample: 5,432 men and women-led businesses
Variables: Industry sector, geographic location, company si

Anna, A. L., Chandler, G. N., Jansen, E. & Mero, N.P. (2000). Women business
owners in traditional and non-traditional industries. *Journal of Business
Venturing, 15* (3), 279-303.

Although the growth in the number of women-owned businesses is
encouraging, the size of such businesses remains small in terms of both
revenues and number of employees, especially in comparison to male-owned
businesses. One explanation for this disparity is that female business
ownership is concentrated primarily in the retail and service industries where
businesses are relatively smaller in terms of employment and revenue as
opposed to high technology, construction, and manufacturing. Social
learning theory, in particular self-efficacy, offers an explanation for this
disparity. This study builds theories of women's career development and
entrepreneurial intentions to examine differences between traditional and
non-traditional women business owners. It examined 170 women business
owners in various traditional and non-traditional businesses in Utah and
Illinois.

The authors develop a theoretical model proposing that venture efficacy,
career expectations and individual context will potentially influence
women's choice to pursue careers in traditional versus non-traditional
industries. MANCOVA analyses showed that women in non-traditional
businesses had higher venture efficacy and higher expectations for profit
than women in traditional industries. Hierarchical regressions showed that
the effects of venture efficacies and career expectancies on sales were
different depending on industry type. Women in traditional businesses had
higher venture efficacy for opportunity recognition and higher career
expectations of life balance and security and placed more importance on the
financial support received from others. On the other hand, the non-traditional
owners had higher venture efficacy for planning and higher career
expectations for money or wealth than the traditional group. The research
supports the construct validity of venture efficacy scales as a means to
differentiate among types of entrepreneurs.

Nature of the study: Empirical
Nature of the data: Qualitative interviews, mail survey
Nature of the sample: 369 women business owners in Illinois, 240 women business
                          owners in Utah
Variables: Entrepreneurs demographics, venture efficacy (technical and
                          managerial competencies), career expectations, support,
                          sales, business type

8. Working for each other: Gender, the household,
ival and growth. *International Small Business*

businesses in two locations in England to discern
venture's survival and growth flexibility and its
ale owner, one female owner, spouse co-owners,
members, especially owner's spouses, were
ce of labor (both paid and unpaid) in the
_ution of a spouse's labor was seen as a vital resource.
wners of growing businesses were more likely to enter into non-
family business partnerships and to actively pursue and achieve human
resources beyond family members. Nearly two-fifths of the businesses were
extensive or moderate participants in business and social networks, but
owners of growing businesses were more active in their network activities
with other business owners and organizations. Nearly half of the
husband/wife partnerships had low growth aspirations. Owners with business
partners other than a spouse were most likely to be growth enthusiasts.

Nature of the study:	Empirical
Nature of the data:	Telephone survey followed by face-to-face interviews.
Nature of the sample:	200 micro-businesses (0-9 employees) located in two communities of northeast and southeast England were contacted by phone (100 in each location). The firms had all been operating for at least two years. Face-to-face interviews were conducted with 104, followed by in-depth interviews with 34 of the owner-managers.
Variables:	Employment change, intentions to grow, enthusiasm for growth, form of ownership, spouse involvement, network participation

Baker, T., Aldrich, H. E., & Liou, N. (1997). Invisible entrepreneurs: The neglect of
women business owners by mass media and scholarly journals in the U.S.A.
Entrepreneurship and Regional Development, 9, 221-238.

This paper examines a paradox: gains in women's business ownership in the
U.S.A. have been extraordinary, but popular press coverage has actually
declined and academic articles on women owners are also exceedingly rare.
The authors demonstrate the extent of the paradox through a detailed
examination of popular newspaper and scholarly coverage of women's
business ownership, then offer explanations for the paradox, and finally
discuss the dissenting voices that are raised by scholars and women's
advocacy groups. The review of periodicals showed that coverage of women
business owners declined between 1982 and 1995. Coverage of women
business owners in academic periodicals also declined, with more than 85%
of entrepreneurship articles making no mention of women. Three
explanations were offered for this: 1) the media no longer considers women's

business "news," 2) scholars are not interested in women's firms because they are mostly small and relatively unimportant, and 3) documented differences between men and women owners are few and thus reporters and scholars no longer look for them. Two dissenting voices complicate these explanations: 1) small but significant gender differences were found in studies of social behavior and leadership, and 2) advocacy groups have asserted that women owners possess unique advantages. Why haven't these voices been heard? The authors argue that androcentrism has clouded our perceptions of gender differences and blinded journalists and academics in two ways: 1) women's distinctive contributions have been muted as they have adapted to institutions of business that were already gendered, and 2) the search for distinctive contributions by women owners has been thwarted by assumptions that traditional ways of doing business are "natural." Future research directions are suggested.

Nature of the study: Empirical
Nature of the data: Archival
Nature of the sample: Articles from newspapers and scholarly journals
Variables: Characteristics of women-owned businesses

Burt

Barr, R. S. (1998). The gender of social capital. *Rationality & Society, 10* (1), 5-47.

Building on the notion that social capital is the contextual complement to human capital, this paper explores how low legitimacy affects returns to social capital. This article begins with the network structure of social capital, explaining the information and control benefits of structural holes. The holes in a network are entrepreneurial opportunities that can add value, and persons rich in such opportunities are expected to be more successful than their peers. Recent empirical research supports this prediction. However, women pose a puzzle. The entrepreneurial networks linked to early promotion for senior men do not work for women. The author poses three common line of arguments used to explain gender differences and then demonstrates how the arguments do not account for those differences: social support (women are more comfortable in a small circle of supportive mutual friends), pink collar jobs (low-opportunity jobs more often held by women), and combat birth (women can better look out for one another's interests-- speaking up for one another in the other's absence, and informing one another of developing opportunities--with dense networks of female colleagues).

The findings showed that promotions came earlier to women with more hierarchical networks, meaning women who borrowed social capital. Early promotion of women was also associated with structural holes and sponsor legitimacy. Women were most likely to be promoted early when they built their network within the entrepreneurial network of a strategic partner beyond their boss. Even working within the limits of a clique network, or their boss's network, was preferable to building their own entrepreneurial network (in terms of early promotion). Women with entrepreneurial networks were actually promoted later. Returns to social capital can be used to sort managers into those accepted as legitimate players in the population versus those deemed suspect. The latter, 'illegitimate entrepreneurs', have to borrow the social capital of a sponsor to benefit from the information and control advantages of structural holes. The fact that women and entry-rank men fall behind when they build their own social capital, and move ahead when they borrow social capital, indicates that they have a legitimacy problem in this firm. Gender was not so much a difference between men and women in particular as it was a generic difference between insiders and outsiders. The author concludes that the network form of social capital varies with legitimacy.

Nature of the study: Empirical
Nature of the data: NA
Nature of the sample: 284 men and women managers
Variables: Network size, density, hierarchy; managers' rank, promotion rate, functional areas of expertise

Barrett, M. (1995). Feminist perspectives on learning for entrepreneurship: The view from small business. In W. D. Bygrave, B. J, Bird, S. Birley, N. C. Churchill, M. Hay, R. H. Keeley, & W. E. Wetzel, Jr. (Eds.), *Frontiers of entrepreneurial research* (pp. 323-336). Boston, MA: Babson College.

This study compares the learning experiences and needs of men and women business owners in Australia. Based on the premise that women's experiences may differ from men's, the study explores how entrepreneurship might mean something different and work differently depending on gender. Using a sample of 812 firm owners from Queensland, the study examined six factors that recur in research about entrepreneurial learning: 1) industry participation of men and women, 2) previous business start-up, 3) continuing operation of a previous business, 4) sources of learning about managing a business, 5) value of particular sources of learning about business management, and 6) perceptions about specific business problems. The sample was stratified based on industry image (male/female) and sector (manufacturing/service). Results showed that men are more likely to participate in female image businesses while very few women participated in male image businesses. The proportion of men and women with previous start-up experience was similar; however, men were significantly more likely to have started more than one previous venture. Findings suggested women business owners had less access to some forms of experience that business owners most value. Despite this, women business owners in this study claimed to experience less difficulty with certain business problems than men did. Women rated many sources of learning more useful than men did, including advice from investors, suppliers, seminars, and business acquaintances. The only learning aspect men found more significantly useful than women did resulted from facing a major setback in the current firm. The author concluded that issues do affect men and women differently and that these derive in part from the industries and sectors in which they are located.

Nature of the study:	Empirical
Nature of the data:	Mail survey
Nature of the sample:	812 men and women business owners from Australia
Variables:	Industry sector, entrepreneurs' experience, education, problems

Belcourt, M. (1990). A family portrait of Canada's most successful female entrepreneurs. *Journal of Business Ethics, 9* (4/5), 435-438.

This study examined the factors contributing to women's decisions to become entrepreneurs. A convenience sample of 36 highly successful women entrepreneurs in Canada was conducted. Their stories illustrated the importance of family dynamics in the decision to become an entrepreneur. Results revealed mirror images of the patterns found to be correlated with male entrepreneurship. The most potent variables influencing the level of entrepreneurial activity were occupational role models and rejection experiences. If women entrepreneurs have an aversion to authority and a desire to be free of controls, incentive programs to increase entrepreneurial activity should minimize reporting or dependency relations. Since male and female entrepreneurs are molded by similar experiences, bankers, venture capitalists, and government policymakers should not assume that female entrepreneurs are operating businesses just for something to do. The diversity of company formation experiences made it difficult to generalize across entrepreneurs.

Nature of the study:	Empirical
Nature of the data:	Personal interviews
Nature of the sample:	Convenience sample 36 successful female entrepreneurs in Canada
Variables:	Business information, life history, career path, self-employment experiences

Bellu, R. R. (1993). Task role motivation and attributional style as predictors of entrepreneurial performance: Female sample findings. *Entrepreneurship and Regional Development, 5,* 331-344.

This study builds on extensive theory and research examining motivations for entrepreneurial behavior. The purpose of this research was to provide evidence, at the gender level, for a predictive model of growth-oriented entrepreneurial performance. The author tests a model adapted from Miner (1993) that focuses on 1) the relationship between role requirements of the entrepreneurial organization and five motivational patterns that fit these roles, and 2) the mediating effect of the individual's attributional style for failure and success, and his/her perception of environmental uncertainty, on two of the five motivational patterns. The Miner Sentence Completion Scale (Form T) and Differential Attribution Questionnaire were used as measures to compare female managers and entrepreneurs. Results show that female entrepreneurs scored significantly higher on self-achievement. Differences in attributions were found, with entrepreneurs attributing failure of entrepreneurial action to unstable (changeable) causes and managers making the attribution to stable causes. While the results of this study corroborated recent findings with male entrepreneurs, some gender differences were indicated. Female entrepreneurs and managers showed propensity for taking greater risks than their male counterparts. The fact that women continue to face more hostile and prejudicial environments seems to suggest that they are willing to accept a greater degree of risk.

Nature of the study: Empirical
Nature of the data: Personal interviews
Nature of the sample: 47 female entrepreneurs and 66 female managers
Variables: Motivational patterns, attributions, entrepreneurial actions

Birley, S. (1989). Female entrepreneurs: Are they really any different? *Journal of Small Business Management, 27* (1), 32-37.

The premise of this article is that the nature of any business (i.e., its trading relationships with customers, suppliers, bankers, and advisors) is "set at the start." The author analyzes current literature on female entrepreneurs using Cooper's (1981) model, which incorporates three broad categories of influence: (1) antecedent influences, including genetic factors, family influences, education, and previous career experiences; 2) incubator organization, which describes the organization the entrepreneur worked in prior to start-up; and 3) environmental factors, including availability of venture capital, role models, and access to support services. From the evidence presented, it is proposed that although Cooper's model of entrepreneurship holds true both for men and women, the factors that contribute to the supply of entrepreneurs are also culturally and situationally bound. For any minority group, its position in society and gender roles (e.g., wife and mother) will be a significant factor in determining individual attitudes to entrepreneurial activity.

Nature of the study: Conceptual
Nature of the data: NA
Nature of the sample: NA
Variables: Antecedent influences, incubator organization, environmental factors

Birley, S., Moss, C., & Saunders, P. (1987). Do women entrepreneurs require different training? *American Journal of Small Business, 12* (1), 27-35.

Few studies to date consider the female entrepreneur. This study was designed to describe the characteristics of male and female participants attending a series of entrepreneurship/enterprise development courses at a college in the U.K. The programs are aimed at those potential entrepreneurs who intend to employ fewer than four people. The study examined the participants' backgrounds and the types of businesses subsequently formed. Findings suggest that significant differences exist between male and female entrepreneurs and the businesses that they form. Specifically, the study finds that: 1) the mean age of the female group was 32.7 years of age, compared to 39.3 for the males; 2) of those in business, 75% of the men ran their businesses from the home, while only 22% of the women were home-based; and 3) female-run businesses used more labor and more female labor than male-run businesses did. There were no significant differences in education levels or previous employment experience.

Nature of the study:	Empirical
Nature of the data:	Telephone interviews
Nature of the sample:	47 men and women participants of employment program in the U.K.
Variables:	Business idea, incubator organization characteristics, customer information, employees, family involvement

Blanchflower, D., & Meyer, B. (1992). A longitudinal analysis of the young self-employed in Australia and the United States. *Small Business Economics, 6* (1), 1-20.

This study is a comparative analysis of the patterns of self-employment among the young (ages 16-25) in Australia and the United States. The research used comparable longitudinal data sets from both countries to assess the movement of young people in and out of self-employment. Findings include: 1) Skilled manual workers, males, and older workers are more likely to choose self-employment. 2) Previous earnings are an important determinant of the transition to self-employment. 3) Additional years of schooling had a positive impact on the probability of self-employment in the U.S. but not in Australia. 4) Factors contributing to leaving self-employment differed in the two countries.

Nature of the study:	Empirical
Nature of the data:	Australian Longitudinal Survey (1985, 1986, 1988); U.S. Survey of Income and Program Participation
Nature of the sample:	Australian and U.S. males and females ages 15-25
Variables:	Demographics (age, sex, locations), education, income, current employment status, employment history, industry

Bliss, R. T., & Garratt, N. L. (2001). Supporting women entrepreneurs in transitioning economies. *Journal of Small Business Management, 39* (4), 336-344.

This article first makes a case for a support organization for women entrepreneurs in transitioning economies and then describes the establishment of the Polish Association of Women Entrepreneurs (PAWE). Data from support organizations are used to establish the "best practices" of such groups. Although focused on Poland, the research yielded several recommendations applicable to support programs for women entrepreneurs in other transitioning economies: 1) clearly define the program's mission; 2) use the 'best practices' approach to overcome cultural differences; 3) select a benchmark sample from countries with cultural, economic, and historical environments similar to the transitioning economy; 4) educate founders about marketing, promotion, and fund-raising, since these activities are critical to the organization's success and these functions are unfamiliar in a planned economy; and 5) gear initial efforts toward membership growth and fund-raising. The article states that understanding the social and economic impact on women of a planned economy and the unique needs of female entrepreneurs in the transition to capitalism were keys to developing effective support organizations.

Nature of the study:	Empirical
Nature of the data:	Telephone interviews
Nature of the sample:	12 support organizations for women from the U.K., France, Poland, Italy, Germany, Slovenia and U.S.
Variables:	Association structure, chapters and affiliations, membership, sponsorship

Boden, R. J. (1996). Gender and self-employment selection: An empirical assessment. *Journal of Socio-Economics, 25* (6), 671-682.

This paper presents an assessment of the factors influencing men's and women's decisions to switch from wage employment to self-employment. New empirical patterns appeared from the longitudinally matched data: 1) relatively strong, positive influence of fertility upon women's selection into self-employment; 2) the greater propensity of small business employees to switch to self-employment; and 3) the significant relationship between wage-sector occupation and predisposition to self-employment.

Nature of the study:	Empirical
Nature of the data:	March Income Supplement of the Current Population Survey
Nature of the sample:	35,000 white men and 32,500 white women who were employed in the wage sector one year and employed in the wage sector or self-employed the following year (for adjacent, paired years between 1987 and 1991).
Variables:	Age, base-year wage, total income of other family members, worker non-wage income

Boden Jr., R.J. (1999). Gender inequality in wage earnings and female self-employment selection. *Journal of Socio-Economics, 28* (3), 351-364.

This paper develops a theoretical model that estimates expected earnings from wage or self-employment. Female self-employment has risen strongly over the last few decades and has become an important labor market development. The few studies that have examined women's decision to become self-employed indicate that this decision is complex. Women are more likely than men to shoulder family-related obligations, especially child rearing, and there is evidence that this affects some women's propensity to become self-employed. Also, women have yet to achieve full economic parity with men in wage employment. How gender inequality in wage earnings may precipitate some women's selection out of wage employment and into self-employment is examined using a probit model. Results showed that evidence of gender-inequality in wage returns (a possible manifestation of employer discrimination) may positively influence some women's decisions to leave wage employment for self-employment. Women's lower wage returns to observed worker characteristics had a positive and significant effect on women's decision to switch from wage employment to self-employment.

Nature of the study: Empirical
Nature of the data: Current Population Survey (CPS Income supplements)
                         1988-1992
Nature of the sample: Female self-employed
Variables: Owner characteristics (age, marital status, education, prior experience, wages, children under 6 years old, total non-wage income), business characteristics (industry)

Boden Jr., R.J. (1999). Flexible working hours, family responsibilities, and female self-employment: Gender differences in self-employment selection. *American Journal of Economics and Sociology, 58* (1), 71-84.

This paper uses cross-sectional data from the Contingent Work Survey of the February 1995 Current Population Survey. Direct evidence is presented to show substantial gender differences in the reasons why individuals become self-employed. In particular, women, especially women with young children, were more likely than men to cite flexibility of schedule and family-related reasons for becoming self-employed. Men's reasons for becoming self-employed showed little association with their parental status. Findings suggest that employers should be encouraged to offer working conditions that are friendly to workers whose family obligations conflict with traditional, 40-hour-per-week jobs.

Nature of the study: Empirical
Nature of the data: Current Population Survey (CPS Income supplements)
                         1988-1992

Nature of the sample: Male & female self-employed
Variables: Owner characteristics (age, marital status, education, prior experience, wages, children under 6 years old, total non-wage income), business characteristics (industry)

Boden, R. J., & Nucci, A. R. (1997). Counting the self-employed using household and business sample data. *Small Business Economics, 9* (5), 427-436

This study compares incidence of self-employment in the U.S. using two data sets, Characteristics of Business Owners (CBO) and Current Population Survey (CPS), for the same reference years, 1982-1987. The purpose was to examine discrepancies in the two data sets and, in particular, to analyze differences by gender and race. The CBO survey data was collected from a mail survey that inquired about age, marital status, personal, and business attributes. The CPS is a monthly survey of about 60,000 households that serves as the major source of information about household labor statistics. An attempt was made to reconcile the different units of analyses in these data sets, based on tax filings and other variables. Six common variables were compared: sex, age, education, marital status, percent income from self-employment, industry, and region. Results show that estimates for the number of self-employed workers diverges between the samples in the years 1982 and 1987. The source of the disparity is gender. The CBO sample reveals a growth rate of 26% for self-employed men, compared to just 3% in the ADF-CPS sample. The CBO data set provides a more authoritative estimate, and is therefore a better source of data about women and minorities.

Nature of the study: Empirical
Nature of the data: Characteristics of Business Owners (CBO) and Current Population Survey (CPS), 1982 and 1987
Nature of the sample: Male & female self-employed; 130,000 owners and 90,000 businesses in U.S.
Variables: Sex, age, education, marital status, percent income from self-employment, industry, region

Boden, R. J., Jr., & Nucci, A. R. (2000). On the survival prospects of men's and women's new business ventures. *Journal of Business Venturing, 15* (4), 347-362.

This study examines the relationship between owner and business characteristics and business survival using the Census Bureau Analyses of 1982 and 1987. The purpose was to compare differential characteristics of male and female-owned businesses and to analyze how these affected business retention or survival rates. The sample was restricted to sole proprietors in retail and service industries in an attempt to select owners with reasonably similar start-up requirements and turn-over rates, and to restrict the study to industries with more equal representation of men and women. Results showed that survival rates were affected by owner experience for both male and female-owned businesses. Multivariate analyses showed that for male-owned businesses the survival rate was higher than for women-owned businesses by 6%. Wage employment provided opportunities to acquire financial and human capital necessary for success in business ownership. Gender differences in the status of wage workers impacted negatively on the survival of female-owned businesses due to lower average wage earning and lack of previous managerial skills. The authors conclude that differences in factors leading to start-up success is somewhat mixed, depending on education and prior experience. However, this study suggests that women are likely disadvantaged in terms of opportunities to accumulate human capital relative to entrepreneurial success through wage employment.

Nature of the study:	Empirical
Nature of the data:	CBO Census Data
Nature of the sample:	130,000 owners and 90,000 businesses in U.S.
Variables:	Owner characteristics (age, marital status, race, gender, education, prior experience, hours worked per week), business characteristics (payroll, industry, receipts, start-up capital, years of ownership tenure)

Brodie, S., & Stanworth, J. (1998). Independent contractors in direct selling: Self-employed but missing from official records. *International Small Business Journal 16* (3), 95-101.

In-depth interview data from respondents who were part of a larger postal survey were analyzed to examine the importance of "entrepreneurial pull" and "economic push" as motives for entry into direct selling. The results follow general trends in the U.K. labor market with females more likely than males to work part-time on their direct selling activity. Males were more likely than females to be economically active at the time of selecting direct selling self-employment, whether working in multi-level or single-level format companies. Females "pushed" into direct selling were significantly more likely than men to have joined a single-level format company.

Nature of the study:	Empirical
Nature of the data:	Survey data from postal questionnaire followed by in-depth interviews
Nature of the sample:	Questionnaires were mailed to 4,050 new independent contractors from 22 direct selling organizations in U.K. Useable responses returned from 722 individuals. From these, data from in-depth taped interviews conducted with 82 individuals over-time, matching males and females on type of organization (multi-level/single-level) were analyzed in this study.
Variables:	Sex, motivation for self-employment

Brophy, D. J. (1989). Financing women owned entrepreneurial firms. In, O. Hagan, C. Rivchun, & D. Sexton (Eds.) *Women Owned Businesses* (pp. 55-76). New York: Praeger.

This chapter examines the financing of entrepreneurially driven, emerging-growth women-owned and operated companies by reviewing past literature. The first section reviews the relevant literature concerning the similarities and differences in characteristics of male and female entrepreneurs. The second section reviews the financing characteristics of emerging growth companies over the business life cycle. The discussion considers the choice between a "life-style" or a low-growth business and an emerging-growth company and also the implications of that choice for the financing of the firm. The third section describes the array of capital sources available to new businesses (e.g., debt, private placement, private equity, alliances and corporate partners). The last section presents findings regarding capital market access for women entrepreneurs and makes recommendations. The author notes that women have encountered significant difficulties in financing their ventures in part because of attitudes held by representatives of male-dominated institutions. A perception that women start hobby or part-time businesses in retail and service primarily for life-style reasons contributes to difficulties women face in acquiring capital. On the other hand, previous research on characteristics of women and men entrepreneurs shows similar characteristics and approaches. Women seeking to grow high potential ventures will encounter challenges, but these are not insurmountable. Only those entrepreneurs who can convince investors that they have strong teams will succeed.

Nature of the study:	Conceptual
Nature of the data:	NA
Nature of the sample:	NA
Variables:	Individual demographics (goals, experience), venture factors (size), environmental factors

Bruce, D. (1999). Do husbands matter? Married women entering self-employment. *Small Business Economics, 13* (4), 317-329.

This study investigates the effects of a husband's self-employment experience on the probability that a wife will enter self-employment. The author proposes that the presence of a self-employed husband may enable intra-family flows of financial and human capital and encourage a woman to become self-employed. Data from the Panel Study of Income Dynamics (PSID) from 1970-1991 was used to examine this premise. The sample was comprised of 3,330 married couples with at least one year of labor market experience from the time period. Economic modeling (probit) techniques showed that women college graduates were less likely to enter the labor market than were non-college graduates. Women with black husbands were less likely to become self-employed. A non-working or wage and salary wife was nearly twice as likely to enter self-employment in any year if her husband was self-employed in the previous year.

Nature of the study:	Empirical
Nature of the data:	U.S. Panel Study of Income Dynamics
Nature of the sample:	3,330 married couples
Variables:	Demographics (age, education), earnings, gender, race, self-employment

Brush, C. G. (1992). Research on women business owners: Past trends, a new perspective and future directions. *Entrepreneurship Theory and Practice*, *16(4)*, 5-30.

This paper proposes a new perspective that offers a basis for interpreting unexplained gender differences between male and female business owners. The author reviewed 57 empirical research studies on women business owners and their ventures, classified the studies into a framework developed by Gartner (1985), and summarized trends emerging from the research. The discussion analyzes the methodology, samples and statistical techniques of current research and concludes that the vast majority of empirical studies were cross-sectional, descriptive, and often not linked to theory. An assessment of findings from research studies concludes that women business owners are similar to males across some basic demographic factors, problems, and business characteristics, but differ widely from male business owners across individual dimensions related to education, work experience, skills, approaches to venture creation/acquisition, business goals, problems and performance. It is suggested that the major reason for these differences is that women conceive of their businesses differently than men do, which in turn leads to different approaches in venture creation and outcomes for performance. To guide future research, a new "integrated perspective" on women-owned businesses is proposed. This perspective is anchored in feminine moral development, psychology, and sociology theories. The author offers feminine interpretations of individual, organizational, process, and environmental factors and proposes research questions for each category of variables. Implications for methodology, measures, and women's entrepreneurial experiences conclude this article.

Nature of the study:	Literature review
Nature of the data:	NA
Nature of the sample:	NA
Variables:	Individual characteristics, environmental factors, organizational characteristics, start-up process

Brush, C. G. (1997). Women-owned businesses: Obstacles and opportunities. *Journal of Developmental Entrepreneurship, 2* (1), 1-24.

This exploratory research investigates factors facilitating and inhibiting growth. The author conducted a focus group with eight successful women entrepreneurs and explored their experiences in growing their ventures. Seven themes emerged, four obstacles and three opportunities. The most prominent obstacles were 1) being taken seriously, 2) child and dependent care, 3) growth and expansion capital, and 4) entrepreneurial education and training. The opportunities were 1) technology, 2) management style, and 3) employee policies. The article concludes with future research directions and four propositions derived from theory.

Nature of the study:	Empirical
Nature of the data:	Focus groups
Nature of the sample:	Successful women business owners
Variables:	Individual characteristics, business characteristics, obstacles, opportunities in growing businesses

Brush, C. G., & Hisrich, R. D. (1991). Antecedent influences on women-owned businesses. *Journal of Managerial Psychology, 6* (2), 9-16.

This study tests elements of Cooper's (1991) framework identifying three groups of influences that affect the start-up and growth of new ventures: individual characteristics, incubator experience, and environmental factors. The study explores the relationship between "antecedent influences" on women entrepreneurs, including personal background, educational and occupational experiences, motivations, skills, and knowledge and the growth of their ventures. Two discriminant function analyses tested the influence of personal factors in predicting high or low growth groupings. Findings from this longitudinal study of 344 women-owned businesses show experience, business skills, and personal factors did affect the future growth of women-owned enterprises. For the woman entrepreneur establishing a venture, previous experience in the field of the venture, financial skills, strength in dealing with people, and idea generation combined with market opportunity motivation were keys to survival. In addition, ability to organize and plan, as well as the educational field of study, were contributing factors to the growth of women-owned enterprises. The antecedent influences of the successful woman entrepreneur were similar to those of successful male entrepreneurs, with the factors contributing to success and survival being the same.

Nature of the study:	Empirical
Nature of the data:	Mail survey
Nature of the sample:	344 women business owners
Variables:	Individual characteristics, business skills, personal factors, business characteristics, growth

Bucar, B., & Hisrich, R.D. (2001). Ethics of business managers vs. entrepreneurs. *Journal of Developmental Entrepreneurship, 6* (1), 59-82.

This research uses a stakeholder perspective of ethical attitudes and standards, specifically, the theory of property, to provide answers to the following questions: 1) How will managers and entrepreneurs react in certain situations? 2) Will they have high ethical standards in their internal and external dealings? 3) Will managers, because of their more bureaucratic environment, have higher ethical standards than entrepreneurs? 4) Will entrepreneurs, because their business practices more closely reflect their personal values, have higher ethical attitudes than managers?

In general, entrepreneurs and managers differed only slightly in their views regarding the ethics of various activities and their ethical perceptions regarding others. There were few differences in the two groups regarding their evaluation of the ethical nature of 12 circumstances and seven scenarios. The similarities in ethical attitudes between the two groups of decision-makers, which can be explained by similar legal, cultural and educational factors that affect ethical attitudes of both groups, seem to be an important finding. However, some significant differences consistently indicated that entrepreneurs are more prone to hold ethical attitudes. Female entrepreneurs and managers were slightly more ethical than their male counterparts, although results were not consistent across all ethical dilemmas.

Nature of the study:	Empirical
Nature of the data:	Detached measuring instrument containing binary, response questions, scenarios, and comprehensive demographic information
Nature of the sample:	165 entrepreneurs and 128 managers
Variables:	Personal characteristics (education, sex, age, income, formal course in ethics, industry experience, professional experience), size of enterprise managed (number of employees, sales), ethical perceptions

Burr, S. G., & Strickland, M. (1992). Creating a positive business climate for women: An approach to small business development. *Economic Development Review, 10* (1), 63-66.

This paper discusses a small business development approach to creating a positive business climate for women in Wisconsin. The authors argue that talented women offer states and communities an avenue for further economic development. They posit that a constructive attitude from business and political leaders towards women business owners will positively affect local economies. Wisconsin has shown that a serious business development program directed towards women produces economic growth. On the premise that state and local development officials are interested to know which services are important to small firms, Wisconsin's Office of Women's Business Ownership surveyed 70,000 women-owned businesses, receiving a response rate of 13.4%. Respondents were asked about a variety of subjects, including trade, procurement, growth, and company demographics. Descriptive statistics show that women were successful in procuring government contracts and were growing their businesses, but were not significantly active in foreign trade. Results show that the government's attitude towards women-owned businesses was as important as tax structure. Avoidance of stereotyping is important to growth of women-owned businesses.

Nature of the study:	Empirical
Nature of the data:	Mail survey
Nature of the sample:	669 Dun & Bradstreet list of women-owned businesses in Wisconsin
Variables:	Business climate, government procurement, business growth, foreign trade, management priorities, financing

Buttner, E. H., Rosen B (1992). Rejection in the loan application process: Male and female entrepreneurs' perceptions and subsequent intentions. *Journal of Small Business Management, 30* (1), 58-65.

This study builds on previous work by this author that examines gender bias in capital acquisition by women business owners. Three hypotheses were developed that suggested bank loan officers did not discriminate against women seeking debt financing. The t-test analyses compared male and female entrepreneurs' expectations about the difficulty of securing start-up loans, perceptions of bankers' evaluation criteria, attributions about rejection and subsequent intentions, and differences in the response to bank loan rejections. Although female entrepreneurs complained of discrimination by bank officials in funding decisions for start up businesses, stating that bank officers viewed them as lacking important entrepreneurial characteristics (leadership, autonomy, readiness for change etc, the analyses fail to support this argument. The findings indicate that women more easily relate rejection of loans to gender bias than men do. The author concludes that gender differences may be based on bankers' and venture capitalists' perceptions and stereotypes rather than reality.

Nature of the study:	Empirical
Nature of the data:	Mail survey
Nature of the sample:	108 male and female entrepreneurs
Variables:	Individual characteristics, factors important to obtaining debt financing (11 item scale), strategies utilized to obtain outside financing (10 approaches), business demographics

Buttner, E. H. (1993). Female entrepreneurs: How far have they come? *Business Horizons, 36* (2), 59-65.

This article summarizes the experiences of entrepreneurial women in North America over the past 20 years, drawing from empirical literature. The article raises discussion questions regarding the uniqueness, success, characteristics, sex-role stereotypes of women entrepreneurs, resources that are available in women's entrepreneurial networks, and work-family conflict experienced by women entrepreneurs. The article compares men and women across these dimensions, suggesting that although these are "obstacles" women must overcome, as women gain experience, build their networks, and establish credibility, their success and longevity will rival their male colleagues and the obstacles will diminish. Women could benefit from supportive male colleagues who might provide advice, information, and resources.

Nature of the study: Conceptual
Nature of the data: NA
Nature of the sample: NA
Variables: Uniqueness, success, characteristics, sex-role stereotypes of women entrepreneurs, resources that are available in women's entrepreneurial networks, and work-family conflict experienced by women entrepreneurs

Buttner, E. H. (2001). Examining female entrepreneurs' management style: An application of a relational frame. *Journal of Business Ethics, 29* (3), 253-270.

This paper builds on previous research about women's management styles and strategies. Anchored in relational theory which posits that women's inner sense of connection to others is a central organizing feature of women's development (Miller, 1976), this study presents results from focus groups of 129 women-owned businesses selected by a convenience method. Qualitative analysis of comments indicated that the women used a relational approach in working with employees and clients. Relational skills included preserving, mutual empowering, achieving, and creating teams. Findings demonstrated that relational theory is a useful frame for identifying and explicating women entrepreneurs' interactive style in their own businesses. Women entrepreneurs using a relational approach with their employees and clients appeared to be using strategies and skills well suited for a more highly educated work force in the new millennium.

Nature of the study: Empirical
Nature of the data: Focus group
Nature of the sample: 129 women business owners from 7 states
Variables: Individual characteristics, dimensions of relational psychology (preserving, mutually empowering, achieving, creating team)

Buttner, E. H., & Moore, D. P. (1997). Women's organizational exodus to entrepreneurship: Self-reported motivations and correlates with success. *Journal of Small Business Management, 35* (1), 34-46.

This study briefly reviews past research on women business owners and asks why women are motivated to start their own ventures. The study focuses on the career aspirations of women in organizations, especially their impact on balancing family and career. A convenience sample of 129 middle level managers participated in focus groups to explore why they left large organizations to become entrepreneurs and how they measured their success. Findings showed entrepreneurial motivations included the desire for challenge and self-determination and the desire to balance family and work responsibilities. Women also left large organizations due to discrimination and organizational dynamics. Self-fulfillment and goal achievement were the primary measures of success, as opposed to monetary (capital) profitability. The authors conclude that factors influencing departure from prior organizations were associated with measures of personal success. Future research directions are suggested.

Nature of the study:	Empirical
Nature of the data:	Focus group
Nature of the sample:	129 women business owners from seven states
Variables:	Individual characteristics, reasons for leaving prior organizations

Buttner, E. H., & Rosen, B. (1988). Bank loan officers' perceptions of characteristics of men, women and successful entrepreneurs. *Journal of Business Venturing, 3* (3), 249-258.

This paper presents anecdotal evidence suggesting that women, compared to similarly situated men, have difficulty securing financing for entrepreneurial endeavors. The authors argue that there is also a tendency to view women in managerial roles in terms of sex stereotypes rather than by their accomplishments. This study investigated whether female entrepreneurs were also viewed in terms of sex stereotypes. Respondents were presented with a business plan and videotape of an interview between a male or female entrepreneur and a loan officer. Actors were employed for this simulation. One hundred and six bank loan officers evaluated entrepreneurs on scales assessing nine attributes of successful entrepreneurs. Sixty-nine undergraduate business students completed the same assessment. It was hypothesized that sex stereotypes influenced perceptions that women, compared to men, did not possess the characteristics necessary for successful entrepreneurship. The results confirmed the hypothesis that characteristics attributed to successful entrepreneurs were more commonly ascribed to men than to women. Mode of presentation did not affect funding decisions, but loan officers were more impartial when only the business plan was evaluated. Loan officers were consistently more conservative than students in their evaluations. The results were also consistent with anecdotal evidence of the difficulties female entrepreneurs encounter in securing working capital. Implications for development of bank officer training materials that reduce sex biases are suggested.

Nature of the study:	Empirical
Nature of the data:	Simulation
Nature of the sample:	60 male and 46 female loan officers of medium-sized southeastern banking institution; 69 undergraduate business students at a large southeastern university
Variables:	Entrepreneurial demographics, entrepreneurial qualities (leadership, autonomy, propensity to take risks, readiness for change, endurance, lack of emotionalism, low need for support, low conformity, and persuasiveness), likelihood of granting a $50,000 loan, likelihood of making a counter-offer of a smaller amount, size of counteroffer

Buttner, E. H., & Rosen, B. (1989). Funding new business ventures: Are decision makers biased against women entrepreneurs? *Journal of Business Venturing, 4* (4), 249-261.

The premise of this study is to explore gender stereotypes of men and women entrepreneurs as perceived by bank loan officers. Loan officers usually make funding decisions on the basis of information gathered from an interview and a business plan. The authors set out to explore the extent to which stereotypes held true as regards these two funding criteria. Questions considered include: 1) Did mode of presentation--business plan versus business plan with interview--increase the male or female entrepreneur's probability of successfully obtaining a business loan? 2) What was the effect of the decision maker's previous experience on funding decisions (i.e., experienced loan officers)?

The study finds no evidence that sex stereotypes influenced business funding decisions. Loan officers made larger counteroffers to females compared to males when they read the business plan and watched the interview. However, women were perceived by loan officers as less entrepreneurial than men. One implication of the findings is that females should seek opportunities to meet with loan officers to present their business proposals. In an interview, they have the opportunity to address questions of motivation and competence.

Nature of the study:	Empirical
Nature of the data:	Mail survey
Nature of the sample:	60 male and 46 female loan officers of medium-sized southeastern banking institution
Variables:	Perceptions of personality characteristics of women and

men, perceptions of personality characteristics of successful entrepreneurs, leadership attributes (Sexton & Bowman's nine-item scale, 1986)

Caputo, R. K., & Dolinsky, A. (1998). Women's choice to pursue self-employment: The role of financial and human capital of household members. *Journal of Small Business Management, 36* (3), 8-17.

This study uses data from the National Longitudinal Study of Labor Market Experience (NLSLME) to investigate the effects of the financial and human capital resources available to a woman in her household on her choice between entrepreneurship and wage employment. The study found that 1) although higher levels of the husbands' earnings from self-employment greatly increased the likelihood of the women being self-employed, the husbands' earnings from wages had no impact; 2) the husbands' business knowledge and experience greatly affected the self-employment status of the women; 3) the presence of young children and the husbands' provision of child care also affected the self-employment status of the women; 4) marital status per se had no impact on women's employment choices; and 5) there were no potential financial and human capital effects for other adults in the household. The authors concluded that role flexibility and other factors play an important role in motivating self-employment choice for women entrepreneurs.

Nature of the study: Empirical
Nature of the data: National Longitudinal Survey of Labor Market Experience for 1988
Nature of the sample: 5,159 men and women self-employed
Variables: Individual characteristics, wages earned, household characteristics, child-care roles, financial capital, human capital, employment choice

Carter, N. M., & Allen, K. R. (1997). Size-determinants of women-owned businesses: Choice or barriers to resources. *Entrepreneurship and Regional Development, 9* (3), 211-220.

This study examined women-owned businesses (WOBs) in the adolescent stage of their life cycle to determine whether the size of WOBs is influenced by their owner's lifestyle intentions and choices or is linked directly to the resources that the entrepreneurs control. The results indicate that having access to financial resources and emphasizing the financial aspects of the business overwhelm the effects of the entrepreneur's lifestyle intention or choice on their chances for having large businesses. For practitioners, the results suggest that women entrepreneurs need to understand the nature of firms in their industry to discover new financial resources that will help them to develop their companies. On a policy level, the research suggests that programs geared towards preparing potential entrepreneurs should focus more on the skills and behaviors that facilitate growth, specifically in the financial management arena.

Nature of the study:	Empirical
Nature of the data:	National Association's of Women Business Owners mail survey
Nature of the sample:	502 women-owned businesses, started by respondents within preceding 2-8 years
Variables:	Choice intention, human capital, financial resources, size of business (gross sales), age of business

Carter, N. M., Williams, M., & Reynolds P.D. (1997). Discontinuance among new firms in retail: The influence of initial resources, strategy and gender. *Journal of Business Venturing, 12* (2), 125-145.

Research in social psychology argues that strategic choice is shaped by experiences to which individuals have been subjected and that females and males have fundamentally different socialization experiences. This study examined whether the performance differences in women-owned and men-owned businesses can be explained by variations in initial resources and founding strategy. Hypotheses tested whether women have fewer start-up resources and, if they do, whether they can compensate for these deficiencies through their founding strategy. The assumption guiding the hypotheses was that the strategy women owners adopt may exploit the unique capabilities they derive from their socialization and improve the performance of their firms, warding off discontinuance. The results offer support for using an integrative model to explain performance. Women-owned firms have higher odds of discontinuing and appear to have fewer resources at start-up. Women owners were less likely than their male counterparts to have instrumental experience from working in the retail industry and tended to start their businesses on a smaller scale. They were no less likely to have access to credit from formal financial institutions. Despite some apparent situational disadvantage, resource deficiencies appear to affect the odds of women-owned businesses discontinuing less than they do men-owned initiatives. The findings indicate support for the supposition that women owners can use founding strategy to decrease the odds of discontinuing business.

Nature of the study:	Empirical
Nature of the data:	Mail survey, telephone verification
Nature of the sample:	203 retail firms listed in Dun's Market Identifier files that between one to six years just before the survey
Variables:	Human capital, financial capital, firm strategy, firm size, gender, survival of business, age of business

Carter, S., & Rosa, P. (1998). The financing of male and female owned-business. *Entrepreneurship and Regional Development, 10* (3), 225-241.

Whether female entrepreneurs are disadvantaged in financing their businesses has been an important policy theme within the gender and enterprise literature. The question remains controversial, as different methodological approaches yield contradictory results. A particular challenge is how to best move from exploratory research to more rigorous methods to separate gender differences from other causative agents. This paper presents new data on the sources and uses of finance by male and female proprietors. The research was part of a three-year study on the impact of gender on small business management. The results show gender differences in certain areas of business financing. Intra-sectoral similarities demonstrate that gender is only one of a number of variables that affect the financing process. Men used significantly larger amounts of capital than women when starting their businesses. The differences found in the size of start-up investment may indicate that female-owned firms will suffer long-term disadvantage as a consequence of under-funding. Women, while similar to men in the use of personal finance, were less prone to use institutional finance such as overdrafts, bank loans, and supplier credit. Factors associated with refusal of capital for men were business sector and educational attainment. For women, refusal was related to their business track record/experience and domestic circumstances.

Nature of the study:	Empirical
Nature of the data:	Mail survey
Nature of the sample:	600 British businesses (300 male-owned, 300 female-owned) in variety of industries
Variables:	Gender, firm age, owner's age, ownership structure, firm size, industry sector, education & training, number and age of children, decision assistance, association membership, prior business experience, financial assets, sources of start-up capital and investment, use of guarantees, ongoing business financing, relationship with lenders

Chaganti, R. (1986). Management in women-owned enterprises. *Journal of Small Business Management, 24* (4), 18-29.

The study contrasts two conceptual models of strategic management in women-owned enterprises: feminine and entrepreneurial. The feminine model posits that women behave differently as entrepreneurs and managers. In contrast, the entrepreneurial model is derived from the assumption that female and male leaders are similar. An exploratory study was used to test whether the models fit the strategic management patterns of women-owned enterprises. Results indicate that successful women-owned enterprises resemble the entrepreneurial model, but this managerial style may be more "feminine" among women entrepreneurs. The study also notes that more women than men were venturing into small businesses, and that the survival rate of their businesses was comparable to those of men-owned enterprises. The authors conclude that large-sample research would be needed to more firmly establish the configurations of strategic elements in successful women-owned enterprises.

Nature of the study: Empirical
Nature of the data: Case profiles developed from face-to-face interviews
Nature of the sample: Eight female entrepreneurs from Pennsylvania whose ventures reached at least break-even level
Variables: Nature of business, age of firm, previous experience, reasons for starting, values, strategies, performance, strategic management style

Chaganti, R., DeCarolis, D., & Deeds, D. (1995). Predictors of capital structure in small ventures. *Entrepreneurship Theory and Practice, 20* (2), 7-18.

This study empirically analyzes financing decisions of small ventures to identify the key determinants of their capital structure. Data was collected in the 1985, 1986, 1987 surveys of members of the National Federation of Independent Business. Six categories of predictors were included in the analysis: goal orientation of the entrepreneur, business outlook for the enterprise, stock of human capital input, strategic changes made, sex of the owner, and life-stage of the enterprise. The study reports that goal orientation, especially the respondents' satisfaction with the business satisfying their economic needs, and the respondents' estimation of the odds of success of the business were among the most important determinants of equity versus debt and internal equity versus external equity financing. Interestingly, the sex of the owner was not an issue in predicting equity versus debt financing. However female owners tended to prefer internal sources of equity versus external sources.

Nature of the study: Empirical
Nature of the data: Mail survey
Nature of the sample: 1,127 (903 responding) National Federation of Independent Business members
Variables: Owner's goals related to challenge, legacy, economic or lifestyle needs; business outlook concerning success for the firm or others' firms; number of hours worked by owner; number of hours worked by family members; number of partners; strategic change related to volume, scale, product line changes, etc.; owner sex; newness of business; equity, debt, internal sources of equity, external sources of equity

Chaganti, R., & Parasuraman, S. (1996). A study of the impact of gender on business performance and management patterns in small businesses. *Entrepreneurship Theory and Practice, 21* (2), 73-75.

This study adds to the extensive comparative research on management patterns in women-owned businesses (WOB) by examining gender differences in firm performance, goals, strategies, and management practices simultaneously. The results indicate that men and women entrepreneurs are similar on prior start-up experience, managerial experience, and parental ownership of business, but differ on the number of years of industry experience. Additionally, women-owned businesses had significantly smaller annual sales and employment growth, but return on assets was similar to that achieved in men-owned businesses. Women business owners rated achievement and financial goals higher and were more likely to develop strategies that emphasized product quality. They were no less likely to emphasize customization, or cost efficiency than men. The discussion compares the study results with those of prior research.

Nature of the study:	Empirical
Nature of the data:	Mail survey
Nature of the sample:	194 male-owned businesses and 178 female-owned businesses listed with Dun's Marketing Services with 4-99 employees and located in northeastern U.S
Variables:	Owner's gender, goals, strategies, management practice, firm performance (sales growth, ROA), prior industry experience, firm size (employees), industry sector

Chan, S. Y & Foster, M. J. (2001). Strategy formulation in small business: The Hong Kong experience. *International Small Business Journal, 19* (3), 56-71.

The nature of strategy formation in small businesses in Hong Kong during the mid-1990s is examined in this study. Development of the hypotheses was guided by a three-part process model that specified the recognition for need for strategic thought, undertaking a strategic audit, and strategic evaluation and choice. Findings reveal that strategy planning is a highly contextual activity. Respondents' planning orientation was both proactive and reactive. Owner-managers were much more likely to rely on internal and personal networks as information sources rather than consult with outside experts, although the overwhelming majority used only sketchy data collection and analysis as the basis for key decisions. Respondents relied extensively on family members, subordinates ("honorary family members"), and outsiders in the respondents' personal network. This collectivist approach is described as a typical reflection of Chinese culture. Gender, education level, and industry experience had no significant effect on most phases of the strategy development process. Women, however, relied more closely on their immediate network/channels for information search than men did.

Nature of the study:	Empirical
Nature of the data:	Mail survey
Nature of the sample:	Questionnaires mailed to 245 owner-managers, members of the Hong Kong Owner-Managers Association. After follow-up phone calls and letters, 44 usable responses returned (18%).
Variables:	Strategy development (strategic need, strategic planning information, strategy formulation, planning involvement), owner-manager and firm characteristics (sex, education, industry experience, managerial position, age, business type, industrial sector, firm age, firm size (employees, sales))

Chell, E., & Baines, S. (1998). Does gender affect business 'performance'? A study of micro-businesses in business services in the U.K. *Entrepreneurship and Regional Development, 10* (2), 117-135.

This study examines the influence of business owners' gender on firm performance by testing whether women's orientation to business differed from men's. Questions of interest include whether women typically adopt an "integrated approach" to their business, whether men tend to operate as if their business/economic lives are separate from their domestic/personal lives, and whether cultural presuppositions of women's and men's roles affect firm performance. The results indicate little support for the supposition that men and women have totally different and distinctive orientations toward business. There were no significant differences in the performance of female sole-owned and male sole-owned businesses in the business services sector, although spouse-owned businesses appear to perform relatively poorly.

Nature of the study:	Empirical
Nature of the data:	Telephone interviews, followed by semi-structured questionnaire administered face-to-face
Nature of the sample:	104 owner-managers (54 from Newcastle, 50 from Milton Keynes, Great Britain) Ninety-four percent of the respondents were business founders with 0-9 employees, business more than two years old, contrasting urban locations; 17 interviews carried out with founder and at least one other person in the firm
Variables:	Owner's gender, form of ownership, business age, business size, firm performance, business turnover, growth orientation, integration of business and family, men's and women's roles in business performance, domestic division of labor, size of business, business sector

Chrisman, J. J., Carsrud, A. L., DeCastro, J., & Heron, L. (1990). A comparison of assistance needs of male and female pre-venture entrepreneurs. *Journal of Business Venturing, 5* (4), 235-248.

The study compares a sample of male and female aspiring entrepreneurs in terms of the problems they encountered during the start-up process, assistance they received from outside advisors, the value of the consulting, and whether the advisory service predicted subsequent start-up activity. Four types of assistance--strategic, administrative, operating, and marketing -- were evaluated. Results indicate that males and females seeking assistance from SBDCs were virtually in terms of the amount of assistance they required and the diversity of their needs. Similarly, there were virtually no differences in their assessment of the value of the consulting. The fact that the proportion of consulted female clients was statistically equal to the proportion of new businesses operated by women also refutes the notion that general assistance programs such as the SBDC are not equally accessible to both sexes. The finding that the proportion of female start-ups was significantly higher than the proportional representation in their region is also seen as supporting this conclusion.

Nature of the study:	Empirical
Nature of the data:	Two mail surveys, telephone follow-ups
Nature of the sample:	162 (94 males, 68 females) clients of Small Business Development Center program in a southern state; 100 clients (61.7%) subsequently started a business
Variables:	Respondent sex, types and amount of assistance, perceived value of the assistance, propensity to start a venture after receiving outsider assistance, industry sector

Clain, S. H. (2000). Gender differences in full-time self-employment. *Journal of Economics and Business, 52* (6), 499-513.

This study investigates gender differences in the propensity for self-employment (vs. wage-and-salary employment) and in the levels of earnings for type of employment. It was assumed that people choose between wage-and-salary employment and self-employment to maximize expected utility. Econometric techniques revealed a gender gap in employment earnings. Women who chose self-employment had personal characteristics that were less highly valued by the marketplace than women who chose wage-and-salary employment. The reverse was true for men. The differences appeared to be related to personal characteristics. Being white and married tended to h᠆ ᠆ a negative impact on the earnings of self-employed women, whereas it ᠆ positive impact on the earnings of self-employed men. Aging tended to ᠆ce the earnings of self-employed men while eroding the earnings of ᠆nployed women. Although the self-employment earnings of both men ᠆ men fell short of their wage-and-salary income, the magnitude of the ᠆ was greater for women. The observed gender differences suggested that women might place a higher value on non-wage aspects of self-employment than men.

Nature of the study:	Empirical
Nature of the data:	Archival
Nature of the sample:	38,015 employed men and 26,667 employed women; 4,025 men and 1,377 women were self-employed. Criteria: age – 65 years old or younger; work at least 35 hrs per week and at least 40 weeks per year; occupation – nonmilitary, nonagricultural
Variables:	Choice of type of employment, income, age, gender, race, marital status, education, occupation, geographical location, health, fluency in English language, presence of one's own children in the household, local market activity, productivity, individual tastes, opportunities

Cliff, J. E. (1998). Does one size fit all? Exploring the relationship between attitudes towards growth, gender, and business size. *Journal of Business Venturing, 13* (6), 523-542.

In an effort to explain why businesses headed by women tend to be smaller in size than those led by men, this study examines entrepreneurs' attitudes toward business growth. Liberal and social feminist theories are used to support hypotheses that female entrepreneurs are less likely to state positive growth intentions. Females were expected to have fewer resources for business expansion, a scarcity that would explain the weaker intentions they placed on growth. Similarly, female entrepreneurs were expected to attach less value to business expansion. The results fail to fully support the hypotheses. Although female participants had less prior business ownership experience and less freedom from domestic responsibilities and were less likely to measure success by the size of their firms, they were just as likely as male participants to desire to grow their businesses. Content analyses of open-ended responses suggest that female entrepreneurs are more likely to establish maximum business size and that these thresholds are smaller than those set by their male counterparts. Female entrepreneurs also seemed more concerned about the risks associated with fast-paced growth and tended to deliberately adopt a slow and steady rate of expansion. For female entrepreneurs, personal considerations appeared to override economic considerations in the business expansion decision. These findings may have important implications for policy-makers, financial capital providers, researchers, and entrepreneurs.

Nature of the study:	Empirical
Nature of the data:	Structured, personal interviews, typically on participant's business premises
Nature of the sample:	229 business owners (141 businesses headed by men and 88 businesses headed by women in the Greater Vancouver area

Variables: of British Columbia, Canada
Gender, resources available for expansion (business education, management experience, industry experience, prior business ownership experience, level of household responsibilities), value placed on growth, growth intentions

Cole, R. A., & Wolken, J. D. (1995). Financial services used by small businesses: Evidence from the 1993 National Survey of Small Business Finance. *Federal Reserve Bulletin, 81* (7), 629-667.

This paper reports preliminary findings regarding the characteristics of the U.S. population of small businesses--firms with fewer than 500 employees-- and their use of credit and other financial services. The main purposes of the survey were to provide information on the use of credit by small and minority-owned firms and to create a general-purpose database on the finances of such firms. The 1993 National Survey of Small Business Finances (NSSBF) collected information on the availability and use of credit by small and minority-owned businesses. Twenty two percent of small businesses were majority-owned by females, 72% by males, and the remaining 6% by males and females equally. Female-owned and minority-owned firms had some characteristics in common that distinguished these two groups from the general population of small businesses. They were somewhat smaller and younger than other firms and more concentrated in the business services industry. They were less likely to be in the construction and mining, primary manufacturing, other manufacturing, and insurance and real estate industries. Female-owned firms had minority owners more often than did male-owned firms, and minority-owned businesses had female owners more often than did non-minority-owned firms. Female-owned firms (as well as the general small business population) were more likely to be organized as S corporations than were minority-owned firms. There was also higher concentration of minority-owned businesses in urban areas.

The preliminary statistics summarized in this article suggest interesting behavior patterns and differences in the use of credits by small businesses. Firm size was a dominant factor in determining the types of financial services that small businesses used. For example, the use of credit lines, loans, and capital leases differed somewhat by sex, race, and ethnicity. Some of these differences may be attributed to size, however. Small businesses differed in their use of financial management services by minority status, but not by sex, of the majority owner. The study also found slight differences in the use of trade credit by female-owned and minority owned firms. The use of non-depository financial services differed by race, ethnicity, and sex of the majority owner. However, the use of depository institutions showed few differences. Finally, differences in the use of trade credit were greater for race than for ethnicity and sex.

Nature of the study:	Empirical
Nature of the data:	1993 National Survey of Small Business Finances (NSSBF)
Nature of the sample:	Small and minority-owned businesses
Variables:	Types and sources of financial services, employment, financial data, firm characteristics, demographic characteristics of primary owner

Coleman, S. (2000). Access to capital and terms of credit: A comparison of men- and women-owned small businesses. *Journal of Small Business Management, 38* (3), 37-52.

The study compares access to capital for men- and women-owned small businesses. Findings reveal that women-owned businesses were significantly smaller, newer, and less likely to use external financing as a source of capital than were those owned by men. Lenders did not appear to discriminate against women on the basis of gender in giving them access to capital. Rather, they discriminated on the basis of firm size, preferring to lend to larger and more established firms. This preference may put women owned firms at a disadvantage, given that on average they are half the size of men-owned firms. The study also examined the terms under which women obtained credit to determine whether they were at a relative disadvantage. Findings revealed that women-owned firms paid higher interest rates for their most recent loans than men-owned firms did and that they were subjected to higher collateral requirements. Taken together, the results suggested that women obtain credit under less favorable terms than men. This difference may affect women's willingness to seek out external credit as well as their perceptions of its availability.

Nature of the study:	Empirical
Nature of the data:	1993 National Survey of Small Businesses survey conducted by the Federal Reserve Board and the U.S. Small Business Administration followed by a telephone survey
Nature of the sample:	Stratified random sample of privately owned small businesses (3,797 men-owned and 840 women owned small businesses) with fewer than 500 employees
Variables:	Gender of the owner, organizational form, SIC classification, bank loans, bank credit products, age and size of the business

Collerette, P., & Aubry, P. G. (1990). Socio-economic evolution of women business owners in Quebec (1987). *Journal of Business Ethics, 9* (4/5), 417-422.

This article presents a descriptive study of female entrepreneurs in Quebec, drawing a general portrait of the female entrepreneur and examining certain features that had not been extensively studied in the past: age, family status, size and type of business, partnerships, motivation, obstacles, financing, and income evolution. The first phase of the study, completed in 1986, drew a profile of the various personal, psychological, and entrepreneurial characteristics of the Quebec female entrepreneur. This study, and the follow-up done in 1987, had two objectives: to examine in more detail some of the characteristics that emerged from 1986 study, and to determine certain trends in the changing situation of the female entrepreneur. The findings suggest that the portrait and the style of the Quebec female entrepreneur had changed; her business was becoming more firmly established and she was gaining self-confidence. She also seemed to be cautious when starting up her business and kept a salaried job for some time before devoting herself full time to her business. She put as much money as possible into increasing her level of equity. This process usually lasted 1-5 years. She appeared to be somewhat uncomfortable when using credit to finance her business. She did not exhibit the desire to take a risk. Rather, she displayed ambition, determination, and a desire for autonomy. The use of a role model appeared to be an important means of learning and finally, she continued to encounter difficulty in combining family and career.

Nature of the study:	Empirical
Nature of the data:	Mail survey
Nature of the sample:	917 businesswomen in the 1986 study and 303 of which in the 1987 follow-up study.
Variables:	Sales volume, gross personal income, change in difficulty in finding money, debt/equity ratio of the business, change in level of debt

Cook, R. G., Belliveau, P., & VonSeggern, K. L. (2001, December). A case study of microenterprise training: Beta test findings and suggestions for improvement. *Journal of Developmental Entrepreneurship, 6* (3), 255-267.

The purpose of this research was to evaluate a specific MEP (Micro-enterprise Program) that was restructured to better serve women and minority entrepreneurs. The MEP was concerned with creating business plans to gain access to lenders for possible funding. The study examines a new curriculum designed for this MEP from the perspective of both graduates and non-graduates. The assessment of the curriculum revealed a number of important findings. Attendance and the effort spent in completing homework assignments made a difference as to whether a participant graduated or not, with on-time homework completion being the more important of the two factors. The research suggests that failure to complete the program was more likely to be a function of personal circumstances that interfered with the ability to attend class and complete the homework on time, rather than problems with program elements. The article suggests improvements in the curriculum.

Nature of the study:	Empirical
Nature of the data:	Survey data captured through questionnaire

Nature of the sample: 107 students (54 graduates and 53 non-graduates) from
                          micro-enterprise training institute established by State
                          Economic Development Agency in New Jersey

Variables: Hours spent per week on homework, quality of textbook,
                          course quality, instructor knowledge and preparedness,
                          percentage attending classes, percentage completing all
                          homework assignments

Cooper, A. C., & Artz, K. W. (1995). Determinants of satisfaction for entrepreneurs.
    Journal of Business Venturing, 10 (6), 439-457.

> This study uses discrepancy theory to examine the determinants of
> entrepreneur satisfaction in the third year of business ownership. The
> premise of the study is that individual satisfaction is determined, in part, by
> whether there is a gap between rewards or performance and the individual's
> goals or expectations. The study finds that satisfaction of entrepreneurs
> emphasizing economic goals was lower than entrepreneurs with non-
> economic goals such as "to do a kind of work I wanted to do."
> Entrepreneurs' initial expectations were positively (not negatively) related to
> the levels of satisfaction realized. This finding is in direct conflict with the
> expectation-reality gap. Contrary to discrepancy theory, women who had
> higher initial expectations were more satisfied later. This may suggest that
> attitudes are, in part, a function of stable individual traits. Women who had a
> positive view of their initial prospects later viewed the experience of
> business ownership more favorably, regardless of subsequent performance.
> The higher levels of satisfaction may reflect a view that they have fewer
> attractive alternatives; it may also be that they discover greater relative
> satisfaction from the day-to-day aspects of business ownership. For
> entrepreneurs and advisors, the findings suggest that particular goals,
> attitudes, and backgrounds are likely to be associated with greater
> satisfaction. For researchers, the study provides insight into discrepancy
> theory by considering its application to entrepreneurs rather than employees
> normally studied.

Nature of the study: Empirical
Nature of the data: Mail survey

Nature of the sample: New businesses (1985, 1986, 1987); 287 (20% women, 4%
                          minorities) owners-managers and members of National
                          Federation of Independent Businesses

Variables: Goal, expectations, age, gender, minority status, satisfaction,
                          takeout (money "draw")

Cooper Maysami, R., & Goby, V. P. (1999). Female business owners in Singapore and elsewhere: A review of studies. *Journal of Small Business Management, 37* (2), 96-105.

This article reviews the literature to assess what motivates women, and Singaporean women in particular, to set up their ventures. Also addressed are various factors contributing to the success of female business owners in Singapore and the problems they may face. Finally, the article examines the business and personal profile of Singaporean female business owners and compares such characteristics to those from other countries. Studies of female owners/managers in Singapore and elsewhere showed remarkably similar results. They started their businesses to become their own bosses and were determined to make the business into a profitable venture. They were mostly well educated, had prior work experience, and enjoyed the support of family in managing the business and coping with the demands of running the business. Having their own business provided them with more freedom and flexibility, which helped them meet the combined responsibilities of family and work. Women business owners generally set up small service and retail industries, since such industries require less initial capital and less technology. For start-up capital, most of them used their personal savings and loans from family and friends rather than bank loans. They faced problems such as work-home conflict, lack of finance and marketing skills, social problems, and competition from others. Many of them were successful, and they mostly attributed their success to personal qualities such as self-discipline, perseverance, and hard work. Also contributing to success were attending business courses, training programs, and education, as well as family support and having a good relationship with people inside and outside their organizations.

Nature of the study:	Empirical
Nature of the data:	Case studies
Nature of the sample:	Women business owners in Asia (Singapore), Canada, Australia, and the U.S.
Variables:	Personal characteristics, major motivating factors, major problems, factors that contribute to success

Covin, T. J. (1994). Perceptions of family-owned firms: The impact of gender and educational level. *Journal of Small Business Management, 32* (3), 29-39.

The prevalence of family-owned firms suggests they represent a substantial career opportunity for university students. This study examines undergraduate and graduate students' perceptions of family-owned firms and whether the perceptions varied by gender and educational level. The findings indicate that students held positive perceptions of managers and employees in family-owned firms but believed that such firms offered limited opportunities for non-family employees. Education level had a significant impact on perceptions of family-owned firms. The graduate students in the sample generally viewed family firms in less favorable light than did undergraduate students. Graduate students viewed family firms to be less competitive, lacking formal procedures, and following policies that provide limited opportunities for non-family members. Gender did not have a significant influence on perceptions of family-owned firms.

Nature of the study:	Empirical
Nature of the data:	Survey data from open-end questionnaire
Nature of the sample:	115 undergraduate, 110 graduate students in upper level business management classes at a large (12,000 students) state college in the Southwest United States,124 males and 101 females, average age 22.3 (undergraduate) and 31.3 (graduate)
Variables:	Sex, educational level, preference for family business employment, family business issues (attributes of family-owned firm employees, competitive weaknesses of family-owned firms, formal performance policies, favoritism in family-owned firms, opportunities for non-family contributions, attributes of managers in family-owned firms), years of full time work experience, previous experience working in a family-owned firm

Cowling, M., & Taylor, M. (2001). Entrepreneurial women and men: Two different species? *Small Business Economics, 16* (3), 167-175

This study identifies differences in the personal and demographic characteristics of women and men in the United Kingdom in four potential labor market states: unemployment, waged employment, single self-employment, and job-creating self-employment. It considers labor market trends in the period 1991-1995. Key findings include: women entrepreneurs are better educated than their male counterparts and considerably less likely to flow in and out of self-employment. Three times as many men as women who were single self-employed in 1991 went on to become job creating self-employed by 1995. The authors' interpretation of this finding is that mature males with more life experience have accumulated more of the human capital essential for business survival and growth.

Nature of the study:	Empirical
Nature of the data:	British Household Panel Survey, 5th Wave. (5,500 households and 9,000 individuals residing in Britain)
Nature of the sample:	Men and women active in the labor market at time of survey
Variables:	Demographics (age, sex, location), education, marital status, children, personal wealth, profession, employment state, prior employment history

Cromie, S., & Birley, S. (1992). Networking by female business owners in Northern Ireland. *Journal of Business Venturing, 7* (3), 237-251.

Using a modified version of the personal contact network instrument developed by Aldrich, Rosen, and Woodward (1987), the authors collected data on the size, diversity, density, and effectiveness of the networks of male and female entrepreneurs in Northern Ireland, in an attempt to discover whether the personal contact networks of women are significantly different from those of men. The results indicate that, with the exception of the gender of the individuals in the personal contact network, female networks were remarkably similar to those of men. For example, women were just as active as men in their networking, their personal contact networks were as diverse as those of men, and they were no more likely to consult family and friends than men were. However, analysis of the cross ties shows that the females tended to rely heavily upon a male colleague as their prime contact but to revert to their own sex for other contacts. In contrast, their male colleagues relied almost entirely on members of their own sex for advice.

Nature of the study:	Empirical
Nature of the data:	Mail survey
Nature of the sample:	274 owner-managers from Northern Ireland
Variables:	Sex, age, marital status, current business situation, time known contact, propensity to network, networking activity, network diversity, cross ties, network density, work environment before starting business

Cuba, R., Decenzo D., & Anish, A. (1983). Management practices of successful female business owners. *American Journal of Small Business, 8* (2), 40-45.

Rejecting the use of personality, leadership, and structural theories to explain why female owners have relatively low levels of financial success, this research focuses on the preparation and daily activities performed by female business owners. The findings indicate three factors are significantly related to financial success: formal education, prior work experience, and the level of task delegation. Financially successful women owners delegated key tasks to employees, were more highly educated, and had more prior work experience than less successful females. The level of mental and physical effort and degree of participative management were not significant criteria for success. This research represents a pilot study intended to encourage future research.

Nature of the study:	Empirical
Nature of the data:	Mail survey
Nature of the sample:	58 women business-owners from Atlanta, Baltimore and Richmond
Variables:	Formal education, prior work experience, level of task delegation in use, financial success

Daily, C. M., Certo, S. T., & Dalton, D.R. (1999). Entrepreneurial ventures as an avenue to the top? Assessing the advancement of female CEOs and directors in the *Inc.* 100. *Journal of Developmental Entrepreneurship, 4* (1), 19-32.

This study examines whether increases in women's leadership experiences in business have paralleled their hiring as CEOs of high growth companies and/or their appointment to Board positions. The authors speculate that women had been gaining ground in middle management corporate positions that would qualify them for CEO positions in smaller growth companies and that women who owned their own businesses would be prime candidates for CEO at other new companies or as directors on boards. The findings reveal that over the 10-year period studied, women had made virtually no progress in ascending to the executive suite and boardrooms of high-growth companies (*Inc.* 100). No more women were serving on boards of directors or CEOs than they had 10 years earlier and there was little evidence that women were being groomed to succeed to CEO positions by serving as inside directors.

Nature of the study:	Empirical
Nature of the data:	Corporate reports filed with SEC
Nature of the sample:	1987 and 1996 Inc.100 firms, independent and publicly traded, with revenues in the year of selection which exceeded those of the previous year
Variables:	Percentage of firms with female directors, number of female directors, number of female CEOs, number of female inside directors, percentage of female outsize directors with corporate backgrounds, percentage of female affiliated directors, average board size

Dant, R. P., Brush, C. G., & Iniesta, F.P. (1996). Participating patterns of women in franchising. *Journal of Small Business Management, 34* (2), 14-28.

Franchising has long been touted as a means of providing opportunities to minorities and women. However, little documentation exists regarding the extent to which this early promise of franchising has been fulfilled. This study considers four questions related to women in franchising: 1) What was the overall pattern of women's participation as franchisors? 2) How was the pattern of women's participation related to the male/female image of the business sectors? 3) How was women's participation pattern related to the industry sectors? 4) How was women's participation pattern related to the size of the franchise systems? The results indicate that women had not yet adequately exploited the franchising route to business. A possible explanation for this finding is that many women-owned businesses were relatively young and therefore a large proportion might not have reached a growth point where franchising could be explored as a viable expansion vehicle. Alternatively, many of the new companies may have been inappropriate for a franchise. Finally, the authors speculate that women may be less aware of, or less attracted to, the franchising option because of their relative inexperience and their historically lower exposure to franchising.

Nature of the study: Empirical
Nature of the data: Mail survey
Nature of the sample: 2,592 franchise systems in North America
Variables: Image of industry (sector), size of franchise system, gender of the president of franchise system, gender of the person in the franchisor's organization, education level, participation rate of presidents and contact executives

Devine, T. J. (1994). Characteristics of self-employed women in the United States. *Monthly Labor Review, 117* (3), 20-34.

The author states that among the more striking aspects of the rise in self-employment has been the increased representation of women among the self-employed. As of 1975, women represented about one out of four self-employed workers. By 1990, they accounted for about one out of three. The research examines who these new self-employed women are and compares them to their wage-and-salary counterparts, their male contemporaries, and self-employed women of the past. The study presents an overview of the characteristics of self-employed women and other worker groups in 1975 and 1990, and discusses major similarities and differences among the groups. The findings reveal that one out of 15 employed women in all age categories and about one out of 10 of those over age 35 were self-employed in their main job in 1990, which appeared to be a part of an upward trend. The data for 1990 suggests that the "average self-employed woman" was older, more likely married, covered by someone else's health care policy, more than a high school graduate, in a managerial or administrative occupation, and worked either a relatively small number of hours or a relatively large number of hours per week, compared to the "average wage-and-salary woman." She was less likely to be black, about as likely to have young children, and, if married, more likely to have a self-employed husband. She also earned less money.

Nature of the study: Empirical
Nature of the data: Current Population Survey Census Data, March 1976, 1991
Nature of the sample: Civilians, aged 16 or older, employed in nonagricultural industries in their longest held jobs
Variables: Race, age, marital status, weeks worked and usual hours, education, occupation, female representation in the U.S. nonagricultural sector, wage/salary, industrial sector

Dolinsky, A. L., Caputo, R. K., Pasumarty, K., & Quazi, H. (1993). The effects of education on business ownership: A longitudinal study of women. *Entrepreneurship Theory and Practice, 18* (1), 43-53.

Drawing upon the theory of the disadvantaged worker, displacement theory, and liquidity constraint theory, this study examines dependence between the level of educational attainment and variations in the likelihood of women entering, sustaining, and re-entering self-employment. The researchers reasoned that self-employment can be integral to improving the status of the less educated and economically disadvantaged. National longitudinal data were used to examine the business ownership experience, an advantage over previous cross-sectional studies. The results support liquidity constraints theory but find the competing disadvantaged worker theory and displacement perspective to be less relevant. Findings indicate that the incidence of initial entry, continuous stayer, and reentry status increased with increasing levels of educational attainment. Less-educated women appeared to face financial or human capital constraints that limited their business pursuits. The results are seen as useful guidelines that could be used to improve the viability of self-employed business ownership for improving the well being of economically disadvantaged and less educated women.

Nature of the study:	Empirical
Nature of the data:	Census data from National Longitudinal Survey of Labor Market Experience (1967-1984)
Nature of the sample:	5,083 women aged 30-44 in 1967
Variables:	Time (years), educational attainment, initial entry into self-employment, continued survivorship in self-employment, re-entry in self-employment

Dolinsky, A. L., & Caputo, R. K. (1994). Long-term entrepreneurship patterns: A national study of black and white female entry and stayer status differences. *Journal of Small Business Management, 32* (1), 18-26.

Adopting a dynamic gross flow approach, the study investigates the long-term self-employment rate differences between black and white women. A decomposition methodology was employed to analyze black/white self-employment rate differences. The results indicated that many of the black/white rate differences in each of the survey years were due to the black women's limited probability of entry into entrepreneurship, which further translates into a limited pool of potential "stayers." The low black self-employment rate found in this study was surprising. Theories pertaining to entrepreneurs as disadvantaged workers would predict a relatively higher self-employment rate for blacks relative to whites. The researchers offer possible explanations for the anomaly: Asset limitations hinder blacks from entering into entrepreneurship and/or black entrepreneurs may encounter discrimination from consumers. The researchers suggest that one solution for increasing the probability of black women entering entrepreneurship would be for the government to increase the opportunities by further underwriting commercial banks, credit unions, state and community micro-loan funds, and other lending institutions and mechanisms that make start-up capital available.

Nature of the study: Empirical
Nature of the data: Census data from National Longitudinal Survey of Labor Market Experience (1967-1984)
Nature of the sample: 5,083 women aged 30-44 in 1967
Variables: Time (years), race, probability of entering entrepreneurship, probability of staying in entrepreneurship, population distribution

Dumas, C. (2001, August). Evaluating the outcomes of micro-enterprise Training for low income women: A case study. *Journal of Developmental Entrepreneurship, 6* (2), 97-128.

The purpose of this research is to document and evaluate the initial outcomes of a pilot program provided to participants in a Community Entrepreneurs Program (CEP), training and education program designed to prepare low-income women to start businesses. Results indicate that the training empowered participants to begin to achieve economic self-sufficiency, helped them to build strong business and develop life management skills, may influence the growth of locally controlled businesses, and helped create new jobs in the inner-city neighborhoods. Results also indicate the need for changes and improvements in the program, such as: revising the level of time spent developing the businesses; providing greater support in the form of additional mentoring, networking and workshops; composing classes with greater diversity; and providing greater access to computers and computer training.

Nature of the study: Empirical
Nature of the data: Interviews in focus groups
Nature of the sample: 55 participants in Community Entrepreneurs Program, Council for Women and Enterprise–Boston
Variables: Annual budget, funding, target population, area served, fee per course, mission statement, clients served

Du Reitz, A., & Henrekson, M. (2000). Testing the female underperformance hypothesis. *Small Business Economics, 14*, 1-10.

This study examines performance of women-owned businesses by comparing a large sample of men- and women-owned businesses in Sweden. Based on previous studies suggesting women had lower performance than their male counterparts, this study sought to comprehensively test this premise. A random sample was drawn from the Statistics Sweden data set, which is the complete population (n=137,000) of all Swedish firms and companies. The sample was stratified by industry, size, and region, and comprised 5,325 firms. Telephone interviews were conducted to assess four aspects of economic performance: sales, profitability, employment, and orders. Comparisons between men- and women-owned businesses showed significant differences. Women-owned firms were smaller, under-represented in manufacturing and over-represented in services, and reported a smaller customer base. Multivariate analyses confirmed under-performance of women-owned firms in sales, but not with regard to profitability, employment, or orders. The study concludes that under-performance is true only if the growth preferences of women are inferior to those of men.

Nature of the study: Empirical
Nature of the data: Statistics Sweden
Nature of the sample: Small firms
Variables: Industry, business size (employees), region, performance, sex, growth prospects, growth rates

Ehlers, T. B., & Main, K. (1998). Women and false promise of micro-enterprise. *Gender and Society, 12* (4), 424-440.

Since the 1980s, micro-enterprise development programs have proliferated in the United States, where they are widely praised as strategies for economic development and poverty alleviation, especially for low-income women and welfare mothers. Using Acker's "disembodied worker" analogy, the researchers suggest that economic, socio-cultural, and gender constraints make it extremely difficult for most women to turn micro-enterprises into viable income producers. The researchers argued that micro-enterprise development is more detrimental and problematic than it is purported to be. The performance of women's small businesses is due in large part to the nature of the businesses women choose. Female micro-enterprises tend to be small, home based, minimally capitalized, and labor intensive, with modest sales volumes and a narrowly defined neighborhood clientele. Women appear to select these kinds of business because they offer easy entry that does not require extensive capital or business background, neither of which they possess. Consequently they are seen as opting to be less profitable and less successful. The researchers contended that existing micro-enterprise training programs reinforce this business segregation by discounting the socio-cultural conditions women bring with them to business and instead emphasized the personal growth of individuals. The result is that women are encouraged to maintain their economic vulnerability and social peripheralization rather than become part of the mainstream business world.

Nature of the study: Empirical
Nature of the data: Qualitative data from interviews and quantitative data from informal survey with ex-clients in a three-year (1994-1996) ethnographic investigation

| Nature of the sample: | Women clients of MicroFem, a private, nonprofit organization, located in a city in the western U.S., providing effective employment and educational programs to assist low-income minority women and youth; staff and members of the various advisory boards of the company |
| Variables: | Race, age, marital status, employment status, income, education, type of self-employment |

Evans, E., & Leighton, L. (1989). The determinants of changes in U.S. self-employment, 1968-1987. *Small Business Economics, 1,* 111-119.

This paper examines changes in self-employment in the U.S. over a period of two decades, focusing on the relationship between the aggregate trends and changes in the economy and population. It identifies similarities and differences by age, race, and sex and assesses the effects on self-employment of changes in the demographic makeup of the economy, the composition of aggregate demand, and other economic factors. Findings include rates of flow in and out of self-employment and differences by age and gender.

Nature of the study:	Empirical
Nature of the data:	Longitudinal data set based on Annual Demographic File from March Current Population Surveys
Nature of the sample:	Full time employed white men and women, non-agricultural
Variables:	Demographics (age, sex, location), employment, time in labor force, education, industry demand, economic policy (tax rates), business form of organization

Fabowale, L., & Orser, B., & Riding, A. (1995). Gender, structural factors, and credit terms between Canadian small businesses and financial institutions. *Entrepreneurship Theory and Practice, 19* (4), 41-65.

This paper reports on an analysis of whether the terms of bank credit differ between men and women business owners. After accounting for structural differences between male-owned and female-owned businesses, no difference remained in the rate of loan rejections, nor did any differences persist in other objective measures of terms of credit. Measures of business risk were closely associated with credit terms. Firms with declining rates of growth were more likely to have their loans rejected, and gender was closely related to this fact. It was also found that women small business owners were significantly more likely than male business owners to perceive disrespectful treatment by lending officers. The findings provide a reconciliation of previous research findings that reported both equality of treatment of genders by financial institutions and a widespread sense of injustice on the part of women business owners. Implications for the training of loan account managers are highlighted.

Nature of the study:	Empirical
Nature of the data:	Mail survey conducted by Canadian Federation of Independent Business (CFIB)
Nature of the sample:	Stratified procedure yield final sample of 1,907 men- and 758 women-owned established small businesses-members of CFIB
Variables:	Gender, measures of capital, firm capacity, internal and external firm conditions, firm character, collateral, probability of loan turndown, co-signatures, amount received/requested ratio, interest rates

Fagenson, E. A. (1993). Personal value systems of men and women entrepreneurs versus managers. *Journal of Business Venturing, 8* (5), 409-430.

This study compares two theoretical perspectives for differences between men and women entrepreneurs and their managerial counterparts: sex-role socialization patterns and situation-centered or occupational role viewpoint. Contrary to expectations, the findings revealed individuals' gender had little influence on their personal value systems. Only a few differences were discerned. Women valued equality more than men and men valued family security more than women.

In contrast, managers and entrepreneurs had vastly different value systems. Entrepreneurs gave significantly greater weight to terminal values such as self-respect, freedom, a sense of accomplishment, and an exciting life, and to instrumental values such as being honest, ambitious, capable, independent, and imaginative. Managers gave greater weight to terminal values such as true friendship, wisdom, salvation, and pleasure, and to instrumental values such as being loving, compassionate, and self-controlled. The results of the study suggest that entrepreneurs want something different out of life than managers. Whereas the latter preferred to enjoy the pleasures that life has to offer, entrepreneurs wanted to be free to achieve and actualize their potential. Men and women who became entrepreneurs or, alternatively, held secure jobs in a management profession were more similar to members of the opposite sex within their profession than they were to members of their own sex in a complementary profession.

Nature of the study:	Empirical
Nature of the data:	Mail survey
Nature of the sample:	255 men and from small towns in New York, New Jersey and Connecticut; women 115 entrepreneurs (68 females, 47 males) and 140 managers (68 females, 72 males)
Variables:	Sex, occupational role (entrepreneur/manager), instrumental and terminal live values, age, education, income, years in current position

Fagenson, E. A., & Marcus, E. A. (1991). Perceptions of the sex-role stereotypic characteristics of entrepreneurs: Women's evaluations. *Entrepreneurship Theory and Practice, 15* (4), 33-47.

The purpose of this study is to explore how women perceive the sex-role stereotypic characteristics of a successful entrepreneur. The authors sought to provide a greater understanding of two factors that may contribute to women's desire to become entrepreneurs: 1) whether women perceive a match between the entrepreneurship profession and feminine traits, and 2) whether this match is more likely perceived if women work in female-headed than in male-headed organizations. The study reveals that women in female-headed companies gave greater weight to feminine attributes than did women who worked in companies headed by men. Women who worked in male-headed firms were predicted to give greater weight to masculine characteristics than women who worked in firms headed by women. This hypothesis was not supported. However, both groups assigned more weight to masculine attributes in the profile of the successful entrepreneur.

Nature of the study:	Empirical
Nature of the data:	Survey completed during a business conference
Nature of the sample:	65 females, 25-69 years old, 91.5% white, from New York, New Jersey, and Pennsylvania with occupations of self employed, upper, middle, and lower management, other
Variables:	Sex of respondents' company head, firm size, personal characteristics (feminine vs. masculine)

Fasci, M. A., & Valdez, J. (1998). A performance contrast of male- and female-owned small accounting practices. *Journal of Small Business Management, 36* (3), 1-7.

Prior research comparing male- and female-owned businesses may be limited by a failure to examine performance on a variety of dimensions, as well as by regional and industry biases. This study was designed to overcome prior limitations by focusing on a specific industry (accounting profession); including business, personal and attitudinal characteristics as predictors of performance; and using a nation-wide sample. Findings reveal that although a male-owned accounting practice can expect a higher ratio of profits to gross revenues than one owned by a female, these differences are mediated by differences in the owner's intentions. Female accountants were more likely to indicate they established their business to attain greater flexibility in their work time and place, whereas higher profitability was associated with achieving challenge and income.

Nature of the study:	Empirical
Nature of the data:	Mail survey
Nature of the sample:	604 small business owners (328 females and 276 males, selected from membership list of the American Institute for

	Certified Public Accountants) with fewer than 5 professional employees
Variables:	Age and size of business, business location, owner's work experience, age, average hours worked in business, education level, marital status, attitudes about establishing the business, gender, performance (productivity ratio or net profit to gross revenue), hours dedicated to business per week

Fay, M., & Williams, L. (1993). Gender bias and the availability of business loans. *Journal of Business Venturing, 8* (4), 363-376.

Two experiments were carried out using a Goldberg type procedure to test whether women were unfairly discriminated against when seeking a loan to establish a business venture. Carefully constructed scenarios of an application for loan to finance a commercial enterprise were mailed to loan officers of major trading bank branches. The scenarios were similar except for sex and education level of applicants. Loan officers were asked whether or not they would approve the loans and the reasons for their decisions. Significant differences in response to male and female applicants were observed. In Experiment I (applicants with university education), both sexes were equally likely to obtain a loan, but education was considered a more important factor for the female applicant than for the male. In Experiment II (applicants with high school education), a female applicant was less likely to obtain a loan than a male applicant. The results support the perception that women can experience gender discrimination.

Nature of the study:	Empirical
Nature of the data:	Mail survey
Nature of the sample:	Loan application scenarios sent to 200 branches of 4 major trading banks operating in New Zealand cities with population less than 15,000
Variables:	Sex, education, probability of receiving a loan

Finnerty, J. F., & Krzystofik, A. T. (1985). Barriers to small business formation. *Journal of Small Business Management, 23* (3), 50-58.

A survey of potential entrepreneurs was conducted to determine differences between individuals who start their own businesses and those who considered starting, but gave up. Demographic profiles of the two groups show that females in managerial positions who have dependents are more apt to go into business than are single males in non-management positions. The factors that were considered the most important for starting a business include 1) market potential for the product, 2) availability of financing, and 3) the rewards and satisfaction of business formation. The factors that were not considered important included the tax climate and present job security.

Although no demographic differences were found for individuals who still wanted to start businesses and those who had given up, differences in opinion existed between the two groups in several areas, including 1) the importance of the business climate, 2) present job security, and 3) family commitments.

Nature of the study:	Empirical
Nature of the data:	Mail survey
Nature of the sample:	161 individuals (112 who had formed and operated a business, 49 who had not formed a business by the time they received the questionnaire) who had received at least five hours of consultation from a Small Business Development Center in 1982-1983
Variables:	Opinions about product, market and environmental conditions, personal considerations (financial risk, security of present employment, rewards and satisfaction, family responsibilities, being the boss), demographic characteristics (age, education, sex, salary, size of family, work experience), starting a new business

Fischer, E. M., Reuber, A. R., & Dyke, L.S (1993). A theoretical overview and extension of research on sex, gender, and entrepreneurship. *Journal of Business Venturing, 8* (2), 151-168.

In this article, liberal and social feminist theories are used to examine differences between male and female entrepreneurs. Prior research findings on sex, gender, and entrepreneurship revealed mixed evidence of sex-based discrimination and meaningful socialized gender differences. However, assumptions about discrimination and gender differences--and their impact on firm performance --persist in the literature. Hypotheses tests were based on the theories and prior findings. For a randomly selected sample of entrepreneurs in manufacturing, retail, and service industries, few differences are found in the education obtained by males and females or in their business motivations. Female entrepreneurs had less experience in managing employees or in helping to start up new businesses. Their businesses were smaller than men's, and had lower growth in income and sales revenue per employee. Implications of both the theoretical frameworks and the empirical findings for future research and for entrepreneurship policy are discussed.

Nature of the study:	Empirical
Nature of the data:	Mail survey
Nature of the sample:	136 (11 female) manufacturing firm owners, 156 (29 female) retail firm owners, 216 (20 female) service firm owners from Dun & Bradstreet listing
Variables:	Sex, education, industry and managerial experience, and prior business ownership, financial motivation, business performance

Gadenne, D. (1998). Critical success factors for small business: An inter-industry comparison. *International Small Business Journal, 17* (1), 36-57.

This study examines several diverse management practices, or business strategies, and their relationship to venture performance. Specific research objectives include: 1) to determine whether management practices of small business owners differ across industries and whether such differences contribute to financial performance; and 2) to determine whether owners' personal characteristics and aspirations influenced successful management practices. Factor analysis identified 12 distinct aspects of management practice. Univariate F tests revealed that each of the management practices significantly influenced return on investment but not growth in return on investment. Additionally, the pattern of successful management practices varied across industry sector. Financial leverage was found to negatively influence return on investment in all sectors, but other practices varied across retail, service and manufacturing. Reliance on professional advice was positively related to firm performance in manufacturing; in retail, "value for money" was positively related to firm performance, and in the service sector, "employee relations" was positively related. Results of two separate MANCOVA analyses revealed no significant effect of owners' personal characteristics on successful management practices across all three industries. Only in the service sector were owners' objectives significantly associated with successful management practices.

Nature of the study:	Empirical
Nature of the data:	Mail survey.
Nature of the sample:	1500 questionnaires were sent to owner-managers of small business, identified through the *Yellow Pages*, in South East Queensland, Australia. Useable responses were returned by 369 (24.7%). Firms represented in the sample included 145 retail, 150 service, 74 manufacturing. Each business employed less than 50 employees with the majority employing less than 10.
Variables:	Firm performance (return on investment, growth in return on investment), management practices, owners' characteristics, industry

Gatewood, E. J., Shaver, K. G., & Gartner, W. B. (1995). A longitudinal study of cognitive factors influencing start-up behaviors and success at venture creation. *Journal of Business Venturing, 10* (5), 371-391.

The purpose of this study is to explore whether certain cognitive factors of potential entrepreneurs can be used to predict their subsequent persistence in business start-up activities and in new venture creation success. Two hypotheses were tested: H1) Potential entrepreneurs who offer internal and stable explanations for getting into business should be more likely to persist in actions that lead to successfully starting a business; and H2) Potential entrepreneurs with high personal efficacy scores should be more likely to persist in actions that lead to successfully starting a business. An analysis of the results found that H1 (internal/stable attributions) was supported for female potential entrepreneurs, whereas external/stable attributions were significant for male potential entrepreneurs. SIC code classifications revealed no significant differences in the sorts of businesses being contemplated by women and men. H2 (personal efficacy) was not supported. Those activities that focused on setting up business operations distinguished potential entrepreneurs who had started businesses from those who had not.

The authors suggest that one of the important features of this research is the use of a longitudinal research design. By measuring attributions before potential entrepreneurs had started (or not started) their businesses, stronger claims for a causal relationship between these initial attributions and the individuals' subsequent success in starting a venture can be made. Men and women do have different reasons for getting into business that appear to be significant indicators of their future ability to start a business successfully. The authors propose that the development of measures focusing on details of the attributional model (i.e., perceptions of skills, abilities, the difficulty of the task, luck, and the value of the opportunity) will likely lead to a more comprehensive and accurate conception of the factors that influence entrepreneurial persistence.

Nature of the study: Empirical
Nature of the data: Mail survey
Nature of the sample: 85 pre-venture clients of a Small Development Center
Variables: Reasons for getting into business, sex, sales, psychological variables, business start-up activities

Green, E., & Cohen, L. (1995). Women's businesses: Are women entrepreneurs breaking new ground or simply balancing the demands of 'women's work' in a new way? *Journal of Gender Studies, 4* (3), 297314

This paper takes as its starting point the androcentricity of existing approaches to entrepreneurship and explores possible ways forward. It considers the growing literature on women entrepreneurs, highlighting in particular the importance of feminist perspectives. Focusing on the issue of motherhood and women's position in the labor market, the authors explore ways in which the respondents' roles and responsibilities as mothers impacted their experiences of moving from employment within organizations to self-employment. The respondents' stories of their experiences as self-employed mothers suggest that while self-employment offers ways of accommodating women's dual roles as mothers and as professionals, it does little to alter their structural positions within the labor market and society more generally; nor does it seem to have any impact on their ideological perspectives.

The findings indicate that self-employment, as a phenomenon, does not appear to significantly alter most women's fundamental position (or world-view). Instead, the move from employment to self-employment seems to represent a retrenchment of these positions, enabling women to more effectively cope with the competing demands of paid and unpaid work, and thus to ensure that they continue to accept responsibility for both.

Nature of the study: Empirical
Nature of the data: In-depth personal interviews
Nature of the sample: 24 women from Sheffield, identified through networking, who left employment within large organizations to set up their own businesses
Variables: Relationship between personal and professional life, the role of husbands and partners, the role of professional and social networks, the development of occupational identity, gender identity, decision to become self-employed

Greene, P. G., Brush, C. G., Hart, M.M., & Saparito, P. (2001). Patterns of venture capital funding: Is gender a factor? *Venture Capital: An International Journal of Entrepreneurial Finance, 3* (1), 63-83.

Since the early 1980s, new ventures with high growth potential and large capital needs have found an ever-increasing pool of venture capital available to support their growth. However, the flow of venture capital investment to women-led businesses remains meager in spite of the fact that in the U.S. and Europe an increasing number of businesses are owned by women. The apparent disparity between potential investment opportunity and actual deals made between venture capital firms and women-led businesses raises the question of whether the sex of the owner/manager is an issue. The majority of venture capital studies to date have investigated the flow of equity funds, investor criteria, and the nature of the investor-investee relationship. Research on women entrepreneurs to date has focused on psychological dimensions, business characteristics, and performance. Questions about the intersection of gender and venture capital financing have been largely unexamined.

This exploratory study utilizes longitudinal data to track U.S. venture capital investments by proportion, stage, industry and gender. The descriptive statistics and the analysis of the findings suggest several hypotheses to explain the apparent gender gap. The data show that venture capital investments in women-led businesses have been very small. In the past 30 years, women-led firms received 2.4% of equity financing. A positive and increasing trend in the late 1990s resulted in women-led ventures receiving 4.1% in 1998. The investigators propose three theoretical approaches: a structural barriers approach suggesting that women might face institutional or network barriers; a human capital approach suggesting leadership skills, background, etc., may be a limiting factor; and a strategic choice approach examining growth aspirations and product/market strategies.

Nature of the study:	Empirical
Nature of the data:	Venture Capital Association data base
Nature of the sample:	All investments in U.S. businesses by venture capital firms 1957-1998
Variables:	Gender, stage of investment, region, business sector, industry

Gundry, L.K., & Welsch, H.P. (2001). The ambitious entrepreneur: High growth strategies of women-owned enterprises. *Journal of Business Venturing, 16* (5), 453-470.

This research focuses on women entrepreneurs whose businesses have exhibited high growth and compares them with businesses exhibiting no growth or low growth. The study attempts to identify the strategic paths chosen by entrepreneurs and the relation of those paths to the growth orientation of the firm. In the process it seeks to answer the fundamental question, what characterizes a high growth oriented entrepreneur?

The study shows that high-growth-oriented entrepreneurs were clearly different from low-growth-oriented entrepreneurs along several dimensions. The former were much more likely to select strategies that permitted greater focus on market expansion and new technologies, to exhibit greater intensity towards business ownership, and to be willing to incur greater opportunity costs for the success of their firms. The high-growth-oriented entrepreneurs also tended to have a more structured approach to organizing a business, suggesting a more disciplined perception of managing the firm. The high-growth-oriented entrepreneurs, labeled "ambitious", were also distinguished by earlier planning for growth of the business; utilization of a team-based form of organization; concern for reputation and quality; adequate capitalization; strong leadership; and utilization of a wider range of financing sources for the expansion of the venture. The aim of uncovering these differences was to enable entrepreneurs and researchers to identify more clearly the attributes of rapid-growth ventures and their founders so as to help delineate the alternative paths to venture growth and organizational change.

Nature of the study:	Empirical
Nature of the data:	Mail survey
Nature of the sample:	832 women business owners across different industries – sourced from Dun's Marketing Database
Variables:	Strategic growth and expansion intentions, degree of entrepreneurial intensity, willingness to incur opportunity costs, organizational structure in use, perceived importance of strategic success factors, financial resources used, demographic characteristics

Gunnerud Berg, N. (1997). Gender, place and entrepreneurship. *Entrepreneurship and Regional Development, 9* (3), 259-268.

This paper proposes that feminist geographies may contribute to new insights about entrepreneurship. First, the implicit masculinity of conventional entrepreneurship research is challenged. Second, different conceptions of place and gender are explored to demonstrate that the way we conceive of place and gender is crucial to our understanding of entrepreneurship. Third, the interweaving of place, gender, and entrepreneurship is discussed. Conclusions include that when studying entrepreneurs one is studying gendered individuals in gendered places. The difference that place makes to gender relations and entrepreneurship should be taken into account. The author argues that the way we think about gender is significant to our understanding of entrepreneurship and that feminist geographies provide useful theoretical frameworks for studying how gender is shaped by, and vice versa, how geographies are shaped by gender, and how this relates to entrepreneurship.

Nature of the study:	Conceptual
Nature of the data:	NA
Nature of the sample:	NA
Variables:	Place (geography and location of economic activity), entrepreneur's personal characteristics, place in geography, gender

Haines, Jr. G.H., , Orser, G. H., & Riding, A.L. (1999). Myths and Realities: An empirical study of banks and the gender of small business clients. *Canadian Journal of Administrative Sciences, 16* (4), 291-307.

This research empirically examines the impact of gender on the relationship between bank lenders and small business borrowers. Both quantitative and qualitative aspects of the relationship are considered. Data are drawn from a national random sample of 1,393 bank loan files. Terms of lending across gender are examined, controlling for covariates such as size and sector. Findings that borrower attributes and terms of lending do not vary by gender of borrower are consistent with the null hypothesis of no discrimination.

Nature of the study:	Empirical
Nature of the data:	Archival
Nature of the sample:	Canadian business owners who obtained bank credit
Variables:	Firm demographics, loan characteristics, borrowers' demographics (gender, background), banks' risk assessment, business performance

Haynes, G.W. (1996). Credit access for high-risk borrowers in financially
concentrated markets: Do SBA loan guarantees help? *Small Business
Economics 8* (6), 449-461.

The U.S. Small Business Administration's (SBA) loan guarantee program
was established in part to improve small business access to financial capital.
This study focuses upon the structure of financial capital markets by
examining the financial characteristics of small business borrowers with and
without SBA loan guarantees. The authors propose a model to evaluate the
behavior of both borrowers and lenders. Gender of the owner is included as a
control variable. Male borrowers represented 87% of the total number of
small businesses and received 89% of the SBA loan guarantees. The authors
conclude that there were no significant differences on business
characteristics of small business borrowers with SBA guarantees and
borrowers without the guarantees.

Nature of the study:	Empirical
Nature of the data:	National Survey of Small Business Finance
Nature of the sample:	3,404 randomly selected U.S. small businesses plus separate sample of 390 small businesses receiving SBA loan guarantees in 1986
Variables:	SBA loan guarantee recipient, measures of financial market conditions, business quality measures

Haynes, G. W., & Haynes, D. C. (1999). The debt structure of small businesses
owned by women in 1987 and 1993. *Journal of Small Business Management,
37* (2), 1-19.

This study uses the National Survey of Small Business Finance (U.S.A.) to
examine the access women-owned small business borrowers had to financial
capital provided by institutional and non-institutional lenders in 1987 and
1993. Non-linear (logit and tobit) multivariate regression models were
employed to examine the probability of holding a debt instrument and the
share of total debt held in each debt instrument by women-owned business
borrowers. While women-owned small businesses still have a higher
probability of borrowing from family and friends, the results suggest that
women-owned small businesses have gained similar access to line-of-credit
loans from commercial banks as men-owned small businesses over the
period of time from 1987 to 1993.

Nature of the study:	Empirical
Nature of the data:	National Survey of Small Business Finance
Nature of the sample:	Non-agricultural, non-financial businesses with less than 500 employees
Variables:	Business debt instruments (size, type, interest rate), business type, business quality, business owner demographics including gender

Haynes, P. J., & Helms, M. M. (2000). When bank loans launch new ventures: A profile of the growing female entrepreneur segment. *Bank Marketing, 32* (5), 28-36.

As women increasingly select entrepreneurship as a path to business ownership, the role and importance of bank loans in initiating these new businesses comes into question. This study examines a group of women-owned businesses, contrasting the profiles of those using bank loans as a primary source of initial capital to the ones relying on alternative funding sources. Firms with bank funding outperformed those without bank funding. Bank loans tended to be more important for owners choosing a corporate form of organizational structure. The additional financial projections required for using a corporate structure may have been key in bank determination of credit potential. In addition, if a woman had a relationship with a bank in place at the launch of her new venture, that relationship continued throughout the life of that business and to a next venture, as women with bank funding tended to start multiple businesses

Nature of the study:	Empirical
Nature of the data:	Mail survey
Nature of the sample:	Women business owners drawn from NAWBO chapter and university affiliated Institute for Women Entrepreneurs
Variables:	Business demographics (form, size, age, industry, sales), entrepreneurs' demographics (age, education, entrepreneurial history), satisfaction with venture, satisfaction with previous employment

Hisrich, R. D. (1989). Women entrepreneurs: Problems and prescriptions for success in the future. In O. Hagan, C. Rivchin & D. Sexton (Eds.), *Women-owned Businesses* (pp. 3-32). New York: Praeger.

Starting and operating a business entails considerable risk and effort-- perhaps even greater for women entrepreneurs who experience the challenges of being in male-dominated arenas, having few role models, and lacking track records in using their business skills. In spite of obstacles, an increasing number of women are becoming entrepreneurs. This chapter looks at the role of women in employment and the entrepreneurial process, reviews research on women entrepreneurs, compares male and female entrepreneurs, and highlights problems and prescriptions for success for present and future women entrepreneurs.

The findings include: 1) More than 90% of women owned-businesses are service-oriented, a fact that reflects their educational and occupational background. 2) Women entrepreneurs tend to have highly educated parents-- particularly fathers--and to have more educated husbands. 3) The start-up process has been identified as different for females. Men are motivated by the drive to control their own destinies. In contrast, women tend to be more motivated by a need for independence and achievement arising from job frustration. Prescriptions for success include the following: 1) Women need to establish track records. 2) Women should compensate for lack of education and experience through continuing education and by hiring experts. 3) Aspiring women entrepreneurs should obtain occupational experience in middle management or technical areas. 4) The woman entrepreneur should assess her family situation before launching a venture. 5) Women entrepreneurs should establish a strong support system of family and friends. 6) Determination and professionalism are important attributes women should cultivate.

Nature of the study: Empirical
Nature of the data: Synthesis of several mail surveys
Nature of the sample: Female entrepreneurs in the U.S.
Variables: Business demographics (form, size, age, industry, sales),
                          entrepreneurs' demographics (age, education,
                          entrepreneurial history), business challenges

Hisrich, R. D., & Brush, C. (1983). The woman entrepreneur: Implications of family educational, and occupational experience. In J. A. Hornaday, J. A. Timmons, & K. H. Vesper (Eds.), *Frontiers of entrepreneurial research* (pp. 255-270). Boston, MA: Babson College.

This nationwide survey of 468 women entrepreneurs establishes a profile of respondents and reports weaknesses in finance, marketing, and business operations. The typical woman entrepreneur is the first born, middle class, a college graduate with a liberal arts major, and married, with children. She has a supportive spouse who is in a professional or technical occupation. Most are in their first entrepreneurial effort and the venture is in a traditional women-business area. The findings indicate that women entrepreneurs should attend seminars on finance, marketing, and planning to improve the success of their ventures. They should be encouraged to study in non-traditional fields such as engineering and science. Banks need to be educated in terms of the credit-worthiness of women entrepreneurs and women should be encouraged early in life to have more dealings with money and negotiations.

Nature of the study: Empirical
Nature of the data: Mail survey
Nature of the sample: Female entrepreneurs in 18 states
Variables: Business demographics (form, size, age, industry, sales),
                          entrepreneurs' demographics (age, education,
                          entrepreneurial history), business challenges

Hisrich, R. D., & Brush, C. (1984). The woman entrepreneur: Management skills and business problems. *Journal of Small Business Management, 22* (1), 30-37.

Women business owners throughout the U.S. were surveyed to develop a profile of the female entrepreneur, to assess the management skills women bring to their business enterprises, and to determine the problems they encounter. The female entrepreneur tended to be between the ages of 35 and 45; married, with children; and well educated. Most had attended college, obtaining degrees in liberal arts and business administration. Almost 90% of the female entrepreneurs operated service businesses, with the majority involved in sales. Most respondents had been in business for themselves for four years or less and had previous experience in their business areas. Respondents typically believed that they lacked management skills in the areas of finance, marketing, and planning. Problems encountered in the start-up phases of businesses included lack of financial training and difficulty in obtaining credit; ongoing problems centered on financial planning. These results suggest that women need to be better prepared to start and operate their own businesses.

Nature of the study:	Empirical
Nature of the data:	Mail survey
Nature of the sample:	Female entrepreneurs in the U.S.
Variables:	Business demographics (form, size, age, industry, sales), entrepreneurs' demographics (age, education, entrepreneurial history), business challenges

Hisrich, R. D., & Brush, C. G. (1985). Women and minority entrepreneurs: A comparative analysis. In J. A. Hornaday, E. B. Shils, J. A. Timmons, & K. H. Vesper (Eds.), *Frontiers of entrepreneurial research* (pp. 566-587). Boston, MA: Babson College.

This paper analyzes the results of a survey of women and minority entrepreneurs that addressed personal characteristics, family background, management skills, the entrepreneurial venture, and problems encountered. Similar characteristics include being a first born, having a college degree, being married with children, starting an entrepreneurial career between the ages of 40 and 45; and previous venture experience. Achievement and job satisfaction were the strongest motivations to starting their own venture. Differences in the profiles are that the typical woman entrepreneur is from a middle- or upper-class family; has a self-employed father, and values independence, whereas the minority entrepreneur is from a lower- or middle-class family, has a blue-collar father, and the decision to start a venture is motivated by opportunity and job satisfaction.

Nature of the study:	Empirical
Nature of the data:	Mail survey
Nature of the sample:	Female entrepreneurs in 18 states

Variables: Business demographics (form, size, age, industry, sales),
                           entrepreneurs' demographics (age, education,
                           entrepreneurial history), business challenges

Hisrich, R. D., & Brush, C. G. (1987). Women entrepreneurs: A longitudinal study.
    In N. C. Churchill, J.A. Hornaday, B.A. Kirchhoff, O.J. Krasner, & K.H.
    Vesper (Eds.), *Frontiers of entrepreneurial research* (pp. 187-199). Boston,
    MA: Babson College.

This paper analyzes the results of a longitudinal study of 344 women
entrepreneurs in the United States. Not only are such areas as personal
characteristics, family background, management skills, the entrepreneurial
venture, and problems investigated, but also the success rate and growth (or
lack thereof) of entrepreneurial ventures. The findings indicate that the
majority of businesses operated by women have been moderately successful
with increases in revenue of about 7% a year. Of the original sample, 30-
40% failed or were no longer in business, a much lower rate than the
frequently mentioned national average of 75% of all new businesses failing
within the first 5 years. Nevertheless the size of the women-owned enterprise
remains small. On the other hand geographic and market scope is expanding
rapidly as women entrepreneurs improve business skills and practice
strategic management.

Nature of the study: Empirical
Nature of the data: Mail survey
Nature of the sample: Re-survey of respondents to 1985 survey. Female
                          entrepreneurs in 18 states.
Variables: Business demographics (form, size, age, industry, sales),
                          entrepreneurs' demographics (age, education,
                          entrepreneurial history), business challenges

Hisrich, R. D., & O'Brien, M. (1981). The woman entrepreneur from a business and
    sociological perspective. In K.H. Vesper (Ed.), *Frontiers of entrepreneurial
    research* (pp. 21-39). Boston, MA: Babson College.

This paper reports the results of an in-depth study of twenty-one women
entrepreneurs. The results indicate that women entrepreneurs have particular
business problems in the areas of obtaining lines of credit, weak collateral
position, and overcoming society's negative beliefs about women. These
problems are related more to the respondent's type of business than to
educational level or background.

Nature of the study: Empirical
Nature of the data: Field observation, interview
Nature of the sample: Self-employed women in Massachusetts

Variables: Business demographics (form, size, age, industry, sales),
                              entrepreneurs' demographics (age, education,
                              entrepreneurial history), business challenges, personal
                              frustrations

Hisrich, R. D., &. O'Brien, M. (1982). The woman entrepreneur as a reflection of the
     type of business. In K.H. Vesper (Ed.), *Frontiers of entrepreneurial research*
     (pp. 54-67). Boston, MA: Babson College.

This paper investigates the differences between women entrepreneurs in non-
traditional businesses and women entrepreneurs in traditional areas of
business. The results indicate that women entrepreneurs in non-traditional
industries are likely to have parents who were business owners and tend to
be slightly better educated, and older than those in retail and wholesale
services. Both groups used their savings to finance the start-up of their
business and had profitable ventures in two years or less. Those in non-
traditional business areas reported a lack of availability of external financing
sources.

Nature of the study: Empirical
Nature of the data: American Management Association data base
Nature of the sample: Women entrepreneurs in the United States
Variables: Business demographics (form, size, age, industry, sales),
                              entrepreneurs' demographics (age, education,
                              entrepreneurial history), business challenges, sources of
                              funding

Holmquist, C., & Sundin, E. (1990). What's special about highly educated women
     entrepreneurs. *Entrepreneurship and Regional Development, 2,* 181-193.

This article deals with Swedish well-educated female entrepreneurs
(Swefees)--that is, entrepreneurs with an education exceeding 12 years. The
Swefees differ from other female entrepreneurs, from male entrepreneurs,
and from other women on the labor market. The analysis found two distinct
categories of Swefees: Loner-Swefees and Family-Swefees. The Loner-
Swefees are single, living in a big city environment, and have experience in
the public or private sector. They are extremely career-oriented. The Family
Swefees are also career-oriented but try to run a family and a firm at the
same time. Swefees are very professional, value customer service, and
personal independence. Although they complain of a lower sales turnover
and low profit, they do not rank these items highest on the list of why they
do business in the first place. Other entrepreneurs of both sexes seem to be
more oriented toward quantitative goals. The population of Swefees was
identified through a questionnaire sent to a sample of 1,440 of the population
of more than 64,000 Swedish female entrepreneurs. The survey produced a

response rate of 70% of the 1,000 entrepreneurs still in business when they received the questionnaire.

Nature of the study: Empirical
Nature of the data: Mail survey
Nature of the sample: Female entrepreneurs in Sweden
Variables: Business demographics (industry, size, location),
                         entrepreneurs' demographics (age, education, experience,
                         skills, motivations)

Holliday, R., & Letherby, G. (1993). Happy families or poor relations? An exploration of familial analogies in the small firm. *International Small Business Journal, 11* (2), 54-63.

This paper explores the relationship of the analogy of "family" businesses in small firms. Using an ethnographic approach, the authors explore authority structures, working relationships, and exploitative practices as these might affect women detrimentally. The authors draw heavily from sociological theory in interpreting women's role in small businesses. In particular, themes about blood ties in the business; size, structure and culture of the firm; and links between home and family life are explored. Evidence shows many examples of compassion and support for women in family firms, particularly as this relates to flexibility of work hours for young children. However, there was also evidence of sexual harassment of women in male-dominated companies. The familial analogy does have relevance in small companies, and, in most cases, has a positive reference. For women who have no prior experience, few authority roles are familiar to them.

Nature of the study: Empirical
Nature of the data: Ethnography
Nature of the sample: Small manufacturing companies
Variables: Relationships, authority structures, culture, policies

Holtz-Eaken, D., Rosen, H.S., & Weathers, R. (2000). Horatio Alger meets the mobility tables. *Small Business Economics, 14* (4), 243-274.

This paper examines income inequality and mobility in the U.S. Based on the premise that entrepreneurship is influenced by income mobility, an economic analysis is undertaken across several populations of entrepreneurs, including minorities and women. Data are from the Panel Study of Income Dynamics (PSID), which includes 5,000 families interviewed between 1969 and 1990. The analysis considers those who make the transition to self-employment. Results show that the number of men and women making the transition was about equal, but that men were more likely to move upward in earnings distribution. Similar results were found for blacks and non-blacks, where non-blacks were more likely to move up in earnings. Mobility patterns differ by the length of the transition time. A detailed multivariate analysis for the entire sample--men, women, and blacks--is conducted for one-year and five-year patterns. In general, results show that self-employment is a successful strategy for moving ahead, in both the short term and the long term, for individuals who start at the bottom of the earnings distribution and are continuously self-employed. On the other hand, for those who start out at the top, continuous experience with self-employment led to a fall in their relative earnings position. For women, the main message seems to be that entrepreneurship has not been a very successful strategy for moving ahead in the earnings distribution. In both the short term and long term, self-employment has led to small gains, and sometimes substantial losses. For blacks, the gains were most significant in the short term, but the earnings losses were more significant in the long term. Further research is suggested to examine whether or not financing patterns impact differences among women and racial and ethnic groups.

Nature of the study: Empirical
Nature of the data: Panel Study of Income Dynamics
Nature of the sample: 5,000 U.S families
Variables: Earnings, self-employment, sex, ethnicity

Honig-Haftel, S., & Martin, L (1986). Is the female entrepreneur at a disadvantage? *Thrust, 7* (1,2), 49-65.

This study compares the problems of female small business owners and entrepreneurs to the problems of their male counterparts. Surveys mailed to business owners in Connecticut were completed by 57 female and 85 male entrepreneurs. Analysis of the data indicates that both male and female entrepreneurs identified the conflict between personal relationships and the business venture as their biggest problem during ongoing business operations. Other findings include; 1) Single women made less revenue than male counterparts. 2) Women entrepreneurs were more highly educated than male entrepreneurs. 3) Few of the women had engineering degrees, while 1/4 of the men had such degrees. 4) Women business owners were more likely than men owners to operate unincorporated businesses. 5) Women, more than men, operated home-based enterprises. 6) Women perceived themselves as having weaker financial management skills than men.

Nature of the study: Empirical
Nature of the data: Mail survey
Nature of the sample: Male and female business owners in Connecticut
Variables: Business demographics (form, size, age, industry, sales),
                         entrepreneurs' demographics (age, education,
                         entrepreneurial history), business challenges

Hyrsky, K. 1999. Entrepreneurial metaphors and concepts: An exploratory study. *International Small Business Journal, 18* (1), 13-34.

Combining ideas from entrepreneurship and linguistics, this study examines definitions of entrepreneurship and entrepreneur. Respondents from Finland, Sweden, Norway, Ireland, Canada and Australia viewed the concepts as equivalents. Five factors for the entrepreneurship concept were determined: work commitment and energy, economic values and results, innovativeness and risk-taking, ambition and achievement, and egotistic features. Three factors were identified for the entrepreneur concept; agent of change, self-serving individualist, and hard worker. An analysis of metaphorical expressions for the concepts generated by the participants were grouped into semantic categories consisting of machinery and other physical objects, warfare and adventure, sports and games, creativity and activity, nature, disease, food items, and special features. Entrepreneurs had more positive attitudes towards entrepreneurial traits and behaviors than other respondents did. Females tended to perceive the concepts more positively than males did. In a cross-country comparison, Scandinavians held more favorable views of the concepts than other respondents.

Nature of the study:	Empirical
Nature of the data:	Professors and lecturers from Business Schools distributed questionnaires to a general sample of informants in their respective countries.
Nature of the sample:	Survey administered to 1,789 economically active adults between 18 and 60 years of age. 751 usable returns (42%). Finnish sample consisted of 474 adults; Sweden and Norway, 96; Australia, 77; Canada, 71; and Ireland, 33. Twenty-five percent of the respondents were either entrepreneurs or small business owners.
Variables:	Entrepreneurial concepts, self-employment status, family business status, age, country affiliation, sex

Kalleberg, A. L., & Leicht, K. T. (1991). Gender and organizational performance: Determinants of small business survival and success. *Academy of Management Journal, 34* (1), 136-161.

This article examines several hypotheses regarding how the survival and success of small businesses headed by men and women are related to industry differences, organizational structures, and attributes of owner-operators. The analysis is based on a group of small businesses in three industries--food and drink, computer sales and software, and health--in South Central Indiana during the period 1985-1987. The study finds that businesses headed by women were not more likely to go out of business or be any less successful than those owned by men. A company's age was positively related to its survival regardless of the gender of its owner-operator. Size was unrelated to survival. There were no differences in earnings growth between businesses headed by men and those headed by women.

Nature of the study:	Empirical
Nature of the data:	Longitudinal telephone survey conducted in three successive years
Nature of the sample:	Male and female business owners in Indiana in food and drink, computer service, and health care businesses
Variables:	Business demographics (form, size, age, industry, products, sales), entrepreneurs' demographics (age, education, gender, need for control), business performance

Kangasharju, A. (2000). Growth of the smallest: Determinants of small firm growth during strong macroeconomic fluctuations. *International Small Business Journal, 19* (1), 28-43.

This paper investigates the determinants of small firm growth in Finland during the strong economic fluctuations of the years 1988-1995. Findings support the life-cycle effect of firm growth. New firms grew more often than older ones, providing that the new firms survived the two-year start-up period. Results also indicated that firm growth decreased with the increasing age of the owner-manager. In addition, higher education was found to affect growth probability. Research findings suggest a gender-based difference in the growth probabilities of firms. The growth probability for firms run by males increased sharply, from 7% during the recession period up to 16% during the recovery period, whereas for firms run by female, growth was below 8% for both periods. For some reason unexplained by the data, male owned/managed firms recovered from the recession sooner than female owned/managed firms.

Nature of the study:	Empirical
Nature of the data:	Archival
Nature of the sample:	26,057 owners-managers and their associated small firms
Variables:	Growth probability, firm age/business cycle, owner-manager age, owner-manager's level of education, gender, sector, industry

Kaplan, E. (1988). Women entrepreneurs: Constructing a framework to examine venture success and failure. In B. A. Kirchhoff, W. A. Long, W. Ed McMullan, K. H. Vesper, & W. E. Wetzel, Jr. (Eds.), *Frontiers of entrepreneurial research* (pp. 643-653). Boston, MA: Babson College.

The goal of this research is to identify key research and theoretical issues in understanding why women make the transition to entrepreneurial careers. Based upon survey data collected from a statewide organization of women entrepreneurs, results indicate that younger women were more disillusioned with corporate life and were motivated by autonomy, the need for employment, and the desire to make money; older women were re-entering the workforce. Younger women were more educated, had better business skills, and were more likely to plan and set business-related goals. The impact of these factors on venture success is not clear.

Nature of the study:	Empirical
Nature of the data:	Mail survey
Nature of the sample:	Women business owners in New Jersey
Variables:	Business demographics (form, size, age, industry, sales), entrepreneurs' demographics (age, education, entrepreneurial history, skills, motivation)

Katz, J. A., & Williams, P. M. (1997). Gender, self employment and weak-tie networking through formal organizations – A secondary analysis approach. *Entrepreneurship and Regional Development, 9* (3), 183-197.

This study analyzes the incidence of social networking and the differences in the level of networking between female entrepreneurs and logical comparison groups--male entrepreneurs and female salaried managers. It notes that most networking theories are developed for strong-tie rather than weak-tie processes. Building on the conceptualizations of Aldrich and colleagues, this study is a secondary analysis of weak-tie network linkage in formal organizations. It uses a representative sample of American self-employed and salaried managers drawn from the General Social Survey (GSS). The results suggest that entrepreneurs' weak-tie network efforts are lower than those of managers, with female entrepreneurs engaging in less weak-tie networking than salaried male managers.

Nature of the study:	Empirical
Nature of the data:	Secondary analysis of General Social Survey data, mail survey
Nature of the sample:	National sample of U.S. households
Variables:	Individual demographics (age, education, employment, gender), membership in social groups, networking

Klofsten, M., & Jones-Evans, D. (2000). Comparing academic entrepreneurship in Europe: The case of Sweden and Ireland. *Small Business Economics, 14* (4), 299-309.

This article examines the entrepreneurial activities of academics in Sweden and Ireland. Based on the premise that educational institutions and universities are increasingly integral to city and regional entrepreneurial development, these authors propose that entrepreneurial activities of Swedish academics will be more highly developed than for Ireland because of greater public policy and government support. A survey of 1,539 academics from five Irish universities and 3,481 academics from four Swedish universities was conducted. Response rates of 34% (Sweden) and 43% (Ireland) were achieved. Results showed the average age of respondents was 42, 22% were female, and the majority had doctoral degrees. There were few differences in demographics across the two countries; however, Irish respondents had more industrial experience and were more likely to have started or owned a small firm. Swedish respondents were more likely to be employed in a small firm or have immediate family members who owned small firms. Nearly 70% of all respondents had some industrial contact, usually in the form of consulting, but the nature of the contact was not statistically different between the two countries. University support of the contact was consistent, and there were no differences between male and female respondents in any area. The study concluded that increased pressures to institutionalize entrepreneurship may result in a decrease in these activities. To date, most academic entrepreneurs are flexibly meeting the needs of small firm owners on an individual basis. On the other hand, formal means of collaboration between high technology firms and universities through technology transfer might be effectively explored.

Nature of the study:	Empirical
Nature of the data:	Mail survey
Nature of the sample:	1,857 entrepreneurial academics; 1,194 Swedish academics & 663 Irish academics
Variables:	Demographics (job classification, education); previous experience, contact with industry, entrepreneurial activities, status, education, occupational status

Kolvereid, L., Shane, S., & Westhead, P. (1993). Is it equally difficult for female entrepreneurs to start businesses in all countries? *Journal of Small Business Management, 31* (4), 42-51.

This study tests the hypothesis that, controlling for the effect of country, female entrepreneurs perceive the business start-up environment to be characterized by greater resource scarcity, turbulence, hostility, and uncertainty than do their male counterparts. There were no significant gender-country interactions, but there were significant national and gender differences. Skilled labor is perceived as being more readily available in Norway than in the U.K. and New Zealand. Norwegian entrepreneurs perceive a more stable sales environment than New Zealand entrepreneurs, who perceive a more stable sales environment than British entrepreneurs. The third factor, hostility/uncertainty, shows significant gender differences on the perception of political uncertainty in the country. Female entrepreneurs perceive higher political uncertainty than do male entrepreneurs. In addition, New Zealand entrepreneurs perceive that there are greater numbers of business failures than Norwegian entrepreneurs, and British female entrepreneurs perceive that there are greater numbers of business failures than Norwegian male entrepreneurs. Overall, there were few gender differences on the influence of the environment on business formation and many more national differences.

Nature of the study: Empirical
Nature of the data: Mail survey
Nature of the sample: Male and female venture initiators in Great Britain, Norway, New Zealand
Variables: Business demographics (form, size, age, industry, sales), entrepreneurs' demographics (age, education, entrepreneurial history), motivations, perceptions of the environment

Kourilsky, M. L., & Walstad, W. B. (1998). Entrepreneurship and female youth: Knowledge, attitudes, gender differences and educational practices. *Journal of Business Venturing, 13* (1), 77-88.

This study uses survey data from a national sample of 1,000 female and male high school students to assess their knowledge of and attitudes toward entrepreneurship. It examines whether there are significant gender differences in this area. The results indicate many similarities between females and males with respect to their knowledge of, and opinions about entrepreneurship; however, there are also significant gender differences. Both males and females exhibit a low level of entrepreneurship knowledge. Females, however, are more aware of their deficiencies in the knowledge area than are their male counterparts. Both sexes believe that further education can correct the knowledge problem. Although very interested in starting a business, females are significantly less likely than males (62% vs. 72%) to want to start a business of their own. Both females and males believe in the importance of giving back to the community, which goes beyond providing jobs. The study findings lead to important curricular implications for entrepreneurship education in the nation's schools, especially in relation to females.

Nature of the study: Empirical
Nature of the data: Telephone survey conducted by Gallup organization for National Center for Research in Economic Education and the Center for Entrepreneurial Leadership
Nature of the sample: National sample (1,000) of male and female high school students
Variables: Knowledge of business (taxation, regulation, supply and demand, profits), knowledge of entrepreneurship (start-up processes, funding, franchising, survival), interest level, motivation

Lee-Gosselin, H., & Grise, J. (1990). Are women owner-managers challenging our definitions of entrepreneurship? An in-depth survey. *Journal of Business Ethics, 9* (4/5), 432-433.

This study examines the characteristics of female owner-managers and their firms, the experience of starting a business, the success criteria used, and their vision of the future of their firms. In the Quebec city area, 400 women owner-managers of businesses in the three industrial sectors answered a detailed questionnaire; 75 of these respondents participated in in-depth interviews. The results suggested the importance of a model of "small and stable business" to these women. The small business is not a transitory phase for their firms; most choose and value such a scale of business and seek recognition for what they do. This model appears to represent an innovative adaptation to their professional, social, family, and personal demands. It also challenges definitions of entrepreneurship and "serious business" in Canada.

Nature of the study:	Empirical
Nature of the data:	Mail survey (400), in-depth interviews (75)
Nature of the sample:	Women business owners in Quebec City
Variables:	Business demographics (form, size, age, industry, sales), entrepreneurs' demographics (age, education, entrepreneurial history, family information), motivations, goals, attitudes, business challenges, perceptions of the environment

Lerner, M., Brush, C. G., & Hisrich, R.D. (1995). Factors affecting performance of Israeli women entrepreneurs: An examination of alternative perspectives. In W. D. Bygrave, B. J, Bird, S. Birley, N. C. Churchill, M. Hay, R. H. Keeley, & W. E. Wetzel, Jr. (Eds.), *Frontiers of entrepreneurial research* (pp. 308-322). Boston, MA: Babson College.

This study investigates Israeli women entrepreneurs, analyzing the relationship between individual factors and business performance. The authors use five theoretical perspectives to understand the relationships: motivations and goals, social leanings, network affiliation, human capital, and environmental factors are examined. Findings show that network affiliation, human capital, and motivation theories have greater explanatory power for performance than social learning or environmental perspectives. Similar to research in the U.S., previous experience in the industry was correlated with sales, and motivations were related to profitability and high personal income. Unique to this research is the finding that membership in an association or network of businesswomen had a highly significant effect on profitability.

Nature of the study:	Empirical
Nature of the data:	Mail survey
Nature of the sample:	Israeli women business owners (220)
Variables:	Business demographics (form, age, industry), entrepreneurs' demographics (age, education, entrepreneurial history), business performance (sales, profit, size, income), networking, socialization, planning horizons

Lin, Z., Picot, G., & Compton, J. (2000). The entry and exit dynamics of self-employment in Canada. *Small Business Economics, 15* (2), 105-125.

This is a study of the extent and cyclicality of self-employment entry and exit flows. It explores transitions in and out of self-employment and investigates the influence of individual characteristics and labor market experience as well as macroeconomic conditions on the probability of these moves in Canada. Gross flows into and out of self-employment averaged approximately half a million per year between 1982 and 1994, amounting to 42% of the population. The study finds no evidence that people are increasingly pushed into self-employment by deteriorating economic conditions. However, it found that younger members of the work force were more likely to enter and leave self-employment. Prior paid experience and prior self-employment were related to increased likelihood to enter self-employment. The longer one was self-employed, the less likely he/she would leave the business. Having a self-employed spouse increased the likelihood that the other spouse would be self-employed. Women's self-employment is more responsive than men's to the national unemployment rate.

Nature of the study:	Empirical
Nature of the data:	T1 files of Revenue Canada Longitudinal data from Survey of Labor and Income Dynamics (SLID) of Statistics Canada (1993, 1994)
Nature of the sample:	Canadian Men and women (ages 15-64) in the labor force
Variables:	Demographics (age, sex, location, marital/family status), current employment status, employment history, spouse's employment status, industry, earnings, macroeconomic conditions

Ljunggren, E., & Kolvereid, L. (1996). New business formation: Does gender make a difference? *Women in Management Review, 11* (4), 3-12.

This study investigates gender differences among Norwegian entrepreneurs in the process of starting a new business. It tests three hypotheses: H1) During the business gestation process female entrepreneurs stress personal expectancies while male entrepreneurs stress economic expectancies; H2) During the business gestation process, women perceive stronger social support than men do and women put more emphasis on such support than men do; and H3) Female entrepreneurs perceive having less control and lower entrepreneurial abilities than their male counterparts. In support of H1 and H2, females were found to emphasize independence as a reason for start-up, and to perceive a high degree of social support during the business gestation process. However, contrary to H3, females were found to perceive themselves as possessing higher entrepreneurial abilities than men.

Nature of the study:	Empirical
Nature of the data:	Mail survey

Nature of the sample: Potential entrepreneurs, self-identified through phone calls to "Green Line for Entrepreneurs."

Variables: Entrepreneurs' demographics, motivations, drive, expectancies, perceptions of social support, perceptions of resource availability

Longstreth, M., Stafford, K., & Mauldin, T. (1987). Self-employed women and their families: Time use and socioeconomic characteristics. *Journal of Small Business Management, 25* (3), 30-37.

The objectives of this study are to describe the socioeconomic characteristics, time use patterns, and employment of hired help of an aggregate group of full- and part-time self employed women and their families. The respondents reported that they spent from 20 to 46 hours per week on their businesses and contributed 30-40% of the family budget.

The results suggest that the desire by women to combine paid work and family responsibilities meant that much more time was spent by females in household work than was commonly spent by male workers. This attempt to fill two "jobs" at once may account for the relatively higher number of female entrepreneurs who work only part-time, and it may also account in part for the lower profitability of women's firms. The findings of this research indicated that female entrepreneurs who were married and had children had problems with allocating time between their businesses and families. Resolving time-related conflicts was an especially challenging task since it required the combined efforts of the entrepreneur and her family. The independent nature of entrepreneurship heightened the difficulties, as potential solutions may come more easily to those who operate in groups.

Nature of the study: Empirical
Nature of the data: Mail survey
Nature of the sample: 114 self-employed women, both full- and part-time
Variables: Socioeconomic characteristics, time use patterns, use of hired help

Loscocco, K. A., & Leicht, K. T. (1993). Gender, work-family linkages, and economic success among small business owners. *Journal of Marriage & the Family, 55* (4), 875-887.

This study investigates work-family connections and economic success among women and men small business owners and examines gender similarities and differences. Analyses of data from a three-year panel survey of 99 women and 312 men owners show more support for the gender similarity than the gender difference model. There is considerable gender similarity in the processes through which business and individual characteristics affect personal earnings, although women owners are disadvantaged in some characteristics critical to business success. Family situation has a direct impact on these owners' business success and indirectly affects personal earnings. The results uncover vestiges of traditional gender roles consistent with the gender difference model, but primarily in the context of marriage. Thus, children are experienced as an incentive to fulfill the good provider role not only among married men but also by single women. The event history analyses show that these effects persist over time.

Nature of the study:	Empirical
Nature of the data:	Telephone survey
Nature of the sample:	Men and women business owners in Indiana
Variables:	Individual demographics, family situations, business demographics, industry demographics, business performance

Loscocco, K. A., Robinson, J., Hall, R.H., & Allen, J.K. (1991). Gender and small business success: An inquiry into women's relative disadvantage. *Social Forces, 70* (1), 65-85.

This article compares the financial success of established female and male small business owners, a topic that merges issues of gender and class. Among 540 successful small businesses in New England, female-owned businesses had lower sales volumes and produced lower incomes than male-owned businesses. The characteristics of the owner and the small business that differ between genders explained the discrepancy in financial success, with the smaller size of women's businesses emerging as the major explanatory factor. Women's lack of experience and their concentration in the least profitable industries contributed strongly to the gender discrepancy as well. The processes through which the female small business owner generates sales and derives income are quite similar to those of her male counterpart, but even successful women are not as well positioned to exploit business opportunities as their male counterparts because of structural disadvantages both within and outside of the business arena.

Nature of the study:	Empirical
Nature of the data:	Mail survey
Nature of the sample:	Male and female members of Small Business Association of New England
Variables:	Individual characteristics including skills and experience, family situation, business demographics, business performance

Loscosso, K. A., & Robinson, J. (1991). Barriers to women's small-business success in the United States. *Gender & Society, 5,* 511-532.

Among 540 successful small businesses in New England, female-owned businesses had lower sales volumes and produced lower incomes than male-owned businesses. The smaller size of women's businesses is the major explanatory factor, followed by women's lack of experience and concentration in less profitable industries. Additional contributing factors are lack of access to capital and government contracts as well as institutional barriers.

Nature of the study: Empirical
Nature of the data: Mail survey
Nature of the sample: Male and female members of Small Business Association of New England
Variables: Individual characteristics including skills and experience, family situation, business demographics, business performance

MacNabb, A., McCoy, J., Weinreich, P., & Northover, M. (1993). Using identity structure analysis (ISA) to investigate female entrepreneurship. *Entrepreneurship and Regional Development, 5* (4), 301-313.

The process of founding a business involves both personal transitions and assumption of new roles, which often results in changes of values and beliefs. Values ascribed to entrepreneurs may conflict with conventional feminine values. Researchers have classified women in accordance with their degree of attachment to entrepreneurial values and conventionally defined masculine-feminine values (Goffee and Scase, 1985; Cromie and Hayes, 1987), but there has been little attempt to examine the process of change in women's values and beliefs as a result of business start-up. This paper uses Identity Structure Analysis (Weinreich, 1980, 1986, 1988) to investigate female entrepreneurship and values. The ISA instrument allows researchers to distinguish core values from those used inconsistently. The findings illustrate that these women do not display all the "classical entrepreneurial" values, specifically rejecting risk taking and profit motivation. This finding is in accordance with other research on female entrepreneurs.

Nature of the study: Empirical
Nature of the data: Self-administered survey, case study
Nature of the sample: Women (12) enrolled in Women in Entrepreneurship Programme in Northern Ireland
Variables: Personal characteristics, self image, role n roles, values, motivations

Mankelow, G., & Merrilees, B. (2001). Towards a model of entrepreneurial marketing for rural women: A case study approach. *Journal of Developmental Entrepreneurship, 6* (3), 221-235

This article develops a model of entrepreneurial marketing for rural women. The research builds on other studies of women entrepreneurs but focuses on rural women entrepreneurs. Using a case study approach, the research develops a model of entrepreneurial marketing by female rural entrepreneurs. The model describes the opportunity seeking, information collection, innovation and marketing strategies used by rural women. The model has a number of similarities to existing entrepreneurial models. The distinguishing feature of the marketing model of rural women entrepreneurs was a grassroots approach to marketing, a local groundedness developed principally through informal social networks that provide the bases for marketing activities.

Nature of the study:	Empirical
Nature of the data:	Case studies
Nature of the sample:	Nine Australian entrepreneurs
Variables:	Age, industry, experience, issues most confident about, method to identify new business, methods to collect information, modifications to product or service, strategy to market

Marlow, S. (1997). Self employed women: New opportunities, old challenges. *Entrepreneurship and Regional Development, 9* (3), 199-210.

This paper argues that the gender of an individual entering self-employment will significantly affect the experience of owning a business. Based on the assumption that women are subject to patriarchal pressures, it argues that being female will affect the experience of self-employment, from initiation of the firm to development of the enterprise and the manner of handling daily management challenges. The author uses a matched study of male and female small business owners to evaluate the effect of gender upon the experiences of small firm ownership. Results suggest conditions under which gender might impinge upon the experiences of small business owners. If women begin new small firms because they feel thwarted as women in their careers, if there are credibility problems for firm owners arising from their gender, if a woman's notion of business success differs from male counterparts because her ambitions are molded by gendered experience, and, finally, if women are utilizing self-employment as a solution to dual demands of domestic and waged labor, then the experience of self-employment is tainted by patriarchal expectations.

ture of the study:	Empirical
e of the data:	Interview

Nature of the sample: Matched pairs (28) of male and female business owners in
                          the United Kingdom
Variables: Business demographics, individual demographics, family
                          situation, social networks, business challenges, personal
                          challenges

Masters, R., & Meier, R. (1988). Sex differences and risk-taking propensity of
     entrepreneurs. *Journal of Small Business Management, 26* (1), 31-35.

     To determine if male and female entrepreneurs in the U.S. differ in risk-
     taking propensity and to replicate Brockhaus' (1980) research comparing
     risk-taking propensity in entrepreneurs and managers, the Choice Dilemma
     Questionnaire (CDQ) of Wallach and Kogan (1961) was mailed to 250
     entrepreneurs and managers in the Midwest. Fifty usable replies were
     received. Entrepreneurs are defined as owning or managing a small business;
     managers are respondents who managed but did not own the business. Data
     were analyzed using statistical analysis of covariance with the CDQ score as
     the dependent variable. Results show no significant differences in the risk-
     taking propensity of entrepreneurs versus managers or male entrepreneurs
     versus female entrepreneurs. Brockhaus and Meier also found that
     entrepreneurs and managers did not differ in risk-taking propensity. This
     finding on male versus female entrepreneurs risk-taking propensity departed
     from findings published prior to the 1970s.

Nature of the study: Empirical
Nature of the data: Mail survey
Nature of the sample: Entrepreneurs and managers in Indiana
Variables: Business demographics, individual demographics, attitudes,
                         behaviors

Mathews, C. H., & Moser, S.B. (1996). A longitudinal investigation of the impact of
     family background and gender on interest in small firm ownership. *Journal
     of Small Business Management, 34* (2), 29-43.

     This study assesses the impact of role models and family backgrounds on
     entrepreneurial career interest, particularly the effects on small firm
     ownership over time. It also explores differences in male and female interest
     in small firm ownership. This study involves an ongoing assessment of
     people in the entry stages of their careers. Results indicate gender has the
     primary influence on interest in small firm ownership, with males showing a
     higher level of interest than females.

Nature of the study: Empirical
Nature of the data: Panel study, 3 waves of mail survey

Nature of the sample: Male and female business administration graduates of Midwestern university

Variables: Individual demographics, family situation, role models, interest in business ownership

McKechnie, S.A., Ennew, C. T., & Read, L. H. (1998). The nature of the banking relationship: A comparison of the experiences of male and female small business owners. *International Small Business Journal, 16* (3), 39-55.

Patterned on early work by Swift and Riding (1988); and Riding and Swift (1990), this research compares business owners having the same form of business, industry, location, size, age, and sales growth, thus holding structural differences of businesses operated by men and women constant. Two studies matched pairs of men and women business owners to examine whether differences exist in the terms and conditions of bank financing, the quality of the service provision, and the overall banking relationship. Results from the quantitative study suggest few differences between male and female business owners, with the exception that females secure larger loans than males, yet are charged higher interest rates on the loans. Results from the qualitative analysis indicate that females may make greater use than males of bank overdraft facilities and loans both at start-up and subsequently for growth and development. These results contradict previous research findings about how female business owners finance their businesses. However, even though female business owners appear to place relatively more importance than males on bank managers' advice and understanding of their marketplace, there appeared to be some evidence of discriminating behaviors in the personal interactions between female business owners and bank managers.

Nature of the study: Empirical

Nature of the data: Large-scale mail survey, smaller scale in-depth face-to-face interviews

Nature of the sample: Quantitative study: 16,000 members of Forum of Private Business in the U.K. sent a mail survey during Spring/Summer, 1992 yielded 6,101 (37.5%) usable responses. Two equally matched samples of male and female respondents were drawn from the total sample (n-282). Qualitative study: 10 women- and men-owned businesses in Southern England matched for size, ownership structure, age, and product/service type.

Variables: Core product of bank (borrowing terms and conditions of loan), perceptions of the nature of the banking relationship (extent relationship was constrained by bank policy, perceptions of service quality and overall relationship with bank manager), sex

Miller, A., & Masten, J. (1993). Integration of micro/small business support agencies and clients to strengthen the private sector in the Dominican Republic. *International Small Business Journal, 11* (2), 26-36.

This study is based on the premise that small business assistance programs facilitate and assist in micro-enterprise development in the Dominican Republic. Based on 13 in-depth interviews with small business assistance programs, results show that the typical client was male (80%), early 30s, with less than eight years of education. The primary motive for the typical client to seek assistance was to improve income and change economic status. Most clients were from low productive employment, agricultural jobs, and lower socio-economic status. The authors draw a comparison between the characteristics of client enterprises and agency organizations by identifying the typical clients, structure and process of assistance. Only one agency served women entrepreneurs with an all female-counseling staff. Recommendations for assistance are made to better serve the people seeking assistance.

Nature of the study:	Empirical
Nature of the data:	Interview
Nature of the sample:	13 small business assistance agency directors in the Dominican Republic
Variables:	Client demographics (age, education, income); agency structure and process

Mirchandani, K. (1999). Feminist insight on gendered work: New directions in research on women and entrepreneurship. *Gender, Work, and Organization, 6* (4), 224-235.

This paper explores research on female entrepreneurs using a feminist theory perspective on gendered work. The analysis suggests that exploring links between social stratification, business ownership, organizational structure, and industry provides useful insights on entrepreneurship. The author argues that it is important to assume a critical view towards the historical exclusion of women from the literature of entrepreneurship. Rather than assuming that this exclusion of women was an "accidental" omission, correctable through replicating studies of male entrepreneurs with female business owners, it would be useful to understand entrepreneurship itself as a "gendered" activity. The author further argues that existing knowledge on women business owners could be enhanced through reflection on two issues: 1) the essentialism in the very construction of the category of "the female entrepreneur," and 2) the ways in which the connections among gender, occupation, and organizational structure differently affect female and male business owners.

Nature of the study:	Conceptual
Nature of the data:	NA

Nature of the sample: NA
Variables: Social stratification, gender, occupation, business ownership, organizational structure, industry

Miskin, V., & Rose, J. (1990). Women entrepreneurs: Factors related to success. In N. C. Churchill, W. D. Bygrave, J. A. Hornaday, D. F. Muzyka, K. H. Vesper, & W. E. Wetzel, Jr. (Eds.), *Frontiers of entrepreneurial research* (pp. 27-38). Boston, MA: Babson College.

This study examines characteristic differences between male and female entrepreneurs, with a primary focus on the relationship of gender to profitability. The success or profitability levels of new business ventures are dependent on type of business, availability of sufficient start-up capital, stage of product development, and the management skills and experiences of the entrepreneur. Socialization is said to have implications for the types of businesses pursued and the financial and technical barriers specific to women entrepreneurs. The results of the study support the interpretation that the traditional socialization of women in the work place does compete for their time, more than is experienced by their male counterparts. It calls for further study of the relationship between performance-related self-confidence and venture success.

Nature of the study: Empirical
Nature of the data: Mail survey
Nature of the sample: Pre-venture clients of Washington State Small Business Development Center, 1986
Variables: Entrepreneurs' characteristics, situational variables, product/service characteristics, venture launch, venture profitability

Moore, D. P. (1990). An examination of present research on the female entrepreneur: Suggested research strategies for the 1990s. *Journal of Business Ethics, 9* (4/5), 275-281.

This study focuses on the state of the art of research on female entrepreneurs and suggests direction for future research. Moore indicates that the field is in an initial stage of paradigm development. Individual studies are fragmented and unrelated and describe only small segments of the female entrepreneurial population. Theoretical tools developed in other areas are frequently applied that are neither valid nor reliable. As female entrepreneurships and business ownerships continue to develop, researchers will be forced to account for the differences between the sexes across a wide range of variables. With the new focus on international markets and cross-cultural comparisons, studies of expatriates as entrepreneurs are needed. Also needed are healthier data sets, more sophisticated statistical techniques, and longitudinal studies. Although the assembled data on the female entrepreneur has not reached the point of theory development, it is at the stage where models can be examined.

Nature of the study: Literature review
Nature of the data: NA
Nature of the sample: NA
Variables: NA

Moran, P. (1998). Personality characteristics and growth orientation of the small business owner manager. *International Small Business Journal, 16* (3), 17-39.

The study reports the development and testing of a procedure for profiling the growth orientation of small business-owner managers using a multi-dimensional approach. A battery of well established instruments was used to tap different aspects of motivation, cognition, and ability to predict owner-managers' perceptions, plans, and needs. The intent of the research is to develop an assessment methodology that could be used to develop and support small business owner's managers and increase their odds of success.

Nature of the study: Empirical
Nature of the data: Multi-dimensional utilizing a wide-range of instruments; included were personality tests and ability-oriented exercises (e.g., in-basket, crisis scenarios).
Nature of the sample: 70 owner-managers enrolled in extended business development programs in north-east and south-west England
Variables: Growth orientation, personality (Myers-Briggs Type Indicator), learning style (Learning Styles Questionnaire), managerial or leadership orientation (Leadership Opinion Questionnaire), preferred team role (Belbin SAQ), values (Gordon's Survey of Personal Values and Survey of Interpersonal Values), creativity (Alternate Uses), ability (in-basket), entrepreneurial orientation (General Enterprise Tendency)

Neider, L. (1987). A preliminary investigation of female entrepreneurs in Florida. *Journal of Small Business Management, 25* (3), 22-29.

This study describes the demographic and personality characteristics of female entrepreneurs and the organizational characteristics of their businesses. A total of 52 women were sampled. Demographic characteristics varied widely with ages from 26 to 62, with a mean of 41 years of age. A majority of the women were firstborns (77%) and had an entrepreneurial parent (54%). Most were currently married (72%) but had been divorced at least once (69%). Over half were college educated (56%) and most owned service businesses (92%). The profile of personality characteristics that emerged indicated that the typical female entrepreneur is very independent, has very high needs for achievement and control over the activities of others, and is clearly action-oriented and persistent. Organizational patterns indicated a relatively informal structure and lack of external funding.

Nature of the study: Empirical
Nature of the data: Field interviews, observation, psychological tests
Nature of the sample: Female entrepreneurs in Florida
Variables: Individual demographics, business demographics, psychological profiles

Nelson, G. (1991). Locus of control for successful female small business proprietors. The Mid-*Atlantic Journal of Business, 27* (3), 213-224.

Surveys were conducted with 97 female business owners to examine the association between perceived control and business success as measured by return on investment (ROI). Relationships were analyzed directly and via hierarchical regression to assess the effects of additional related independent variables. The negative relationship between age and ROI was anticipated, but the positive correlation between time in business and performance is contrary to some previous research. The possibility that the association between locus of control and certain forms of achievement may be curvilinear, in particular, logarithmic, indicates an aspect of internality that warrants further examination. The analysis also implies a discontinuity because the data suggest such great differences in locus of control internality between those who have barely achieved moderate success and those who have achieved phenomenal success.

Nature of the study: Empirical
Nature of the data: Mail survey
Nature of the sample: Female business owners
Variables: Individual demographics, individual motivations, individual attitudes, individual behaviors, business demographics, business performance

Nilsson, P. (1997). Business counseling services directed towards female entrepreneurs: Some legitimacy dilemmas. *Entrepreneurship and Regional Development, 9* (3), 239-258.

This paper examines and evaluates perceptions of a three-year-old governmental business support program directed towards female entrepreneurs in the rural districts of Sweden. The implementation of a gender-segregated business counseling (GSBC) service is discussed from a neo-institutional perspective. The intention is to explore the components of the counseling service's identity formation and then to discuss the responses from the local management. The dilemmas mainly concern two issues: first, the GSBC services were perceived as alien in comparison with conventional business support. Due to the tasks and procedures (economic advice, educational programs and seminars) within the GSBC, it differed from the business support services conducted by the local government. Secondly, the GSBC service was perceived as salient, in its ability to receive legitimacy among actors outside the local government.

Nature of the study: Empirical
Nature of the data: Interview
Nature of the sample: Female business counselors affiliated with GSBC
Variables: Counselors' resources (education, experience, business
                         background), perceptions of services, perceptions of
                         legitimacy, perceptions of relationships with Local
                         Enterprise Boards and Swedish National Board for
                         Industries and Technical Development

Olson, S. F., & Currie, H. M. (1992). Female entrepreneurs: Personal value systems and business strategies in a male-dominated industry. *Journal of Small Business Management, 30* (1), 49-57.

The relationship between the personal values of female entrepreneurs and their chosen business strategies is examined in this survey research of women business owners in the construction industry. (All companies are certified under the Federal Surface Transportation Assistance Act.) The responses are classified using the Miles-Snow typology consisting of four strategy classifications: 1) defender, 2) reactor, 3) prospector, and 4) analyzer. Forty percent of the female entrepreneurs placed their strategies in the defender category, 20% in the analyzer category, 20% in the prospector category, and 8% in the reactor category. In addition, comparison to earlier studies examining male entrepreneurs in the same industry indicated that women in male-dominated areas may feel forced into allowing external factors to dictate their strategies, regardless of their personal values. In contrast, the male entrepreneurs' strategies mirror their personal values.

Nature of the study: Empirical
Nature of the data: Mail survey
Nature of the sample: Women business owners in construction industry, in
                         operation for a minimum of two years
Variables: Individual demographics, business demographics, business
                         strategy choices, personal values

Parasuraman, S., Purohit, Y. S., Godshalk, V. M., & Beutell, N. J. (1996). Work and family variables, entrepreneurial career success, and psychological well-being. *Journal of Vocational Behavior, 48,* 275-300.

The paper investigates the influence of work and family variables on the career success and psychological well-being of both men and women entrepreneurs. The results showed that work-domain variables accounted for significant variation in time commitment to family. Time commitment to work and time commitment to family played an important role, mediating the effects of role demands and gender, work, and family characteristics on work-to-family conflict and family-to-work conflict. These two types of work-family conflict in turn mediated the effects of time commitment to work and family, along with other selected work and family variables, on entrepreneurs' career success and life stress.

Nature of the study:	Empirical
Nature of the data:	Survey
Nature of the sample:	111 business owners enrolled in continuing education courses for small business owners in two eastern universities
Variables:	Entrepreneurial career success, autonomy, schedule inflexibility, work-role overload, job involvement, parental demands, instrumental support, informational/emotional support, family involvement, time commitment to work, work to family conflict, career satisfaction, family satisfaction, life stress, time commitment to family, family to work conflict

Pellegrino, E. T., & Reece, B. L. (1982). Perceived formative and operational problems encountered by female entrepreneurs in retail and service firms. *Journal of Small Business Management, 20* (2), 15-25.

Women in small business have been viewed as facing special problems and unique obstacles to success in establishing and managing small businesses. This study uses semi-structured interviews to collect formative, operational, and demographic information as well as offer a set of open-ended questions pertaining to the role of women in small business. The overall findings do not support the contention of unique problems for women in starting or operating a small business. However, obtaining funds to start and operate the business, as well as operational concerns with record keeping, financial management, and advertising are reported. The authors recommend replication of the study in a similar SMSA and future research with a comparable population of males and females.

Nature of the study:	Empirical
Nature of the data:	Interview (semi-structured)
Nature of the sample:	20 randomly selected female entrepreneurs from the population of female entrepreneurs in the Roanoke, VA SMSA

| Variables: | Industry (USOE codes), years as business owner, problems in obtaining information and assistance, estimating business potential and profitability, selecting a location, obtaining funds to finance and operate the business firm, managerial planning, human resources, record keeping, financial management, marketing |

Price, C., & Monroe, S. (1992). Educational training for women and minority entrepreneurs positively impacts venture growth and development. In N. C. Churchill, S. Birley, W. D. Bygrave, D. F. Muzyka, C. Wahlbin, & W. E. Wetzel, Jr. (Eds.), *Frontiers of entrepreneurship research* (pp. 216-230). Boston, MA: Babson College.

This study reports on women and minority participants in six years of the Premiere "Fast Trac" training programs offered in Denver, Colorado. A literature review provides contextual information on the demographics of U.S. women- and minority-owned small business activities. The study uses a control group of selected Fast Trac participants (prior to their training) in Denver and Kansas City, Missouri. The study concludes that the training had a positive impact on the success of women- and minority-owned firms. Writing sound business plans, counseling, networking, capital and financial planning, along with support from the Denver community, were effective in converting potentially high risk ventures into more stable and growing enterprises.

Nature of the study:	Empirical
Nature of the data:	Mail survey, interviews; longitudinal
Nature of the sample:	Questionnaire A: 125 female and minority graduates of Denver Fast Trac programs prior to 1991 plus 20 additional respondents in 1993; Questionnaire B: 82 participants of Denver Fast Trac programs from 1987- 1992; Questionnaire C: 72 Denver and 49 Kansas City pre-Fast Trac business owners
Variables:	Characteristics of the respondent and the business, sources of financing, Fast Trac program outcomes

Read, L. H. (1994). Raising finance from banks: A comparative study of the experiences of male and female business owners. In W.D. Bygrave, S. Birley, N. C. Churchill, E. Gatewood, F. Hoy, R. H. Keeley, & W. E. Wetzel, Jr. (Eds.), *Frontiers of entrepreneurship research* (pp. 361-372). Boston, MA: Babson College.

This study addresses the perception that women business owners face greater difficulties in raising capital than men business owners do. Issues explored include how businesswomen use their banks, the problems experienced, how problems are dealt with, and attitudes towards banks. Matched pair samples are made for gender comparisons. The findings indicate more similarities than differences between male and female entrepreneurs in their use of banking facilities and experiences of dealing with banks. Although neither men nor women used banks often for advice, women were more likely to do so, while men were more likely to respond to the banking advice. Nevertheless, 12.5% of women business owners did feel that they had experienced unfair or discriminatory treatment from their bank because of their gender.

Nature of the study: Empirical
Nature of the data: Interviews
Nature of the sample: 40 matched pair samples (female/male) in South England
Variables: Characteristics of the business, characteristics of the owner, use of banks, banks as source of advice, frequency of banking contact, involvement of others in the banking relationship, problems in the banking relationship, manner in which problems addressed

Renzulli, L.A., Aldrich, H., & Moody, J. (2000). Family matters: Gender, networks, and entrepreneurial outcomes. *Social Forces, 79* (2), 523-546.

Gender differences are one of several factors posited to have an effect on business start-ups. This article focuses on information and social support networks as specific components of social capital. The authors conceptualize social capital as inherent in people's relations with others and examine the association between men's and women's social capital and their likelihood of starting a business. Two aspects of respondents' social capital are highlighted: the extent to which their business discussion networks are heterogeneous and the proportion of kin included. Findings indicate that a high proportion of kin and homogeneity in the network, rather than being female or having a high proportion of females in the network, are critical disadvantages facing potential small business owners.

Nature of the study: Empirical
Nature of the data: Telephone interviews (Research Triangle Entrepreneurial Development Study)
Nature of the sample: 353 male and female nascent entrepreneurs and business owners, Research Triangle, NC
Variables: Life stage of firm, employment status, human capital characteristics of entrepreneur, network characteristics

Riding, A. L., & Swift, C.S. (1990). Women business owners and terms of credit: Some empirical findings of the Canadian experience. *Journal of Business Venturing, 5* (5), 327-340.

A pervasive perception exists that women business owners face discrimination by bankers. This study analyzes that perception through a gender comparison of debt financing. Findings show that the financing conditions for women principals are less favorable than those for male business owners; however, female-owned firms tend to be both younger and smaller than male-owned firms. The authors posit that such findings suggest alternative explanations of perceived gender bias. After controlling for business characteristics, differences remained as to the amount of collateral requirements for a line of credit.

Nature of the study:	Empirical
Nature of the data:	Mail survey
Nature of the sample:	3,217 business principals (153 women); Canadian Federation of Independent Business (CFIB)
Variables:	Business characteristics, financing conditions, perceptions of bank competition, perceptions of bank service, concerns about bank service

Robinson, S. (2001). An examination of entrepreneurial motives and their influence on the way rural women small business owners manage their employees. *Journal of Developmental Entrepreneurship, 6* (2), 151-167.

This research is based on projection theory (Cohen et al., 1996; Feldman, 1992), which, in this context, posits that entrepreneurs will offer their employees job characteristics consistent with those that the proprietors themselves desired before starting their businesses. The study uses the qualitative quasi-deductive research method to determine if, and in what way, some rural women entrepreneurs' management styles were influenced by their motives for starting businesses. As suggested by projection theory, these women were at least somewhat influenced by their own desires and experiences to offer their employees work situations and opportunities consistent with the entrepreneurs' own needs and desires. It was also discovered that each of the women placed great importance on relationships. They created and maintained corporate cultures with minimal interpersonal conflict among employees.

Nature of the study:	Empirical
Nature of the data:	Case study
Nature of the sample:	Female entrepreneurs in rural Pennsylvania
Variables:	Business owner, flexible hours, independence and control of work, financial reward, provide a ministry

Robinson, P. B., & Sexton, E. A. (1994). The effect of education and experience on self-employment success. *Journal of Business Venturing, 9* (2), 141-156.

The impact of education on the business success of an entrepreneur is the subject of much discussion and speculation in both the popular and academic press. This study examines the effect of education, experience, and gender on the probability of being self-employed, as well as the relationship between years of formal education and the earnings potential of the self-employed vs. wage-and-salary workers. Three hypotheses are supported, that the self-employed have more years of formal education than wage-and-salary workers, that the number of years of formal education will increase the probability of becoming self-employed, and that a relationship exists between years of formal education and self-employment or wage-and-salary success. A positive but weaker relationship is found between experience and self-employment success. The authors conclude that a general education has a strong positive influence on entrepreneurship in terms of becoming self-employed and successful.

Nature of the study:	Empirical
Nature of the data:	Database. Public Use-B sample of 1980 U.S. Census of Population
Nature of the sample:	Limited to 23- to –64-year-old non-student workers who either worked for wages or salary in 1979 or who were self-employed in that year
Variables:	Human capital characteristics, business ownership status, number of hours and weeks worked, total family income, industry

Romano, C. (1994). It looks like men are from Mars, women are from Venus. *Management Review, 83* (10), 7.

This study analyzes how entrepreneurs define and achieve success. Using data from the National Foundation for Women Business Owners, the authors posit that money is an important component of success for both sexes but that differences are also a factor. For women, success is reported as having control over their own destinies, building ongoing relationships with clients, and doing something fulfilling. Men describe success in terms of achieving goals. The men who mention happiness and satisfaction link those terms to gaining self-satisfaction for a job well done.

Nature of the study:	Empirical
Nature of the data:	National Foundation for Women Business Owners data base
Nature of the sample:	127 male and female entrepreneurs
Variables:	Definitions of success, sex of the respondent

Rosa, P., Carter, S., & Hamilton, D. (1996). Gender as a determinant of small business performance: Insights from a British study. *Small Business Economics, 8* (4), 463-478.

This study examines the relationship between gender and small business performance, exploring the proposition that women business owners perform less well on quantitative financial measures. Using a sample stratified by gender and industry, the authors find differences by sex in quantitative economic and financial performance measures. Female businesses were found to under-perform in terms of the number of employees, VAT registration, sales turnover, capital assets, and range of markets. Female business owners were also less likely to own multiple businesses and less likely to plan expansion. Those female business owners who did plan to expand also selected different expansion strategies than male business owners. However, the authors emphasize that the complexity of the patterns of results requires careful interpretation.

Nature of the study: Empirical
Nature of the data: Mail questionnaire
Nature of the sample: 600 owner managers, stratified by sex and industry sector
                         (200 each from textile/clothing, business services,
                         hotel/catering)
Variables: 650 variables representing business and owner
                         characteristics and entrepreneurial performance

Rosa, P., & Hamilton, D. (1994). Gender and ownership in U.K. small firms. *Entrepreneurship Theory and Practice, 18* (3), 11-27.

This paper examines the impact of gender on small business ownership in regard to the gender composition of the founding team, the relationships among the founding team, and management roles of business owners. The authors report difficulties in interpreting sex differences as "gender" trends, owing to significant sectoral variation. Nevertheless, some marked gender differences were identified as to differential patterns of kinship with the respondent, the allocation and perception of specialist roles within the business, and the fact that female owners are less likely to be associated with more than two businesses. Overall sole traders were in the minority in both sexes, implying that most owners shared responsibility and management in some way with other owners. The paper concludes with methodological implications of co-ownership for the sampling and analysis of small business owner/managers from a gender perspective.

Nature of the study: Empirical
Nature of the data: Interview/structured questionnaire
Nature of the sample: 602 male and female business owners in U.K.
Variables: Industry, characteristics of owners, relationships among
                         owners, roles

Rozier, C. K., & Thompson, M. (1998). Female entrepreneurs in a female-dominated health profession: An exploratory study. *Journal of Developmental Entrepreneurship, 3* (1), 149-164.

While 74% of physical therapists are female and opportunities exist for self-owned practices, the number of men who open physical therapy practices exceeds the number of women. This paper uses a qualitative approach to identify processes and conditions for women in physical theory to become entrepreneurs and presents an explanatory model relating internal and external factors and self-employment consequences. Role models and mentors are identified as important elements of external conditions, with all participants reporting role models as female and mentors as male (if a mentor exists). The identified patterns support the importance of positive external conditions as related to positive self-employment consequences.

Nature of the study:	Empirical
Nature of the date:	Interview
Nature of the sample:	9 female physical therapists
Variables:	Personal characteristics, family backgrounds and careers, role models, mentors, issues relating to work or family

Scherer, R. F., Brodzinski, J. D., & Wiebe, F. A. (1990). Entrepreneur career selection and gender: A socialization approach. *Journal of Small Business Management, 28* (2), 37-44.

Career selection literature focuses upon gender differences in the relationship between early social learning experiences and career decisions. This paper explores whether gender is the basis for differences in entrepreneurial career preference, particularly as related to social learning variables, education and training aspirations, expectations for entry, and career self-efficacy. The authors conclude that males have a higher preference for entrepreneurship than females do. Differences are ascribed primarily to self-efficacy and expectations of entering an entrepreneurial career. The authors suggest that social learning differences have a strong impact on shaping preferences for an entrepreneurial career. Practical suggestions to support entrepreneurship by women are offered.

Nature of the study:	Empirical
Nature of the data:	Survey
Nature of the sample:	216 male and 165 female undergraduate business administration students, southern U.S.
Variables:	Demographic characteristics, education and training aspirations, career entry expectations, self-efficacy measure

Scherr, F. C., Sugrue, T. F., & Ward, J. B. (1993). Financing the small firm start-up: Determinants of debt use. *Journal of Small Business Finance, 3* (1), 17-36.

> The study empirically investigates the initial (start-up) capital structures of small firms. Research hypotheses concern the relationship between the ratio of debt to total capitalization and three sets of explanatory variables: human capital, risk preferences, and business and firm operation attributes. Myer's Pecking Order Hypothesis is used to support arguments that owners/managers will finance new ventures in a hierarchical fashion, first using internal equity, followed by debt and, finally, external equity. Because external equity is extremely costly for small firms, debt financing was expected to be the preferred external source of financing. Findings reveal a positive relationship between the use of debt and business income expectations and marital status. Owner's age and race was a significant negative predictor of debt financing, whereas educational and experience-based characteristics did not appear to be important to outside lenders. Firms that used debt capital financing utilized multiple sources of borrowing, but the single largest source of debt was bank financing, with borrowing from other members of the family (quasi-equity) being the second most important source. Male owners were found to use significantly more debt, leading the authors to speculate that female owners may be more risk averse or that lenders may discriminate against female owners. Industry was an important factor in debt financing.

Nature of the study:	Empirical
Nature of the data:	Mail survey
Nature of the sample:	Two samples extracted from the 1982 Characteristics of Business Owners (CBO) database); One sample included firms regardless of source of debt financing; one only firms' borrowing from financial institutions
Variables:	Ratio of business start-up debt to total capital, owner's age, owner's education, owner's business education, owners' family business experience, owner's managerial experience, owner's business experience, percent of owner's income expected from the business, owner's marital status, owner's gender, owner's ethnicity, industry, expected firm size, expected profitability

Schiller, B. R., & Crewson, P.E. (1997). Entrepreneurial origins: A longitudinal inquiry. *Economic Inquiry, 35* (3), 523-531.

> The question of who is an entrepreneur and what factors breed entrepreneurial success is longstanding. This paper explores the profile of those who pursue self-employment in their youth and those who succeed, emphasizing the importance of studying entry and exit rates. Using data from the National Longitudinal Surveys of Youth, the authors find a high incidence of self-employment, but low success rates. Significant correlates of

entry into self-employment and eventual success differ markedly by gender. Role models, self-assurance, and marriage are more relevant to the supply of female entrepreneurs. Education and experience are negatively correlated with female entrepreneurship while work experience is positively correlated with performance. The authors suggest that different strategies are needed to develop entrepreneurship among men and women.

Nature of the study:	Empirical
Nature of the data:	National Longitudinal Surveys of Youth database
Nature of the sample:	12,000 youths
Variables:	Socio-economic background, education, work history, long-run goals, years self-employed, self-employment income, industry/occupation

Schwartz, E. (1976). Entrepreneurship: A new female frontier. *Journal of Contemporary Business, 5* (1), 47-76.

This paper explores sets of characteristics, motivations, and attitudes of female entrepreneurs, as well as the barriers they face. The research was motivated by the small amount of attention paid to date to female entrepreneurs. Motivations for female entrepreneurs are reported as the need to achieve and to have job satisfaction, as well as economic necessity and a desire for independence. Strong egos and the need for achievement are also seen to be relevant personality traits. Findings suggest that the major barrier to success for women entrepreneurs is credit discrimination during the capital formation stage and that the most frequent mistakes made are in pricing practices. The author concludes that there is little difference in the makeup of female and male entrepreneurs.

Nature of the study:	Empirical
Nature of the data:	Interviews for women business owners and literature review for information on male entrepreneurs
Nature of the sample:	20 female entrepreneurs
Variables:	Personal characteristics, motivation for starting a business, industry, prior work experience, perception of entrepreneurial behavioral traits, management style, barriers faced

Scott, C. E. (1986). Why more women are becoming entrepreneurs. *Journal of Small Business Management, 24* (4), 37-44.

This paper explores why women are turning to entrepreneurship in increasing numbers, as well as the characteristics of women business owners and how successful they have been. Hypotheses include motivations related to "glass ceiling" issues and desired flexibility for family concerns. Drawing from two separate surveys, the author concludes that women business owners are better educated than the average woman and have previous experience as managers. Comparatively few, however, have the type of background usually deemed appropriate for male business managers, such as business administration, science, or engineering. Men and women also report different priorities as entrepreneurs; men stress being their own boss, while women place more emphasis on personal challenge and satisfaction.

Nature of the study: Empirical
Nature of the data: Mail survey
Nature of the sample: 154 women business owners from the Georgia Women Business Ownership Educational Council; 80 women business owners from the Georgia Women Business Ownership Educational Council plus supplement of male-owned businesses from the Atlanta telephone book.
Variables: Personal and business characteristics, reasons for going into businesses, disadvantages and advantages of being a women business owner, chief problems, importance of business income, expectations

Servon, L. J. (1996). Microenterprise programs and women: Entrepreneurship as individual empowerment. *Journal of Developmental Entrepreneurship, 1* (1), 31-55.

Combining policy analysis with program evaluation, this paper argues that the Women's Initiative for Self Employment (WISE), like many micro-enterprise programs, uses credit as a springboard for simple access to business funding as well as to support individual empowerment. The history and philosophy of WISE is presented, along with a description of program services, outcomes, and policy implications. The majority of low-income women are considered as not equipped to start businesses without first gaining access to other resources and skills. Programs like WISE accommodate this recognition by shifting the focus of their missions to include a broader range of acceptable outcomes. While these programs may not meet traditional economic development goals such as creating many new businesses with multiple employees, programs are reported as performing important functions that are often more closely aligned with the social welfare field. Specifically, these programs are shown to be functioning as social training programs, with a desired outcome of empowering women to manage their lives within the constraints of the new economy.

Nature of the study: Empirical
Nature of the data: In-depth interviews, existing program data, non-participant observation, and survey data of WISE participants
Nature of the sample: WISE organizational materials and program borrowers
Variables: Historical and philosophical descriptions, program descriptions, loan fund characteristics, loan portfolio, borrower characteristics, staff activities, qualitative indicators

Sexton, D. L., & Bowman, N. B. (1986). Validation of a personality index: Comparative psychological characteristics analysis of female entrepreneurs, managers, entrepreneurship students and business students. In R. Ronstadt, J. A. Hornaday, R. Peterson, & K.H. Vesper (Eds.), *Frontiers of entrepreneurship research* (pp. 40-51). Boston, MA: Babson College.

This paper proposes a model of new venture creation that is intended to identify psychological characteristics unique to the entrepreneur, provide additional information on female entrepreneurs, and contribute to the validation of a modified JPI/PRF-E test instrument (Jackson Personality Inventory and Personality Research Form – E). The authors acknowledge that many psychological measures common to successful people are not unique to entrepreneurs but further propose that there are sets of psychological measure levels that are indeed unique to entrepreneurs. The traits measured are conformity, energy level, interpersonal affect, risk-taking, social adroitness, autonomy, change, harm avoidance, and succorance. Findings show significant differences on all nine scales between female students in entrepreneurship and female students in other business majors. Similar differences were found between female entrepreneurs and managers. Age-related differences are also noted.

Nature of the study:	Empirical
Nature of the data:	Test instrument
Nature of the sample:	127 female, Texas business students (54 entrepreneurship, 73 other business major), 201 Texas businesswomen (105 entrepreneurs, 96 managers).
Variables:	Jackson Personality Inventory, Personality Research Form-E

Sexton, D. L., & Bowman-Upton, N. (1990). Female and male entrepreneurs: Psychological characteristics and their role in gender related discrimination. *Journal of Business Venturing, 5* (1), 29-36.

This paper explores the psychological traits of growth oriented male and female entrepreneurs using the Jackson Personality Inventory and the Personality Research Form-E. Comparative findings between male and female business owners reveal no significant differences in five of the nine traits. Females did score significantly lower on traits related to energy level and risk taking and significantly higher on traits related to autonomy and change. The authors conclude that the psychological propensities of male and female entrepreneurs are more similar than they are different.

Nature of the study:	Empirical
Nature of the data:	Test instrument
Nature of the sample:	Convenience samples of 105 female entrepreneurs from Texas and 69 male entrepreneurs from Ohio
Variables:	Conformity, energy level, interpersonal affect, risk-taking, social adroitness, autonomy, change, harm avoidance, succorance

Sexton, D. L., & Kent, C. A. (1981). Female executives and entrepreneurs: A preliminary comparison. In K. H. Vesper (Ed.), *Frontiers of entrepreneurship research* (pp 40-55). Boston, MA: Babson College.

Previous studies of the psychological characteristics of entrepreneurs have largely been based upon male samples. This study reports upon a comparative study of psychological and demographic characteristics of female entrepreneurs and executives. The project hypothesis is that female entrepreneurs would be found to differ from female executives. Findings show that female entrepreneurs and executives tend to be more similar than different. However, differences are reported showing the entrepreneurs as slightly less educated and ranking hard work and persistence as more important than for female executives.

Nature of the study:	Empirical
Nature of the data:	Personal interviews and mail survey
Nature of the sample:	Convenience sample of 48 female entrepreneurs plus 45 female executives drawn from Standard and Poor's Corporate Directory. All respondents located in Texas.
Variables:	Sibling position, motivation for working, parent's occupation, education, age, work experience, personal priorities, success ingredient, self-concept, business industry

Shabbir, A., & Gregorio, S.Di. (1996). An examination of the relationship between women's personal goals and structural factors influencing their decisions to start a business: The case of Pakistan. *Journal of Business Venturing, 11* (6), 507-529.

Adopting a symbolic interactionist approach, this study explores women's experiences in starting a business, focusing on women's perceptions and interpretations of their business goals and the advantages and constraints they face in starting a business at a micro level. The study revealed that women wanted to start a business to achieve three types of personal goals: personal freedom, security, and satisfaction. The impact of structural factors on the ability of women to start a business varied according to their dominant personal goals. A proposed framework acts as an explanatory framework of the relationship between the goals and structural dimensions. Caution is given as to the unique nature of the Pakistani context. Case excerpts are included.

Nature of the study:	Empirical
Nature of the data:	Interviews
Nature of the sample:	33 female participants in an entrepreneurial development program (EDP), Pakistan
Variables:	Motivation, access to resources, technological constraints, professional and occupational constraints, government regulations, role of family/friends, start-up activities, business characteristics

Shane, S., Kolvereid, L., & Westhead, P. (1991). An exploratory examination of the reasons leading to new firm formation across country and gender. *Journal of Business Venturing, 6* (6), 431-446.

The model of reasons for start-up developed by Scheinberg and MacMillan (1988) is used in an international research project on new business formation conducted by the Society of Associated Researchers in International Entrepreneurship (SARIE). Factor analysis reveals four robust reasons for start-up: independence, recognition, learning, and roles. The authors find significant differences by country, gender, and country-gender interactions. The only reason for start-up that applies across country and gender is the ability to develop one's own approach to work.

Nature of the study:	Empirical
Nature of the data:	Mail survey
Nature of the sample:	Business owners in New Zealand (138), Great Britain (209) and Norway (205)
Variables:	Country status, gender, 21 items for measuring reasons (from the SARIE questionnaire), two added reasons about tax considerations

Shaver, K. G. (1995). The entrepreneurial personality myth. *Business and Economic Review, 41* (3), 20-23.

Research in entrepreneurship debunks the idea of an entrepreneurial personality. The author reviews research comparing entrepreneurs to non-entrepreneurs on achievement motivation, locus of control, risk taking, and creativity and concludes that only achievement motivation shows a clear relationship to entrepreneurial activity. This study focuses on the reasons for starting a business, defined as either internal or external to the person and stable or variable over time, representing dimensions of attribution theory. Two primary findings are that individual beliefs about entrepreneurial potential are changeable and that entrepreneurial careers of women differ from those of men.

Nature of the study:	Empirical, longitudinal
Nature of the data:	Interview
Nature of the sample:	31 female and 54 male pre-venture clients of a Houston Small Business Development Center
Variables:	Reason for starting a business, time spent on business organizing activities, individual characteristics

Shaver, K. G., Gartner, W. B., Gatewood, E.J., & Vos, L.H. (1996). Psychological factors in success at getting into business. In P. D. Reynolds, S. Birley, J. E. Butler, W. D. Bygrave, P. Davidsson, W. B. Gartner, & P. P. McDougall (Eds.), *Frontiers of entrepreneurship research* (pp. 77-90). Boston, MA: Babson College.

This study is described as the preliminary phase of a longitudinal design to assess the relationship between psychological characteristics and business organizing activities. Measures of achievement motivation, locus of control, risk perception, and creativity are assessed among participants in an SBDC-based course on how to get into business. Respondents were asked to indicate their chosen business and their reasons for entry. Reasons for going into business were coded according to measures representing attribution theory and results of this coding were examined for demographic differences. Results indicate that it is possible to obtain reliable measures of psychological characteristics without having to employ complete scales. There is a surprising lack of differences based on demographic characteristics, except for sex. Scale interaction shows that the innovation scores and achievement/activity scores are greater among male than female respondents.

Nature of the study:	Empirical, longitudinal
Nature of the data:	Interview
Nature of the sample:	116 participants of a southeastern U.S. SBDC training program (60 female, 56 male)
Variables:	Measures of achievement motivation, locus of control, risk perception, creativity, reasons for starting business, industrial sector

Shragg, P., Yacuk, L., & Glass, A. (1992). Study of barriers facing Albertan women in business. *Journal of Small Business and Entrepreneurship, 9* (4), 40-49.

This study investigates the real and perceived barriers facing Albertan women in business relative to those facing men in business. Six of seven barriers to female entrepreneurship previously attributed to gender, as identified in the literature review (e.g., access to financing, support and information networks, lack of business management training and experience, negative effects on personal and family relationships, hostile environment and other barriers), may not be supported by this study. The findings suggest that the barriers to female entrepreneurship were issues of negative self-perceptions. The majority of barriers faced by female entrepreneurs were also faced by male entrepreneurs.

Nature of the study:	Empirical
Nature of the data:	Mail survey
Nature of the sample:	245 entrepreneurs (142 male; 103 female)
Variables:	Barriers to female entrepreneurs, gender, length of

association with the business, previous experience in a similar type of business, previous business ownership experience, the degree of dependence on the business as a source of income

Singh, S.P., Reynolds, R.G., & Muhammad, S. (2001, April). A gender-based performance analysis of micro and small enterprises in Java, Indonesia. *Journal of Small Business Management, 39* (2), 174-182.

This article attempts to examine the micro- and small-scale enterprises in Java, Indonesia, at two levels: the individual and the enterprise. The specific objectives of this study are: 1) to present a descriptive profile of enterprises in Java by gender, 2) to examine the rate of growth of employment in Indonesia by gender and type, and 3) to determine the performance of female enterprises in Java. The survey revealed that female-operated businesses were concentrated in more traditional and less dynamic markets than businesses operated by men. Female businesses were concentrated in low-income informal sectors, where prospects of growth were limited. Employment growth rates of female enterprises were, for the most part, significantly lower than those of male enterprises. The article suggests that, to the extent that women do have different business objectives than men, programs and policies need to be gender-differentiated. It also suggests that theory and results derived from research in developed countries be examined and tested before they are applied to developing countries.

Nature of the study:	Empirical
Nature of the data:	Personal interviews
Nature of the sample:	200 entrepreneurs in Java, Indonesia
Variables:	Growth rate of employment, size of employment, profit, age, marital status, age of business, number of family workers, industry grouping, business history, goals, sex of the owner

Smeltzer, L. R., & Fann, G. L. (1989). Gender differences in external networks of small business owner/managers. *Journal of Small Business Management, 27* (2), 25-32.

External networks are posited to lead to power for small business owners through access to information. Previous research indicates that women are not a part of formal male-dominated networks. This study investigates potential gender differences between the personal information sources used for decision making by men and women small business owners/managers. Data obtained through semi-structured interviews reveal that women were more likely to use other women for information sources and that women were more likely to gain social as well as instrumental forms of support through their networks. No gender differences are reported regarding degree or type of business planning or the perceived turbulence of the business environment.

Nature of the study:	Empirical
Nature of the data:	Interviews
Nature of the sample:	58 female and 59 male business owners in Missouri and Arizona
Variables:	Business characteristics, types of decisions made, business planning issues, sources of information, perception of business environment, gender

Smith, N. R., McCain, G., & Warren, A. (1982). Women entrepreneurs really are different: A comparison of constructed ideal types of male and female entrepreneurs. In K.H. Vesper (Ed.), *Frontiers of entrepreneurship research* (pp. 68-77). Boston, MA: Babson College.

This study builds on previous work proposing patterns of entrepreneurial types. Craftsman-Entrepreneur (rigid) and Opportunistic-Entrepreneur (adaptive) are posited to represent extreme types based upon the manner in which the firm is operated. Female entrepreneurs are compared to a previous studied sample of male entrepreneurs and are found to differ in behavior and attitudes with a clear tendency to be more in the opportunistic range. Suggested explanations are offered, including geography, industrial sector, and sex.

Nature of the study:	Empirical
Nature of the data:	Mail survey
Nature of the sample:	76 members of a women's entrepreneurship club in San Francisco
Variables:	Entrepreneurial types instrument, respondent characteristics, business characteristics

Spilling, O. R., & Berg, N. G. (2000). Gender and small business management: The case of Norway in the 1990s. *International Small Business Journal, 18* (2), 38-59.

This article presents a statistical picture of gender differences in small business management in Norway. Responding to the growing awareness of the importance of gender relations in entrepreneurship, the paper focused on the importance of understanding female managers of SMEs in the Norwegian context through the presentation of more comprehensive statistics than have previously been applied. Among the self employed, women accounted for 24% and men 76%. Compared to the total working population, however, self-employed men accounted for 10.8% of the total labor force, while self-employed women accounted for 4.2%. The percentage participation of women self-employed varied widely by sector. Women have the highest share in public, social, and private services, and above average share in retailing, hotel and restaurant sectors, and below average shares in all other industries. The age distribution of female self-employed was slightly younger than men, a possible indication that the share of women choosing self-employment is increasing. A higher share of self-employed men than women work full-time, which appeared to impact the income generated. Women were virtually absent as top executives at larger firms. Only 16% of firms had women as top executives. Only 21% of all managers are women.

Nature of the study:	Empirical
Nature of the data:	Statistics Norway 1990 Population Census and the Central Register of Firms and Establishments
Nature of the sample:	2,124,452 population of working men and women; of this 165,261 are self-employed
Variables:	Occupation classification, industry, age, residential area, family status, number of working hours, personal income, main income generator for family, total number of firms recorded, corporate form, managerial status or board status for men and women, turnover rates for men and women

Srinivasan, R., Woo, C. Y., & Cooper, A. C. (1994). Performance determinants for male and female entrepreneurs. In W.D. Bygrave, S. Birley, N.C. Churchill, , E. Gatewood, F. Hoy, R.H. Kelley, & W. E. Wetzel, Jr. (Eds.), *Frontiers of entrepreneurship research* (pp. 43-56). Boston, MA: Babson College.

This paper explores longitudinal, performance determinants and outcomes of firms started by male and female entrepreneurs. Success is measured at levels of survival and venture growth. The authors hypothesize that women-owned firms have a higher probability of discontinuance and a lower probability of growth than those owned by men. Determinants of survival and growth are posited to include attributes of the entrepreneur, processes of venture start-up, and industry membership. Findings show significant gender differences for both survival and growth of businesses. Women-owned ventures are found to under-perform in regard to both survival and growth, with motivational variables playing a more significant role for women than for men.

Nature of the study:	Empirical
Nature of the data:	National Federation of Independent Businesses database
Nature of the sample:	2994 members of the National Federation of Independent Businesses
Variables:	Performance measures of survival and growth in employees, motivation for starting, characteristics of business owner, source of start-up funds, sources of advice

Stanworth, C., & Stanworth, J. (1997). Reluctant entrepreneurs and their clients: The case of self-employed freelance workers in the British book publishing industry. *International Small Business Journal, 16* (1), 58-74.

The study examines employment trends in the publishing industry in the U.K. to trace whether freelancers who left employment in the industry were pushed or pulled into self-employment as freelancers. Based on type of entry into self-employment four "causation" types were developed: 1) refugees, 2) trade-offs, 3) missionaries, and 4) converts. The sample was predominantly female (75%). Males in the sample had a higher propensity to have been propelled reluctantly into self-employment (refugees), whereas women showed a stronger propensity to the "trade-off" group, where they could combine paid work with domestic duties. Women were more likely to be found in the "missionary" group, where individuals had left employment voluntarily to avoid a stifling or unsatisfactory work situation. Males and females equally represented the "convert" group, where they initially saw self-employment as only a stop-gap strategy but later showed little interest in returning to the workplace ("pull strategy"). Loveridge's typology of segmented labor markets was adapted to explain the movement in the industry. The trend is characterized as PE (primary external) labor market and SE (secondary external).

Nature of the study:	Empirical review and integration of previous multi-stage project.
Nature of the data:	Mail survey followed by in-depth interviews
Nature of the sample:	800 U.K. freelance editors and proof-readers conducted during early to mid-1990s. Useable questionnaires returned by 371. Subsequent recorded in-depth interviews were conducted with a representative sample of 40 respondents. Finally, 14 publishing establishments were chosen for more extensive case studies and key staff were interviewed.
Variables:	Self-employment without employees, work rewards (function of work, income, work activity, personal development, temporal, contextual variety, social interaction, personal identity)

Stevenson, L. A. (1986). Against all odds: The entrepreneurship of women. *Journal of Small Business Management, 24* (4), 30-36.

The number of women owning businesses in North America is increasing and the extent of women's participation in nontraditional fields is broadening. This paper reviews the existing literature on women as business owners. Findings are cited regarding gender differences in educational and experiential backgrounds, marital differences, and career influences. Males and females are more alike than different regarding their motivation for business entry, psychological characteristics, and the perception of business problems encountered. The author recommends increased research in the field, the development of a database on women business owners, and the application of female-centered notions of entrepreneurship.

Nature of the study: Literature review
Nature of the data: NA
Nature of the sample: NA
Variables: Education, work experience, motivation for business entry, psychological characteristics, perception of business problems encountered

Stevenson, L. (1990). Some methodological problems associated with researching women entrepreneurs. *Journal of Business Ethics, 9* (4/5), 439-446.

There is a need to feminize the research on entrepreneurs in order to include the experiences of women in what is known about entrepreneurs and the entrepreneurial process. Male bias is posited as one of the main problems in the research on women as entrepreneurs. This paper explores methodological problems associated with conducting research on women entrepreneurs, including the exclusion of women from the research design, sexual imperialism in interpretations, and a reliance on structured, quantitative research approaches. The author recommends the development of a data base to allow for more generalizeable findings, the broadening of the list of topics to be pursued regarding women entrepreneurs, expanding venues for publication, promoting research on women entrepreneurs, and applying a feminist perspective to the overall topic.

Nature of the study: Conceptual
Nature of the data: NA
Nature of the sample: NA
Variables: Methodological approaches

Stoner, C. R., Hartman, R. I., & Arora, R. (1990). Work-home role conflict in female owners of small business: An exploratory study. *Journal of Small Business Management, 28* (1), 30-38.

This study examines the content and nature of work-home role conflict for female small business owners in order to better understand the social and psychological significance of the resultant tension. The authors test a set of work-home role dimensions drawn from the 1977 Quality of Employment Survey. Role conflict dimensions of fatigue, difficulty in relaxing, inability to pursue personal interest, and schedule conflicts were reported most often. The authors conclude that women business owners are likely to experience role conflict regardless of family structure or time spent at work. Role conflict is associated with levels of business satisfaction and perceived success. Home-work conflict is more prevalent in owners with lower self-esteem or self-worth. In turn, self-esteem is affected by business satisfaction and financial health.

Nature of the study: Empirical
Nature of the data: Mail survey
Nature of the sample: 92 female business owners from Illinois and California drawn from Dun & Bradstreet and association membership lists
Variables: Work-home role dimensions, number of hours worked, other work activities, constructs related to aspects of personal and business life

Storey, D. (1994). New firm growth and bank financing. *Small Business Economics, 6* (2), 139-150.

This paper examines the impact of human capital and learning on the availability of debt capital to new firms. Findings from two surveys indicate that bank lending to new firms is unrelated to many of the personal characteristics of founders. It is more closely related to whether or not the founder uses personal savings and to legal status of the business.

Nature of the study: Empirical
Nature of the data: Surveys of new firm founders in County Cleveland, England, in 1979 and 1990
Nature of the sample: Random sample of all non-farm, non-retail businesses in the county
Variables: Demographics (age, sex, location), education, experience, firm characteristics (size, age, industry), financing history

Sullivan, P., Halbrendt, C., Wang, Q., & Scannell, E. (1997). Exploring female entrepreneurship in rural Vermont and its implications for rural America. *Economic Development Review, 15* (3), 37-42.

The number of females in the U.S. living in poverty has grown significantly, particularly in rural areas. Entrepreneurial activities are proposed as a means for women to move out of poverty into economic self-sufficiency. The authors select personal and structural level characteristics posited in previous literature as related to business success, focusing upon motivations, perceptions of success, and institutional contributions toward success. The findings show that the major reasons for starting a business were flexibility in work hours and location, economic necessity, and the lack of job security. The respondents' definition of business success focuses upon personal rewards and satisfaction, and economic self-sufficiency or independence. Local community support is seen as crucial to the business.

Nature of the study:	Empirical
Nature of the data:	Focus Groups
Nature of the sample:	Four groups of women business owners in rural northeastern Vermont (selected from Dun & Bradstreet list)
Variables:	Motivations for starting business, perceptions of success, family background, business training programs used, participation in public assistance programs

Terborg, J. R., & Ilgen, D.R. (1975). A theoretical approach to sex discrimination in traditionally masculine occupations. *Organizational Behavior and Human Performance, 13* (3), 352-376.

An in-basket simulation was designed to examine occupational sex discrimination at the time the employee sought access to the organization, and again once the employee was on the job. Two access variables--the hiring decision and starting salary--were used to identify access discrimination; five treatment variables--employee development, delegation of work assignments, employee evaluation, distribution of rewards, and promotion--were used to identify treatment discrimination. Although females were hired as frequently as identically qualified males, the female was offered a significantly lower starting salary, and once within the organization was assigned to routine tasks more frequently than to challenging ones in comparison to the male. Second year salary raises increased the initial salary discrepancy between males and females at the time of hiring. The results are discussed in the light of attribution theory, equity theory, and the role of stereotypes.

Nature of the study:	Empirical
Nature of the data:	Experimental simulation
Nature of the sample:	36 male and 7 female undergraduates
Variables:	Sex of stimulus person, sex of respondent, hiring decision, starting salary, job assignments, training program assignment, overall performance, promotability, bonus money, percent raise, second year salary, promotability to West Coast; attribution of performance to luck, ability, effort, internal or external constraints; use of the WAMS to measure stereotypes

Ufuk, H., & Ozgen, O. (2001). Interaction between the business and family lives of women entrepreneurs in Turkey. *Journal of Business Ethics, 31* (2), 95-106.

This paper examines the relationships between the multiple business and family roles of the female married entrepreneur in Turkey. The concept of role is presented as a view of social relations as part of the orderly structure of society. The respondents reported that being entrepreneurs affected their roles in family life negatively, while positively affecting their roles in their social, economical and individual life. In addition, respondents suffer from conflicts between the entrepreneur role and other roles in the family; the role of entrepreneur mostly conflicted with the roles of housewife, mother, and wife.

Nature of the study:	Empirical
Nature of the data:	Interviews
Nature of the sample:	220 female members of the Ankara Union of Tradesmen and Craftsmen Chambers, Turkey
Variables:	Characteristics of the business owner and her family, characteristics of the respondent's business life, interaction between business and family life

Verheul, I., & Thurik, R. (2001). Start-up capital: Does gender matter? *Small Business Economics, 16* (4), 329-345.

This study examines the direct and indirect effects of gender on ways in which male and female entrepreneurs finance their businesses. It examines differences in types of business, types of management, and entrepreneurial experience. It also examines barriers that may be gender-specific. A 1994 panel study of 2,000 Dutch entrepreneurs (500 females, 1,500 males) was used to test for direct and indirect effects of gender differences on financing. Findings indicate that female entrepreneurs have a smaller amount of start-up capital, but that they do not differ significantly with respect to types of capital. On average, the proportion of debt and equity capital in the businesses of female entrepreneurs was the same as in those of their male counterparts.

Nature of the study:	Empirical
Nature of the data:	Panel study, 1st wave mail survey
Nature of the sample:	2,000 Dutch entrepreneurs who started their businesses in the first quarter of 1994. Panel was set up and implemented by EIM Business and Policy Research in Zoetermeer.
Variables:	Demographics (age, sex, location), education, experience, industry, full/part-time work status, risk tolerance, financing methods

Walker, D., & Joyner, B. E. (1999). Female entrepreneurship and the market process: Gender-based public policy considerations. *Journal of Developmental Entrepreneurship, 4* (2), 95-116.
This article explores the theoretical aspects of gender-based public policy programs specifically designed to increase the number of women creating and developing new ventures. The authors propose a conceptual framework of four kinds of gender discrimination based upon access to financial capital: pure, institutional, statistical, and economic. An analysis of four Small

Business Administration programs reveals the potential for discrimination to be decreased in each category. However, the analysis also reveals a potential increase in pure gender discrimination due to resentment of preferential treatment in programs targeted toward women. The paper concludes with a summary of potential for changes in resource allocation due to public policy programs.

Nature of the study: Conceptual
Nature of the data: NA
Nature of the sample: NA
Variables: Gender discrimination types, government assistance programs

Watkins, J. M., & Watkins, D. S. (1983). The female entrepreneur: Her background and determinants of business choice: Some British data. In J. A. Hornaday, J. A. Timmons, & K. H. Vesper (Eds.), *Frontiers of entrepreneurship research* (pp. 271-288). Boston, MA: Babson College.

This paper presents the extent and nature of female entrepreneurship in Britain, including individual characteristics and motivations, as well as interactions with others. In addition, the authors attempt to identify systematic or random biases against women business owners that have the potential to be addressed through political action. The results of the gender comparison reveal that women are largely restricted to the formation of stereotypically "female" businesses by both involuntary factors and conscious decision. Educational levels are seen to be similar for males and females but substantial gender differences are seen in the cumulative educational and work experience patterns.

Nature of the study: Empirical
Nature of the data: Semi-structured interviews
Nature of the sample: 58 female and 54 male entrepreneurs in the U.K.
Variables: Family history, educational background, previous employment history, extent of entrepreneurial endeavors

Weinstein, A., Nicholls, J.A.F., & Seaton, B. (1992). An evaluation of SBI marketing consulting: The entrepreneur's perspective. *Journal of Small Business Management, 30* (4), 62-71.

The Small Business Institute (SBI) is a vehicle through which U.S. college and university students assist small firms. This study provides a literature review on student business consulting and further explores entrepreneurs' perceptions of the effectiveness of such students as marketing consultants. The results indicate that the majority of clients are satisfied with the assistance provided, finding student reports important for the development of their marketing strategies. In addition, entrepreneurs view students' professionalism, business knowledge, practicality of recommendations, and their overall analysis favorably. Finally, a regression model indicates that client satisfaction can be predicted based on students' business knowledge and practicality. The conclusion is that many entrepreneurs find SBI services offer objectivity and planning insight to their marketing activities. No gender differences are found for either client satisfaction or business/entrepreneurial characteristics.

Nature of the study: Empirical
Nature of the data: Telephone survey
Nature of the sample: 58 former SBI clients receiving marketing assistance between 1985 and 1989
Variables: Respondent demographics, business characteristics, Keisner's scale for client satisfaction

Welbourne, T. M. (1999). Wall Street likes its women: An examination of women in the top management teams of initial public offerings. *Center for Advanced Human Resource Studies. Working Paper Series.* Ithaca, New York: Cornell University. Online: Retrieved October 15, 2001, from http://www.ilr.cornell.edu/depts/cahrs/WPapers.html.

How women in the top management teams of corporations affect organizational performance is largely unknown. Trend data indicate IPO firms are gaining in the number of women they employ in top management teams. This paper focuses upon the determinants of initial public offering (IPO) firm success by examining the effect of women's membership on the top management teams upon the organizations' short- and long-term financial performance. Findings show the percentage of women on the top management team is related to the Tobin's Q (measure of short term firm performance), union presence, and CEO ownership but not to the stock price or earnings per share in 1996. The author posits that having women on a firm's top management team may provide signals to investors about the firm itself regarding management issues. The author further concludes that the actual benefit is not solely from the presence of women, but from the perspectives gained with a diverse gender mix on the team.

Nature of the study: Empirical
Nature of the data: Prospectuses of IPO firms, COMPUSTATA database, and database from Securities Data Corporation (1993-1996)
Nature of the sample: 476 firms that went public in 1993
Variables: Characteristics of firm, percentage of women on top team, stock price, earning per share, paragraphs in risk section, net income per share, unionization, percentage owned by CEO prior to IPO, geographic area

Westhead, P., & Cowling, M. (1995). Employment change in independent owner-managed high-technology firms in Great Britain. *Small Business Economics, 7* (2), 111-140.

This study explores the potential for small technology-based firms to achieve substantial employment growth in the U.K. Given that technology-based firms are responsible for a significant portion of innovations, factors leading to increased employment size are of interest. Theories explaining this growth derive from resource exchange, population ecology, and economics. Factors specifically associated with employment change have to do with the personal background and work experience of the founder, as well as business characteristics (e.g., customer base, networking, financial base, technology, management functions). A survey of high-technology-based firms engaged in hard manufacturing was obtained by contacting Science Park managers in the U.K. A longitudinal survey of 227 firms was carried out in 1986 and 1992. During this time, 50 of the firms closed. Multivariate analysis was used to examine employment creation. Work experience of the founder was significant; however, only two firm variables were significant (age and leased premises). None of the networking or customer base variables were significant, nor were the technology-based variables. Growth in employment was associated with highly educated founders and larger sized firms. Gender was not significant.

Nature of the study:	Empirical
Nature of the data:	Survey
Nature of the sample:	U.K. technology manufacturing firms
Variables:	Founder demographics, business characteristics (customer base, financial base, technology, management functions), employment growth

Zapalska, A.M. (1997). A profile of women entrepreneurs and enterprises in Poland. *Journal of Small Business Management, 35* (4), 76-82.

Poland was an early leader in moving from a centrally planned economy toward political pluralism and economic transformation. The economic situation includes an increasing number of women starting businesses. This study assesses the psychological characteristics, motives, and objectives of Polish female entrepreneurs, as well as the types of businesses they start. Findings reveal the female respondents as better educated than the male respondents and possessing similar or greater amounts of business experience. No significant gender differences are found in personality attributes. Female respondents were more likely to consider innovation and the creation of something new as important factors for the success of the business and were substantially more likely to report a commitment to long-term capital accumulation and investment.

Nature of the study:	Empirical
Nature of the data:	Telephone survey
Nature of the sample:	110 male and 40 female entrepreneurs in three urban centers in Poland
Variables:	Characteristics of the entrepreneurs, motives for starting the business, psychological factors, type of venture, business strategies, short and long term objectives

PART 3

Annotations Venture Capital

Amit, R., Brander, J., & Zott, C. (1998). Why do venture capital firms exist? Theory and Canadian evidence. *Journal of Business Venturing, 13* (6), 441-467.

This article proposes that the value of venture capitalists is their ability to reduce the cost of informational asymmetries, i.e., "hidden information" (leading to adverse selection) and "hidden action" (leading to moral hazard). The authors make four observations: 1) Venture capitalists operate in environments where their relative efficiency in selecting and monitoring investments gives them a comparative advantage over other investors. They are, therefore, prominent in industries where informational concerns exist. 2) Within the class of projects providing venture capitalists an advantage, they prefer projects where monitoring and selection costs are relatively low or where the costs of informational asymmetry are less severe. They favor later stage investment to start-up investment. 3) If informational asymmetry is important, then the ability of the venture capitalist to exit may be significantly affected. Most exits will therefore be through "insider" sales, particularly management buyouts, and acquisitions by third parties, rather than IPOs. 4) Informational asymmetries suggest that owner-managers perform best when they have a large stake in a venture.

Nature of the study: Empirical
Nature of the data: Two surveys by Macdonald & Associates
Nature of the sample: Canadian venture capital firms
Variables: Type of industry, age of venture-backed companies, number of investments by stage and year, average size of investments by stage and year, average debt and equity by investment stage, type of venture capital exit, estimated return by exit type, effect of venture capital share on performance

Amit, R., Glosten, L., & Muller, E. (1990). Does venture capital foster the most promising entrepreneurial firms? *California Management Review, 32* (3), 102-112.

The investment decisions of venture capitalists are often made at a time when they cannot accurately assess the entrepreneur's capacity to develop a successful venture. Because of this inability and the resulting high risk, venture capitalists must charge high rents to produce adequate returns on their investment portfolios. This results in high-ability entrepreneurs deciding to develop their ventures on their own, because the price offered

80does not reflect their true ability and is judged unattractive. This study uses scenarios of high, medium, and low ability entrepreneurs deciding to develop prototypes under different cost conditions and making their choice to use venture capital funding. The study also suggests that higher failure rates can be expected among venture-capital-backed firms than in the population of new firms.

Nature of the study:	Conceptual
Nature of the data:	NA
Nature of the sample:	NA
Variables:	Entrepreneurial ability, effort, required return

Amit, R., Glosten, L., & Muller, E. (1990). Entrepreneurial ability, venture investments, and risk sharing. *Management Science, 36* (10), 1232-1245.

This study investigates a number of issues relating to the desirability and implications of new venture financing within a principal-agent framework, attempting to capture the essence of the relationship between entrepreneurs and venture capitalists. The proposed model suggests that 1) as long as the skill levels of entrepreneurs are common knowledge, entrepreneurs will choose to involve venture capital investors, since the risk sharing provided by outside participation outweighs the agency relationship that is created; 2) less able entrepreneurs will choose to involve venture capitalists, whereas the more profitable ventures will be developed by those who can succeed without external participation, given the adverse selection problem associated with asymmetric information;] 3) if a costly signal is available that conveys the entrepreneur's ability, some entrepreneurs will invest in such a signal and then sell to investors; these entrepreneurs, however, need not be more able ones. The study found that while the equilibrium price paid for a new venture is the one for which the expected NPV equals zero, less skillful entrepreneurs will still receive funding.

Nature of the study:	Conceptual
Nature of the data:	NA
Nature of the sample:	NA
Variables:	Venture profit, skill level of entrepreneur and effort, investment magnitude, potential sources of funding, cost of raising funds, buyer bid price

Benaglia, R., Giudici, G., & Paleari, S. (1999). *The conflict of interests between venture capitalists and entrepreneurs: What happens if private benefits and information asymmetries do exist?* Milan, Dipartimento di Economia e Produzione, Politecnico di Milano.

There is an inherent conflict of interest in the venture capitalist (VC)/entrepreneur agency relationship. This paper develops a theoretical model of the agency relationship between the VC and the entrepreneur, taking into account both the value added by the VC in the post-investment phase and the incentives for the VC to allocate scarce time between improving current ventures and evaluating new investment opportunities. The model shows that there is an optimal level of attention for the VC to devote to a portfolio's ventures, measured by the length and the number of financial rounds. The VC's optimal choice does not match the entrepreneur's expectations, whose objective function depends both on the firm's ownership share retained and the value of private benefits extracted from the venture. A VC's involvement in the venture is a function of environmental conditions. In specific, an increase in agency costs and in investment risk leads to an increase in the level of attention dedicated to the firm; an increase in the VC's experience reduces the frequency of interactions.

Nature of the study:	Conceptual
Nature of the data:	NA
Nature of the sample:	NA
Variables:	VC time and interaction, length and number of financial rounds, ownership share, venture benefits, agency costs, investment risk, VC experience

Boocock, G., & Woods, M. (1997). The evaluation criteria used by venture capitalists: Evidence from a U.K. venture fund. *International Small Business Journal, 16* (1), 36-58.

In the early 1990s Midland Bank introduced 11 regional enterprise funds in order to plug a perceived equity capital gap. This paper evaluates the activities of one of these funds, the Midland Enterprise Fund for the East Midlands. The focus includes consideration of the source and function of the fund as well as the investors' decision-making process. The authors use a systematic review of applications for funding to find a multi-stage decision-making process. Selection criteria found include specific individual fund requirements, product markets, and the management skills and commitment of the entrepreneur. In addition, the authors conclude that the academic debate over the relative significance of criteria used by venture capitalists to evaluate opportunities has little real relevance for practitioners.

Nature of the study:	Empirical
Nature of the data:	Semi-structured interviews plus archival research of working notes and reports
Nature of the sample:	232 applications received during the first two years of the fund
Variables:	Characteristics of investments made, reasons for rejection

Bowden, R. J. (1994). Bargaining, size, and return in venture capital funds. *Journal of Business Venturing, 9* (4), 307-331.

The terms of agreement by venture capitalists are the results of cooperative bargaining between the project originators and the financiers. This study investigates the conditions under which bargains are made, the nature of the bargains, and the way in which they are influenced by fund size. A bargaining framework is proposed that predicts agreements are likely to be successfully concluded when owners and funds (or fund managers) have different approaches to the rates of return they require on their investments-- for example, because they have different attitudes or possibilities for investment diversification or because they have different expectations about the likely success of the project. Contracts can result in asymmetric outcomes, where the fund's share of project earnings exceeds its share of the financing. Bargaining power and fund size are related as well.

Nature of the study:	Conceptual
Nature of the data:	NA
Nature of the sample:	NA
Variables:	Financing amount, required rate of return, portfolio diversification, risk aversion, expected returns, fund size

Brophy, D. J. (1981). Venture capital investment, 1981. In K.H. Vesper (Ed.), *Frontiers of entrepreneurial research* (pp. 246-280). Boston, MA: Babson College.

This paper provides insight regarding trends and characteristics of the investment patterns of National Venture Capital Association (NVCA) member firms from 1974 to 1980 and the outlook for 1981. Investments during this time were directed principally toward "new" venture capital positions, primarily in the computer and medical technology fields, and to start-up situations. During 1980, investment NVCA member firms--mostly closely-held, private venture capital organizations--reached historically high levels. The volume of investment increased substantially from 1977, with 1980 dollar volume exceeding the 1979 and 1978 levels by a significant margin and almost doubling the 1977 level. This study concludes that the increase in investment and available funds clearly reflected the strong and positive effect of the capital gains tax revision of 1978. The expected impact of this change was, among other things, an increase in the flow of venture capital investments.

Nature of the study:	Empirical
Nature of the data:	Mail survey
Nature of the sample:	73 member firms of the NVCA
Variables:	Number of investments, amount of investment, venture capital/non-venture capital investment, old/new venture capital investment

Brophy, D. J., Amonsen, E., & Bontrager, P. (1982). Analysis of structuring and pricing of venture capital investment proposals. In K. H. Vesper (Ed.), *Frontiers of entrepreneurial research* (pp. 358-395). Boston, MA: Babson College.

This paper illustrates the potential usefulness of a computerized simulation model (e.g. Monte Carlo), incorporating sensitivity analysis and probability estimation, to help entrepreneurs, venture capitalists, and other interested parties determine the implied pricing of venture capital funding and estimate the associated risk of achieving the expected pricing in a private-placement rather than auction market setting. The model, as applied to a case study of a venture capital investment proposal, is shown to significantly increase the efficiency of the negotiating process and made make it possible to determine optimal or "fair" structure and pricing arrangements.

Nature of the study: Empirical
Nature of the data: Simulation
Nature of the sample: NA
Variables: Financing structure, price of venture capital funding (rate of return), variations in returns (risk), firm performance, inflation rate, sales and costs, cash flow assumptions, terminal value assumptions

Brophy, D. J. (1992). Financing the new venture: A report on recent research. In D. L. Sexton, & J. D. Kasarda (Eds.), *State of the Art Entrepreneurship* (pp. 387-401). Boston, MA: PWS Kent.

Entrepreneurship researchers have acquired a better understanding of the funding of new ventures, including a better conceptualization of the positions of the founder/manager and the venture capital investor in project structuring, valuation, and development over time. This chapter reviews the literature and suggests directions for continued efforts.

The review of research is organized according to the following topics: 1) characteristics of new venture investors; 2) new venture factors found to be used by investors as *ex ante* criteria for investment decisions or associated with the success or failure of new ventures either to obtain financing or to succeed operationally over time; 3) the investment process, including the negotiation, structuring, and valuation of new venture financing deals; 4) monitoring new ventures and later-round investments in the company; and 5) transitions and exits, including the sale of all or part of the new venture by strategic alliance, merger, outright sale, leveraged buyout, or initial public offering.

Nature of the study: Literature review
Nature of the data: NA
Nature of the sample: NA

Variables: Investors, investment criteria, investment process, investment monitoring, exits

Bruno, A. V., & Tyebjee, T. T. (1983). The one that got away: A study of ventures rejected by venture capitalists. In J. A. Hornaday, J. A. Timmons, & K. H. Vesper (Eds.), *Frontiers of entrepreneurial research* (pp. 289-306). Boston, MA: Babson College.

This paper focuses on ventures that were denied funding by venture capitalists. Denied entrepreneurs were surveyed for their perceptions of the reasons for denials and their perceptions of venture capitalists. Reasons for denial were categorized as venture related, venture capitalist related, deal structure, or other. Denied entrepreneurs most frequently mentioned venture-related reasons. The top three perceptions of venture capitalists held by denied entrepreneurs were that they demanded too much equity, provided easy access to capital, and provided management assistance. Entrepreneurs' preferred form of financing was equity and their preferred source was venture capitalists. Denied entrepreneurs who were subsequently successful in raising capital raised approximately $1.9 million and gave up an average of 45.1% of equity.

Nature of the study:	Empirical
Nature of the data:	Telephone survey, mail survey
Nature of the sample:	62 ventures
Variables:	Age and industry sector, reasons for denial, perceptions of venture capitalists, time spent seeking financing, preferred sources and forms of financing, investment size by round and source, ownership relinquished, results of being unsuccessful in raising capital

Bruno, A. V., & Tyebjee, T. T. (1985). The entrepreneur's search for capital. *Journal of Business Venturing, 1* (1), 61-74.

Five studies were undertaken to identify and evaluate the factors that impinge upon the entrepreneur's search for venture capital. Results imply the need for 1) division of ownership among multiple founders in a way that reflects past, present, and future contributions to success; 2) significant previous experience on the part of founders; 3) a management team that is well rounded in technical and management skills; 4) early planning; 5) recognition of the significant cost of outside capital in terms of relinquished equity; 6) recognition of the dramatic effect of outside capital on growth; and 7) realization of the possibilities for raising venture capital besides the venture capital firm. Venture capital can supply a far greater infusion of capital than can other sources, but it is more expensive in terms of the share of equity that must be given up.

Nature of the study:	Empirical
Nature of the data:	Mail survey, telephone survey
Nature of the sample:	Venture capitalists, California high–technology companies
Variables:	Venture firm characteristics, decision-making criteria and process, entrepreneurial expectations, extent of venture capital involvement in start-ups

Busenitz, L. W., & Fiet, J. O. (1999). Venture capital firm resources and their long-term effect on venture disposition. In P. D. Reynolds, W. D. Bygrave, S. Manigart, C. M. Mason, G. D. Meyer, H. J. Sapienza, & K. G. Shaver (Eds.), *Frontiers of entrepreneurial research* (pp. 407-418). Boston, MA: Babson College

This study investigates the resources possessed by venture capital firms prior to funding deals to determine if they were significant predictors of venture exits. The three intangible resources that may be sources of comparative advantage and lead to more profitable investments in new enterprises are: 1) informational capital, 2) human capital, and 3) organizational capital. Informational capital may be viewed as useful knowledge that may help VCs in evaluating prospects of investing in a new enterprise. Human capital consists of valuable, tacit knowledge that seems to be positively correlated with the experience of a firm's principals and the long-term value of the venture at the time of its disposition. Organizational capital, which is an intangible resource developed among the principals of a VC firm, promotes specialization and coordination of information among specialists that is positively related to long-term venture performance. This study confirms that a firm's resources matter and may in fact be sources of sustainable competitive advantage.

Nature of the study:	Empirical
Nature of the data:	Mail survey
Nature of the sample:	196 ventures and the VC firms that first funded them
Variables:	Industry specialization, size and age of the VC firm, type of VC entity, stage of financing, venture performance, venture outcome

Busenitz, L. W., Moesel, D. D., Fiet, J. O., & Barney, J. B. (1997). The framing perceptions of fairness in the relationship between venture capitalists and new venture teams. *Entrepreneurship Theory and Practice,* 21(3), 5-21.

This paper investigates how conditions in place at the time of first-round funding can frame a new venture team's perception of the fairness of its relations with its venture capitalists. The authors assumed that a team's perception of whether its treatment by its venture capitalist was procedurally just will affect a team's receptivity to venture capitalists' advice. An analysis of data showed that some governance mechanisms put in place by venture capitalists during the funding process and the background of the venture team significantly framed perceptions of fairness in their relationship. The current financial conditions of the venture firm, which was also a variable of interest in this study, were not factors in the framing of a team's perception of fairness.

A major finding of this study was that the indiscriminant use of contractual covenants can adversely frame a team's perception of fairness, which ultimately could inhibit its receptivity to venture capitalists' advice.

Nature of the study:	Empirical
Nature of the data:	Mail survey
Nature of the sample:	116 venture-capital-backed firms
Variables:	VC board seats, constraining covenants, earn-out arrangements, industry experience, new venture average firm tenure, overall team tenure, sales, innovation, rounds of funding, employees, perception of VC procedural fairness

Bygrave, W. D. (1988). The structure of the investment networks of venture capital firms. *Journal of Business Venturing, 3* (2), 137-157.

In this study, the joint investment networks of venture capital firms are examined. A sample of portfolio companies was taken randomly from the Venture Economics database of all companies known to have received first rounds of venture capital. The venture capital firms were classified into three categories: 1) the top 61 firms in terms of the most investments, 2) the top 21 high innovative venture companies (HIVC), and 3) the top 21 low innovative venture companies (LIVC). HIVCs face the highest degree of risk because their portfolio companies have significant unknowns concerning the abilities of their entrepreneurs, the market for their products, the potential for developing saleable products, the expectations of raising additional financing rounds, competitive responses, etc. It was found that the HIVCs had a higher incidence of connectedness as measured by the percentage of pairs with one or more co-investments. This suggests that co-investing is a vehicle to reduce uncertainty by gathering information. The implications are that 1) venture capital firms' links to other venture capital firms are extremely valuable; 2) entrepreneurs should submit proposals for funding to a limited number of targeted firms; 3) HIVCs concentrate in the high-technology firms in California and the Northeast, whereas LIVCs are evenly spread throughout the U.S.; and 4) the model for co-investment networks also will apply to investors and lenders in general.

Nature of the study:	Empirical
Nature of the data:	Venture Economics database
Nature of the sample:	464 venture capital firms and 1,501 portfolio companies
Variables:	Number of single investments; number of pairs of investments; stage, innovativeness, industry segment, and location of venture capital firms

Bygrave, W. D. (1987). Syndicated investments by venture capital firms: A networking perspective. *Journal of Business Venturing, 2* (2), 139-154.

Venture capital firms have networks through which they share information on the portfolio companies in which they invest. An analysis of the networking was conducted by assessing the venture capital firms' joint investments in portfolio companies during the period 1966-1982. Factors that influence the amount of networking included the innovativeness, technology, stage, and industry of the portfolio companies. The top 61 venture capital firms were found to have extensive networks. Three out of four portfolio companies had at least one of the top 61 venture capital firms as an investor. Sharing of information was shown to be a stronger reason for networking than was spreading the financial risk. Venture capital firms are expected to become even more specialized in the future. Implications for companies seeking financing are that entrepreneurs should seek financing from venture firms that are known to invest in their industries, should not hawk their business plans, and should know the "going rate" by staying up to date on investment deals happening in their industries.

Nature of the study: Empirical
Nature of the data: Venture Economics database
Nature of the sample: 464 venture capital firms and 1,501 portfolio companies
Variables: Number of single investments, number of pairs of investments, stage, innovativeness, industry segment

Bygrave, W. D., Fast, N., Khoylian, R., Vincent, L., & Yue, W. (1988). Rates of return of venture capital investing: A study of 131 funds. In B. A. Kirchhoff, W. A. Long, W. Ed McMullan, K. H. Vesper, & W. E. Wetzel, Jr. (Eds.), *Frontiers of entrepreneurial research* (pp. 275-289). Boston, MA: Babson College

This paper examines the compound annual internal rates of return (IRR) of venture capital funds started between 1978 and 1984. The rates of return were broken down according to the years in which the funds were started. When funds of the same age were compared, the more recent a fund's starting date, the lower its rate of return, all other things being equal. The findings appeared to substantiate a trend that was being talked about in the industry at that time: rates of return of venture capital funds had, in general, been declining. In fact, the authors conclude that overall returns on venture capital had been declining since 1983. However, the pool of venture capital continued to swell because long-term investors who invest in venture capital knew that over the entire history of the industry, returns on venture capital funds had, on average, outperformed those of the S&P 500 stocks.

Nature of the study: Empirical
Nature of the data: Existing databases
Nature of the sample: 131 funds

Variables: Level of investment, internal rate of return computed at the
                       end of each calendar year, age of funds

Bygrave, W. D., Johnstone, G., Lewis, J., & Ullman, R. (1998). Venture capitalists'
    criteria for selecting high-tech investments: Prescriptive wisdom compared
    with actuality. In P. D. Reynolds, W. D. Bygrave, S. Manigart, C. M. Mason,
    G. D. Meyer, H. J. Sapienza, & K. G. Shaver (Eds.), *Frontiers of
    entrepreneurial research* (pp. 544-555). Boston, MA: Babson College.

This study investigates the characteristics of venture-capital-backed Internet,
software, hardware, and semiconductor companies that floated initial public
offerings between 1994 and 1997, to see if it was possible to develop a
universal profile. Findings showed no standard profile for a high potential
venture; however, industry segment and the life-cycle stage of the industry
were critical variables. If there was a universal prescription it was on the
qualitative criteria of management and directors. The study further
discovered that the actual profiles did not match the prescribed profile for a
high potential venture that is widely disseminated in textbooks and trade
books.

Nature of the study: Empirical
Nature of the data: IPO prospectuses
Nature of the sample: 122 venture-backed technology companies
Variables: Industry segment, management team experience, market
                        size, growth share, distribution channels, life cycle stage,
                        uniqueness of product and proprietary protection, financial
                        performance measures

Bygrave, W. D., Johnstone, G., Matchett, M., & Roedel, J. (1999). Venture capital
    high-tech investments: Can we differentiate the best from the worst? In P. D.
    Reynolds, W. D. Bygrave, S. Manigart, C. M. Mason, G. D. Meyer, H. J.
    Sapienza, & K. G. Shaver (Eds.), *Frontiers of entrepreneurial research* (pp.
    433-445). Boston, MA: Babson College.

This study investigates venture-capital-backed Internet, software, hardware,
and semiconductor companies that had an IPO between 1994 and 1997 to
address two questions: Was the market value of the companies at the time of
their IPOs correlated with any of the variables in the data set? Were the
returns on the first round of venture capital at the IPO correlated with any of
the variables? The results showed that the market capitalization correlated
with quality of management, R&D expenses, sales revenue growth, industry
segment, and the life-cycle stage of the industry. In general, the message to
entrepreneurs and their venture capital backers is to have the highest quality
management team, spend heavily on R&D, build revenue as rapidly as
possible, be in an early-stage industry and not worry too much about
profitability, as neither gross margin nor net income was a significant factor.

Nature of the study: Empirical
Nature of the data: 117 venture-capital-backed high-tech firms
Nature of the sample: IPO prospectuses
Variables: Market value, quality of management, R&D expenses, sales revenue growth, industry segment, life-cycle stage of the industry, gross margin, net income

Camp, S. M., & Sexton, D. L. (1992). Trends in venture capital investment: Implications for high-technology firms. *Journal of Small Business Management, 30* (3), 11-19.

This study assesses trends in venture capital disbursement that occurred from 1980 to 1990 in the United States. Investment trends examined include 1) movement toward later stage investments; 2) a shift away from technology-related ventures, and 3) changes in the industry placements for initial or first-round investments. Since 1985, researchers have speculated that venture capital disbursements are shifting away from high technology. This study empirically documented such a shift, and the theoretical support for such a transition is reviewed. Conceptually, the shift has been attributed to increased competition for investment opportunities, changing risk preferences among venture capitalists, poor exit mechanisms, and declining rates of return. As a result, researchers have suggested the need for a new paradigm for understanding venture capital investment.

Nature of the study: Empirical
Nature of the data: Venture Economics database
Nature of the sample: 600 venture funds
Variables: Industry segment, stage of investment, size and percent of investment, follow on financing

Carter, R. B., & Van Auken, H. E. (1994). Venture capital firms' preferences for projects in particular stages of development. *Journal of Small Business Management, 32* (1), 60-72.

This article examines how important the stage of development of venture-seeking firms is to potential investors and the relationship to project evaluation criteria used by venture capital firms. The respondents are shown to have preferences for projects in particular stages of development. Early stage investors are less concerned with the management of risks and more concerned with liquidity than later stage investors. Early stage investors are more interested in control, spend more time, and are willing to replace management if necessary. Early stage investors prefer an initial public offering as an exit strategy.

Nature of the study: Empirical
Nature of the data: Mail survey
Nature of the sample: 69 venture capitalists
Variables: Size of projects, percentage ownership required, preferred stage of investment, historical percent of investment stage, evaluation criteria, risk factors, management involvement

Chesbrough, H. (2000). Designing corporate ventures in the shadow of private venture capital. *California Management Review, 42* (3), 31-50.

Private venture capital casts a long shadow over corporate ventures, in part because they compete for the same entrepreneurial talent. Corporate venturing may improve its performance by emulating certain practices of private venture capital but will never achieve the structures that private venture capital can create. Instead, the design principles for corporate ventures should embrace potential structural advantages of corporate venturing and leverage those advantages. Four potential advantages are discussed: time horizon, scale of capital invested, coordination of complementarities, and retention of learning group. Lucent's New Ventures Group adopts many useful practices of private venture capital, but retains some of the potential structural advantages of venturing within an established firm.

Nature of the study: Conceptual
Nature of the data: NA
Nature of the sample: NA
Variables: Incentive intensity, financial discipline, monitoring, creativity in developing business models, time horizon, scale of capital invested, coordination of complementarities, retention of learning group

Cyr, L. A., Johnson, D. E., & Welbourne, T. M. (2000). Human resources in initial public offering firms: Do venture capitalists make a difference? *Entrepreneurship Theory and Practice, 25* (1), 77-91.

Venture capitalists' preference for complete, well-balanced founding teams is well established. In addition, the strategic human resource management literature posits that superior performance might accrue to firms that have a member of the top management team responsible for human resources. This paper tests whether or not venture capitalist backing affects the likelihood that initial public offering firms will report having a vice president of human resources. It also examines the combined effect on performance as a result of being venture-capital-backed and having a vice president of human resources. Results indicate that VCs do influence their portfolio firms' approaches to human resources; VC-backed firms are more likely to have VPs of HR than are non-VC-backed firms. Additionally, post hoc analyses reveal that VC backing does not affect the likelihood that the portfolio firm will have another member of the top management team (e.g. the CFO or VP of Administration) responsible for human resources. This suggests that VCs might prefer that, when a member of the top management team holds responsibility for human resource activities, s/he focus specifically and solely on HR rather than be saddled with additional responsibilities.

Nature of the study: Empirical
Nature of the data: IPO prospectus, COMPUSTAT, Going Public – The IPO reporter & Securities Data Corporation
Nature of the sample: 402 IPO firms, less than 25 years old, fewer than 10,000 employees, with market values less than one billion dollars.
Variables: Venture capital backing, vice-president of human resources, firm risk, firm performance, age, and size of firm, CEO ownership, stock price

De Clercq, D., Kumpulainen, M., Makela, M., & Goulet, P. (1999). A longitudinal study of portfolio investment strategies in the Finnish venture capital industry. In P. D. Reynolds, W. D. Bygrave, S. Manigart, C. M. Mason, G. D. Meyer, H. J. Sapienza, & K. G. Shaver (Eds.), *Frontiers of entrepreneurial research* (pp. 446-460). Boston, MA: Babson College.

This study identifies relationships between venture capital firms' portfolio investments and strategic decision making as they pertain to realized strategies. These relationships were studied at both an industry and firm level over a four-year period. After the second year of the study, the results indicated that industry scope provided a significant specialization effect. Moreover, venture capital firms increased geographic diversification throughout the four years of the study. In addition, venture capital firms diversified stage of growth scope through the first two years of the study before entering a period of equilibrium where the level of diversification held relatively constant for the remaining two years. The macro-level process of strategy evolution in the venture capital industry regarding geographic scope diversification, industry scope specialization, and stage-of-growth diversification followed by equilibrium also occurred on a micro-level as individual venture capital firms followed this same process based on firm-level experience.

Nature of the study: Empirical
Nature of the data: Mail survey
Nature of the sample: Investments made by 15 Finnish venture capital firms, 1994-1997
Variables: Number of portfolio companies, average ownership, investment risk/return relationship, geographic diversification, industry diversification, and stage-of-growth diversification, VC experience

Dubini, P. (1989). Which venture-capital-backed entrepreneurs have the best chances of succeeding? *Journal of Business Venturing, 4* (2), 123-132.

This study was conducted to determine which entrepreneurial team characteristics are useful predictors of performance. A sample of 151 ventures rated by venture capitalists was cluster analyzed according to product-service and market characteristics. Four very different clusters were identified: 1) high-powered followers, 2) high-technology inventors, 3) low-technology distribution players, and 4) dream merchants. It was expected that different entrepreneurial team characteristics would be significant for each cluster, and the results indicate that this was generally the case. The capacity for sustained and intense effort was especially important for ventures operating in established markets. The ability to assess and manage risk is crucial in those product-market combinations where environmental turbulence implies difficulties in objectively predicting the evolution of the industry, such as in high-tech companies.

Nature of the study:	Empirical
Nature of the data:	Mail survey
Nature of the sample:	151 ventures
Variables:	Product characteristics, market characteristics, entrepreneurial team characteristics

Dunkelberg, W. C., & Cooper, A. C. (1983). Financing the start of a small enterprise. In J. A. Hornaday, J. A. Timmons, & K. H. Vesper (Eds.), *Frontiers of entrepreneurial research* (pp. 369-381). Boston, MA: Babson College.

A large number of factors undoubtedly affect the financing decisions of firms. This study examines patterns of financing of small firms in 1979. Both primary and secondary sources of funds were considered, with personal savings being the most important single method of financing. Patterns of financing varied according to how ownership was achieved, years of ownership, initial size of firm, and industry classification. Overall, individuals were major sources of funds for 64 percent of the firms, whereas venture capital was the smallest with only one-half percent of companies resorting to it. Fifty-four percent of the firms relied on two major capital sources. Firms that were founded by present owners and financed primarily through private sources were found to have distinctive characteristics associated with industry membership, years since founding, primary goals of the founder, nature of previous organization, initial size, and whether they started with partners.

Nature of the study:	Empirical
Nature of the data:	Mail survey
Nature of the sample:	1,805 small firms, members of the National Federation of Independent Business

Variables: Source of financing, years since founding, hours worked by
                           owners and unpaid family, primary goals of the founder,
                           nature of previous organization, initial size, industry,
                           previous job experience, partners at start-up

Ehrlich, S. B., De Noble, A. F., Moore, T., & Weaver, R. R. (1994). After the cash
    arrives: A comparative study of venture capital and private investor
    involvement in entrepreneurial firms. *Journal of Business Venturing, 9* (1),
    67-83.

    Equity-funded entrepreneurs were surveyed about their relationship with
    their primary investors. Activities associated with levels of involvement,
    reporting and operational controls, and types of expertise sought by the
    entrepreneur were investigated. The results indicate important distinctions
    between venture capitalists (VC) and private investors (PI) in terms of the
    value-added benefits they bring to entrepreneurial firms. While VCs demand
    higher performance standards for their investments, they also provide more
    frequent and detailed feedback than do PIs when the firm is not achieving
    these standards. VCs provide assistance in selecting the venture's
    management team significantly more often than do PIs. These findings
    suggest that a formalized VC approach may be needed by entrepreneurs with
    a strong technical background and limited managerial experience, while
    entrepreneurs with strong managerial experience may prefer PIs, who are
    less likely to alter the makeup of the team that has been assembled.

Nature of the study: Empirical
Nature of the data: Mail survey
Nature of the sample: 70 Southern California equity-funded entrepreneurs
Variables: Level of investor involvement, reporting and operational
                         controls, expertise sought by investors

Elango, B., Fried, V. H., Hisrich, R. D., & Polonchek, A. (1995). How venture
    capital firms differ. *Journal of Business Venturing, 10* (2), 157-180.

    This study examines differences among venture capital firms: 1) venture
    stage of interest, 2) amount of assistance provided by the venture capital
    firm, 3) venture capital firm size, and 4) geographic region where located.
    This research focused on what venture companies look for in evaluating
    investments and how they work with portfolio companies following
    investment. The desired qualities of management showed no differences by
    stage. However, after the investment was made, earlier stage investors
    attached more importance to spending their time evaluating and recruiting
    managers. Earlier stage investors sought ventures with higher potential
    returns — a 42% hurdle rate of return for the earliest stage investors versus
    33% for the late-stage investor. Late stage investors spent more time
    evaluating potential investments. There was little difference in the time spent

after the investment. Firms were split into three groups based upon the amount of time spent with a portfolio company after an investment was made as lead investor. The most active group averaged more than 35 hours per month per investment, and the least active group averaged less than seven hours. Venture capital firms varied in the amount of capital they managed and size of investment, with differences in the size of investment by geographical region.

Nature of the study:	Empirical
Nature of the data:	Mail survey
Nature of the sample:	149 venture capitalists general partners
Variables:	Stage of investment, firm size, time spent with portfolio firms, geographic region, entrepreneur, product, market, return criteria, importance of the services

Fiet, J. O. (1991). Network reliance by venture capital firms and business angels: an empirical and theoretical test. In N. C. Churchill, W. D. Bygrave, J. G. Covin, D. L. Sexton, K. H. Vesper, & W. E. Wetzel, Jr. (Eds.), *Frontiers of entrepreneurial research* (pp. 445-455). Boston, MA: Babson College.

Venture capital firms and business angels have been shown to utilize networks of similar co-investors as sources of investment information. However, it had not been shown whether they actually relied upon the investment information that they received from their network contacts. This study finds that business angels rely more upon themselves for investment information than upon their network of other business angels. On the other hand, venture capital firms rely more upon a network of other venture capital firms than they do upon themselves to gather information regarding market risk. When the degree of network experience and trust was high, opportunism was controlled.

Nature of the study:	Empirical
Nature of the data:	Mail survey, interviews
Nature of the sample:	83 business angels and 141 venture capital firms
Variables:	Informal network, formal network, investor type, market risk, and agency risk

Fiet, J. O. (1995). Reliance upon informants in the venture capital industry. *Journal of Business Venturing, 10* (3), 195-224.

Do venture capitalists and angel investors rely on informants or are they concerned about self-serving behavior? The results of this study suggest that the more venture capitalists or angel investors are concerned with market or agency risk, the less likely they will be to use informal network informants. Investors with risk concerns consult formal network informants. Venture capitalist and angel investors view market risk as equally important.

However, angel investors view agency risk as more important than do venture capitalists. Venture capital firm investors consult formal network sources more frequently than do business angels. They enjoy a more efficient information flow, and as they become more experienced, they increase their reliance on formal sources. Informal sources are seen as less reliable and present more difficulties in determining self-interested behavior.

Nature of the study: Empirical
Nature of the data: Mail survey
Nature of the sample: 141 venture capitalists and 83 business angels
Variables: Investor type, importance of market risk in decision-making, importance of agency risk in decision-making, degree and use of formal and informal network

Fiet, J. O. (1996). Fragmentation in the market for venture capital. *Entrepreneurship Theory and Practice, 21* (2), 5-20.

This study examines two types of venture capital networks angels and venture capital firms (VCFs) to determine if there is fragmentation in the equity capital market. Market fragmentation creates opportunities for entrepreneurs to tap at least two separate sources of funding. If it is not fragmented, entrepreneurs would have very limited opportunities to present their deals to more than one source for funding. The study finds evidence to support some market fragmentation, based on the sources of information utilized by each network. Friends were infrequently used by either networks as sources of information. However, angels use friends more often than do venture capitalists. Both venture capitalists and angels contacted business associates. Venture capital firms contacted other venture capital firms more frequently than did angels.

Nature of the study: Empirical
Nature of the data: Mail survey, telephone survey
Nature of the sample: 141 venture capitalists and 87 angel investors
Variables: Frequency of consultation with business associates, friends and venture capital firms

Flynn, D. (1991). The critical relationship between venture capitalists and entrepreneurs: Planning, decision-making, and control. *Small Business Economics, 3,* 185-196.

This study examines the relationship between venture capital investors and new venture organizations. It investigates the post-investment relationship in the areas of technological core and administrative needs. Findings include a recommendation that venture capitalists become more involved in the administrative component of the new venture organization. The addition of a solid administrative component to the technical core provides for the continued innovation necessary to the long term survival and growth of the organization.

Nature of the study: Empirical
Nature of the data: Interviews (20), mail survey (40 additional venture capitalists)
Nature of the sample: Venture capitalists in San Francisco, Los Angeles, and New York
Variables: VC fund characteristics (size, specialty, experience), methods for screening new ventures (industry, technology, stage, entrepreneur's experience, reputation), post-investment control methods (level of control, areas of concentration, measures used to monitor progress), outcomes.

Flynn, D. (2001, April). Life Cycles of New Venture Organizations: Different Factors Affecting Performance. *Journal of Developmental Entrepreneurship, 6* (1), 41.

This study seeks to extend previous work indicating a relationship between new venture organization (NVO) performance and demographic, decision-making, structural, information processing, and environmental factors on the part of the venture capitalist (VC). The focus of the research was to address a key moderating variable: the stage in the life of the venture when the VC decides to become involved. The behavior of VCs and their affiliated NVOs was investigated in the context of the life cycle construct by assessing the differences that existed for firms that invested earlier versus later in the organizational life cycle.

The study provides evidence that the requirements for a positive impact on new venture performance vary based on when the VC involvement occurred in the life cycle of the new venture organization. The study further supports the contention that some imprinting occurred by the VCs (Boeker, 1989), altering the direction but not necessarily the level of future performance. This analysis contributes to the empirical literature of the life cycle construct as called for by Hanks et al. (1993) and Randolph et al. (1991).

Nature of the study: Empirical
Nature of the data: Questionnaire, including items designed to determine timing of VC investment and demographic variables of NVO and VC
Nature of the sample: Random sample of 76 VCs
Variables: Sex, age, education, experience, mean investment, crisis situations, future situations

Florida, R., & Kenney, M. (1988). Venture capital and high technology entrepreneurship. *Journal of Business Venturing, 3* (4), 301-319.

This article asks whether venture capital complexes are important to innovation and entrepreneurship. Venture capital complexes can be classified into three types: 1) finance-oriented complexes, such as New York and Chicago, 2) technology-oriented complexes, such as San Francisco-Silicon Valley, and 3) hybrids that exist in Boston, Minneapolis, Connecticut, and Texas. Venture capital complexes have a relatively high proportion of venture capital subsidiaries of financial institutions, and export their funds. Technology-oriented complexes contain large proportions of limited partnerships, favor local investment, and attract venture capital from other areas. Enormous incentives for venture capital firms to locate in established technology centers are created by a high concentration of good deals. Technology and finance-oriented venture capital complexes have a symbiotic relationship. Well-developed capital networks provide tremendous incentives for start-ups and help create a self-reinforcing cycle of new enterprise formation, innovation, and economic development.

Nature of the study:	Empirical
Nature of the data:	Venture capital industry database
Nature of the sample:	Venture capital investors, portfolio companies, investment syndication partnerships
Variables:	Capital base, number of venture firms, number of top venture capital firms, number of venture capital subsidiaries, number of limited partnerships, instate/out of state investments, venture capital investment by region, investments and co-investments

Frederiksen, O., Klofsten, M., Landstrom, H., Olofsson, C., & Wahlbin, C. (1990). Entrepreneur-Venture capitalists relations: The entrepreneurs' views. In N. C. Churchill, W. D. Bygrave, J. A. Hornaday, D. F. Muzyka, K. H. Vesper, & W. E. Wetzel, Jr. (Eds.), *Frontiers of entrepreneurial research* (pp. 251-265). Boston, MA: Babson College.

This study explores the relationship between venture-capital-backed companies and venture capital firms in Sweden as to the formation of the cooperation, details of cooperation and communication, the perceived influence of the venture capital partner, and the outcome of the cooperation, all from the perspective of the portfolio company. The focus is on the situation in early 1990 and on the development since the mid-1980s. The results confirm that venture capitalists provide more than the capital that is an important motive for almost every entrepreneur. VCs are also the main source for complementary management resources. They provide competence, support and access to networks. They work on the strategic level, guide economic reporting, and complement the management team, mainly by being active on the board of the portfolio company.

Nature of the study: Empirical
Nature of the data: Mail survey
Nature of the sample: 136 Swedish venture-capital-backed firms.
Variables: Forming of relationship, frequency of contacts, ways of
                        cooperation and communication, use of and need for
                        external competence, perceived influence from venture
                        capital partner, perceived outcome of the cooperation, age,
                        size, industry, stage, type of start-up

Frederiksen, O., Olofsson, C., & Wahlbin, C. (1991). The role of venture capital in
    the development of portfolio firms. In N. C. Churchill, W. D. Bygrave, J. G.
    Covin, D. L. Sexton, K. H. Vesper, & W. E. Wetzel, Jr. (Eds.), *Frontiers of
    entrepreneurial research* (pp. 435-444). Boston, MA: Babson College.

This study explores the degree to which the influence of venture capital firms
impacts the development of portfolio companies. The approach was to link
characteristics of the cooperation and the influence of the venture capital
firm on the development of the portfolio company to the subjective outcome
of the cooperation. The study finds that the only clear influence exerted by
venture capital firms is the control and capital dimension. Otherwise, the
development of the portfolio companies in terms of economic development
or growth is found to be unrelated to the perceived influence.

Nature of the study: Empirical
Nature of the data: Mail survey
Nature of the sample: 50 Swedish venture-capital-backed firms
Variables: Characteristics of the cooperation (age, frequency of contact,
                        effort, means of cooperation), perceived influence of venture
                        capital firm, portfolio firm development, and subjective
                        outcome

Freear, J., Sohl, J. A., & Wetzel, Jr., W. E. (1990). Raising venture capital:
    Entrepreneurs' views of the process. In N. C. Churchill, W. D. Bygrave, J. A.
    Hornaday, D. F. Muzyka, K. H. Vesper, & W. E. Wetzel, Jr. (Eds.),
    Frontiers of entrepreneurial research (pp. 223-237). Boston, MA: Babson
    College.

The study investigates how new technology-based firms (NTBFs) perceive
their external equity investors, particularly private individual investors and
venture capital funds. Data obtained from respondents, who were the CEOs
or other senior officials of the firm, include 1) the process of finding
investors and raising funds; 2) investors' expectations of annual rates of
return and the timing and method of liquidation; and 3) the role of investors
and their working relationship with the firm. The majority of NTBFs that
raised funds from private individuals had also approached venture capital

funds, but with limited success. Only about one-third of the NTBFs that raised funds from venture capital funds had also approached private individuals, but more than 80 percent were successful. NTBFs were able to raise funds more rapidly from private individuals than from venture capital funds. Board membership was the most common role for both groups, closely followed by a consulting role. Approximately 80 percent of the private individuals and venture capital funds had some sort of working relationship with the NTBFs, with 75% of the NTBFs finding the working relationship to be productive.

The lessons learned by NTBFs in seeking external equity funding were that they should have 1) raised more money earlier; 2) prepared and presented their cases for funding more effectively; 3) sought more and a broader mix of investors; and 4) defined their relationship with individual investors more carefully before the deal was concluded.

Nature of the study: Empirical
Nature of the data: Database, mail survey
Nature of the sample: 284 NTBF firms founded in New England (177 were funded
                         with outside equity financing)
Variables: Length of search process, expected annual rate of return,
                         expected time and method to liquidate investments, investor
                         role in management, working relationship

Freear, J., Sohl, J. E., & Wetzel, Jr., W. E. (1992). The investment attitudes, behavior and characteristics of high net worth individuals. In N. C. Churchill, S. Birley, W. D. Bygrave, D. F. Muzyka, C. Wahlbin, & W. E. Wetzel, Jr. (Eds.), *Frontiers of entrepreneurial research* (pp. 374-387). Boston, MA: Babson College.

This study reports on the preliminary results of a survey of high net worth individuals (a net worth of $1 million or more) for the purpose of discovering their attitudes toward investing in entrepreneurial ventures, their history of venture investing, and their demographic characteristics. The discussion is limited to the yield from investment referral sources, the significance investors attach to venture location, and trends in their investment activity. For non-investors, the discussion includes their interest in venture financing and the incentives that would induce them to become investors. The findings show that 1) the three most productive referral sources are friends, business associates, and lead investors, as opposed to "gatekeepers" (attorneys, accountants, and bankers; 2) investors are inclined to expand, rather than contract, the geographic scope of their portfolios; 3) from 1987 through 1991, the rate of venture investing by the respondents dropped by almost 50 percent; and 4) with the right enticements, it is conceivable that three quarters of the potential investors would become venture investors.

Nature of the study: Empirical
Nature of the data: Mail survey
Nature of the sample: 184 high net worth individuals from the 1990 Real Estate Transfer Database, with 146 individuals who have made venture investments (business angels) and 38 non-investors/potential investors
Variables: Yield of investment referral sources, venture location, trends in angel investing, interest in venture financing, incentives to become investors

Freear, J., Sohl, J. E., & Wetzel, Jr., W. E. (1995). Angels: Personal investors in the venture capital market. *Entrepreneurship & Regional Development, 7,* 85-94.

According to the authors, the invisible angel segment of the venture capital market appears to play a central role in maintaining the vitality of the U.S. entrepreneurial economy. For new technology-based ventures (NTBVs), angels are the most common source of seed and start-up financing if the round of financing was less than US$500,000. This paper examines the role of private investors in the equity financing of NTBVs as well as the entrepreneur's perceptions of raising venture capital. The authors describe the venture capital market from a demand and supply perspective and contrast the role of the private investor with that of the more visible venture capital funds. Entrepreneurs reported that it took less time to find and close a deal with angels than with venture capital funds and the financing was perceived to be less expensive. The value angels placed on the non-financial characteristics of the ventures they back was a distinguishing feature of the angel segment of the venture capital market in the U.S. Entrepreneurs who understand the distinctive roles of angels and venture capital funds can save time and increase the odds of raising capital from the right source at the right time.

Nature of the study: Empirical
Nature of the data: Database, mail survey
Nature of the sample: 248 new technology-based firms
Variables: Source, amount, and stage of financing; process of raising funds; characteristics of investors

Freear, J., & Wetzel, Jr., W. E. (1989). Equity capital for entrepreneurs. In R. H. Brockhaus, Sr., N. C. Churchill, J. A. Katz, B. A. Kirchhoff, K. H. Vesper, & W. E. Wetzel, Jr. (Eds.), *Frontiers of entrepreneurial research* (pp. 230-244). Boston, MA: Babson College.

Of 283 firms (26 percent response rate) receiving venture capital funding, 83 (35 percent) raised $73.818m of external equity capital in 108 financing rounds from individuals prior to being financed by venture capital funds. Seventy-seven percent were "early stage" rounds, of which 65 percent were for under $1,000,000, with a median of $350,000. Of significance is that 128 respondents' firms (54%) did not raise equity capital from individual investors prior to financing from venture capital funds.

Nature of the study: Empirical
Nature of the data: Mail survey
Nature of the sample: 283 venture-funded firms from the Venture Economics data base
Variables: Sources of funding prior to venture capital funding, sources of funding, amount of funding, stage of funding

Fried, V. H., & Hisrich, R. D. (1988). Venture capital research: Past, present and future. *Entrepreneurship Theory and Practice, 13* (1), 15-29.

This paper is a literature review of academic articles on venture capital since 1981. The authors have developed a simple yet detailed model of the venture capital process based on the academic literature that has been done on this subject. In turn, the model is suggested as a foundation for future research in the field of venture capital. The review found 16 articles, 18 proceeding papers, and five book chapters, which is a significant increase over previous reviews. The research from 1981 to 1987 focuses on six primary topics: 1) the portfolio of venture capital firms, 2) the investment decision, 3) operations, 4) strategy, 5) impact on the entrepreneur, and 6) public policy. The heaviest research emphasis has been on the portfolio and investment decision topics. The primary source of data for these articles was mail and telephone surveys. Most of the studies used frequency counts, percentages, or means. A descriptive model of the venture capital process is developed to serve as an organizing framework for research in the field. This research is mainly in the areas of the linkage between investor and venture capital firm, the relationship between the venture capital firm and the investee, and the operation of the venture capital firm.

Nature of the study: Literature review
Nature of the data: NA
Nature of the sample: NA
Variables: Venture capital

Fried, V. H., & Hisrich, R. D. (1989). Venture capital from the investors' perspectives. In R. H. Brockhaus, Sr., N. C. Churchill, J. A. Katz, B. A. Kirchhoff, K. H. Vesper, & W. E. Wetzel, Jr. (Eds.), *Frontiers of entrepreneurial research* (pp. 258-273). Boston, MA: Babson College.

The paper investigates the venture capital process from the institutional investor's perspective and discusses 1) the reasons for investing in venture capital (high return on investment and portfolio diversification); 2) the criteria used in selecting venture funds (people, teamwork, performance, discipline, and strategy); 3) reference checking with entrepreneurs as an important procedure in the selection of funds; 4) the post-investment relationship between investor and venture capitalist; and 5) the potential for culture clashes between venture capitalist and investor.

Nature of the study:	Empirical
Nature of the data:	Interviews
Nature of the sample:	18 venture capital investors (7 pension funds, 3 insurance companies, 3 corporations, 1 endowment fund, 1 individual investor and 3 independent investment advisors specializing in venture capital)
Variables:	Reasons for investing, criteria in selecting venture funds, reference checking, post-investment relationship between investor and venture capitalist

Fried, V. H., & Hisrich, R. D. (1994). Toward a model of venture capital investment decision making. *Financial Management, 23* (3), 28-37.

This paper describes how venture capitalists make investment decisions. Generic criteria that venture capitalists use are classified into three categories: concept, management, and returns. A six-stage process model is proposed: 1) origination, 2) venture capital firm-specific screen, 3) generic screen, 4) first-phase evaluation, 5) second-phase evaluation, and 6) closing. The venture capitalist investment decision-making process is designed to reduce the risk of adverse selection. Different activities occur in each stage. It is argued that the venture capitalist provides both supply-side and demand-side benefits to the market.

Nature of the study:	Empirical
Nature of the data:	Interviews, mail survey
Nature of the sample:	23 venture capitalists in various regions in the U.S.
Variables:	Investment criteria, investment stages, time

Gifford, S. (1997). Limited attention and the role of venture capitalist. *Journal of Business Venturing, 12* (6), 459-482.

In prior literature, venture capital research has modeled the entrepreneur as the agent of the venture capitalist. In this article the venture capitalist is seen as an agent of the entrepreneur. The problem is analyzed by considering the allocation of a venture capitalist's limited attention between current ventures and acquiring new ventures. The optimal allocation of the venture capitalist's attention determines the optimal frequency of meetings with the entrepreneur and the optimal termination date at which the venture goes public. The opportunity cost of attending to an incubating venture is the foregone evaluation of new ventures. This opportunity cost implies that the venture capitalist wants to have fewer and less frequent consultations with the entrepreneur than is required to maximize the entrepreneur's return. This action is rational when viewed from the perspective of the venture capitalist confronted with allocating time and capital among various projects. The most striking implication of this application is that the venture capitalist's optimal allocation is socially efficient. Since the venture capitalist is exhibiting what is commonly called moral hazard, this implies that moral hazard is efficient.

Nature of the study: Conceptual
Nature of the data: NA
Nature of the sample: NA
Variables: Number and frequency of consultations, growth in value, loss on investment, age of the venture, total profit, abandonment of the venture, opportunity costs

Gorman, M., & Sahlman, W. A. (1989). What do venture capitalists do? *Journal of Business Venturing, 4* (4), 231-248.

This study investigates the relationship between venture capitalists and their portfolio companies. The results of the study show that the venture capitalists spent about half their time monitoring, on average, nine portfolio investments. Of these, five were firms they helped found and on whose board of directors they served. For the companies on whose boards they served, the venture capitalists usually invested 80 hours of on-site time and 30 hours of telephone time per year in direct contact with the companies. The most frequently performed service by the venture capitalists for the portfolio companies was to assist in fund raising, in strategic analysis, and in management recruiting. In cases of company failure, the venture capitalists occasionally dismissed and replaced current management. Usually, failures were attributed to problems in senior management; among non-managerial causes, product development was cited in half the cases.

Nature of the study: Empirical
Nature of the data: Mail survey
Nature of the sample: 49 venture capitalists
Variables: Number of active partners per venture capital firm, number of investments managed, number of board seats per partner, number of hours spent, assistance provided to ventures, causes of failures

Goslin, L. N., & Barge, B. (1986). Entrepreneurial qualities considered in venture capital support. In R. Ronstadt, J. A. Hornaday, R. Peterson, & K.H. Vesper (Eds.), *Frontiers of entrepreneurial research* (pp. 366-378). Boston, MA: Babson College.

The study focuses on identifying entrepreneurial qualities and experiences that venture capitalists consider critical to a favorable decision to support a start-up venture. The three locations for the sample concurred on the importance of the management team and product. However, differences in the definition of the management team and the innovativeness of the product were observed for the three locations of venture capital firms.

Nature of the study: Empirical
Nature of the data: Mail survey
Nature of the sample: 42 venture capital firms in Portland, Seattle, and San
                         Francisco
Variables: Location of venture capital firms, management team criteria
                         for success

Greene, P. G., Brush, C. G., Hart, M. M., & Saparito, P. (2001). Patterns of venture capital funding: Is gender a factor? *Venture Capital, 3* (1), 63-83.

There is a disparity between the number of women-led firms in the U.S. and the proportion of venture capital those firms receive. This paper uses longitudinal data from 1953 to 1998 to track U.S. venture capital investment by proportion, stage, industry, and sex of entrepreneur. Since 1953, 2.4% of investments went to identifiable women-led firms, while 46.8% went to identifiable men-led firms. In the period 1988-1998, identifiable women–led firms received 3.5% of investments; male-led received 48.4%. Women-led firms that received venture financing were more often in the service sector; male-led firms were more often in manufacturing. Significant differences were also found for stage of investment. Women-led firms received early stage financing, while men more often received buyout/acquisition financing.

Nature of the study: Empirical
Nature of the data: National Venture Capital Association database
Nature of the sample: Venture capital investments
Variables: Sex of firm owner or top management, year of first
                         investment, stage at first investment, industrial sector

Gupta, A. K., & Sapienza, H. J. (1992). Determinants of venture capital firms' preferences regarding the industry diversity and geographic scope of their investments. *Journal of Business Venturing, 7* (5), 347-362.

Competition has intensified in the venture capital industry in the U.S. Venture capital firms (VCF) have faced increased pressure to seek lower risk investments, improve rates of return, and provide value to new venture development. Building on the premise that decisions regarding product-market scope are a key component of firm strategy, this study identified factors that might explain variations in VCFs' preferences regarding industry diversity and geographic scope of their investments. The study identifies four basic results: 1) VCFs specializing in early stage ventures prefer less industry diversity and narrower geographic scope relative to other VCFs; 2) corporate VCFs prefer less industry diversity but broader geographic scope related to non-corporate VCFs; 3) larger VCFs prefer greater industry diversity and broader geographic scope than do smaller VCFs; and 4) VCF firms that primarily provide small business investment companies (SBIC) financing have no preference for industry diversity but prefer a narrower geographic scope.

Nature of the study: Empirical
Nature of the data: Pratt's Guide to Venture Capital Sources
Nature of the sample: 169 domestic VCFs
Variables: Industry preference, geographic scope, stage of financing, ownership structure, size of the VCF, type of financing, age, stage of investment

Hall, J., & Hofer, C. W. (1993). Venture capitalists' decision criteria in new venture evaluation. *Journal of Business Venturing, 8* (1), 25-42.

This study examines the criteria used by venture capitalists to evaluate actual venture proposals. Sixteen verbal protocols--in which the participants think aloud as they review business proposals--were constructed from the venture evaluation decisions. The findings suggest that venture capitalists screen and assess business proposals very rapidly. A surprising finding involves the lack of importance venture capitalists attached to the entrepreneurial team and the strategy of the proposed venture during the early stages of the venture evaluation process. Key criteria identified include fit with the venture firm's lending guidelines and the long-term growth and profitability of the industry in which the proposed business will operate.

Nature of the study: Empirical
Nature of the data: Interviews
Nature of the sample: 16 venture capitalists
Variables: Time to decision, decision criteria

Hambrecht, W. R. (1984). Venture capital and the growth of Silicon Valley. *California Management Review, 26* (2), 74-82.

This article examines the growth of the venture capital industry in the early 1980s, specifically in Northern California. It traces the history and origin of the (modern) venture capital world, which is generally considered to have begun after World War II. Also described are the major events that propelled the U.S. into a position of technological leadership. In 1981, California venture funds raised nearly three times the amount of capital raised by those of any other state and accounted for more than one-third of the capital raised nationwide. California also accounted for 36% of the new venture financings during 1981, more than half of which were located in Santa Clara County alone. The author also forecast the outlook of the venture capital industry in the 1980s, suggesting that the rate of returns would decrease as new money continued to flow in. The efficient perfect market for equities would continue to spread downward until only the truly high risk, early stage financings would still carry the same risk/reward ratio that all of venture capital experienced during the 1970s. The article concludes with the author encouraging entrepreneurs with innovative, unique ideas and a sense of commitment to consider venture capital financing.

Nature of the study: Conceptual
Nature of the data: NA
Nature of the sample: NA
Variables: Rate of return, geographic dispersion

Harrison, R. T., & Mason, C. M. (1990). Informal risk capital in the United
    Kingdom. In N. C. Churchill, W. D. Bygrave, J. A. Hornaday, D. F. Muzyka,
    K. H. Vesper, & W. E. Wetzel, Jr. (Eds.), *Frontiers of entrepreneurial
    research* (pp. 266-280). Boston, MA: Babson College.

The authors assert that the difficulty of obtaining external finance on reasonable terms constituted a major constraint on new venture formation and growth in the U.K. In light of this, the paper has four objectives: 1) to summarize the evidence for the existence of a financing gap in the U.K., particularly as it affects the supply of institutional or formal sources of equity finance; 2) to assess the significance of informal investors in the U.K.; 3) to explore the role of investor clubs and financial marriage bureaus in linking potential investors and investee businesses; (4) to define a research agenda for further study of informal risk capital investment in the U.K. This paper reviews the nature of the equity gap facing new and growing ventures in the U.K. and assesses the contribution of both demand-related and supply-related explanations for this gap. The use of informal equity investment (sources of risk capital other than professionally managed venture funds, institutional investors, and public equity markets), is one possible resolution of the new venture equity gap. This study suggests that, based on a preliminary analysis of the U.K. situation, informal sources of equity were used by a significant proportion of those small ventures in the U.K. that sought external equity funding at some stage. Informal investors did play a role in the provision of equity capital in the U.K. On the basis of the experience of one informal investment network (Metrogroup), the study finds that informal investors in the U.K. may differ in their characteristics and attitudes from those in the U.S. However, because of the diverse and fragmentary nature of the available evidence, it was impossible to reveal more on the operation of the informal risk capital market in the U.K.

Nature of the study: Empirical
Nature of the data: Previous research, case study
Nature of the sample: An informal investment network
Variables: Role of informal investors in the provision of equity capital, role of investor clubs in linking potential investors and investees

Harrison, R. T., & Mason, C. M. (1991). Informal venture capital in the U.K. and the U.S.A.: A comparison of investor characteristics, investment preferences and decision-making. In N. C. Churchill, W. D. Bygrave, J. G. Covin, D. L. Sexton, K. H. Vesper, & W. E. Wetzel, Jr. (Eds.), *Frontiers of entrepreneurial research* (pp. 469-481). Boston, MA: Babson College.

It had been widely accepted in the U.K. that there was a shortage of risk capital for ventures seeking external equity finance. In the U.S., a well-developed informal venture capital market played a major role in filling the equity gap. This paper reports on the preliminary results of a study of informal investors in the U.K. and compares these with evidence on the characteristics and behavior of informal investors in the U.S. The research suggests that informal investors were indeed playing an important role in the financing of small businesses in the U.K. in two ways: 1) they contributed to the filling of the equity gap by making investments, typically £50,000 or less, with a significant portion invested in new and recently established businesses; and 2) it is easier for entrepreneurs to raise finance from informal investors than from venture capital funds. Compared with venture capital funds, informal investors had a lower rejection rate, were more patient investors, and had lower rates of return targets; and (3) informal investors appeared to be contributing to the closing of a regional equity gap that results from the over-concentration of venture capital investments in the South East and adjacent regions, as the majority of the investments made by informal investors were in companies located close to their home or office.

The paper also indicates that in comparison to the "typical" U.S. informal investor, U.K. informal investors appeared to 1) have more investment opportunities brought to their attention; 2) consider more proposals but invest in a smaller proportion of these; 3) operate independently, reducing the average total investment per financing round available to investee ventures; 4) fail to identify entrepreneurs themselves as a primary source of information on investment opportunities; 5) have slightly higher rate of returns and capital gains expectations for all investment types; 6) be rather less patient investors, with a median exit horizon of 3 to 5 years; and 7) be

161

less satisfied with the overall performance of their informal investment portfolios.

Nature of the study: Empirical
Nature of the data: Mail survey
Nature of the sample: 63 actual and potential informal investors in the U.K.
Variables: Differences between U.K. and U.S. informal investors, investor characteristics, informal investor activity, deal acceptance rate, investment size and syndication, risk and return, exit routes, portfolio performance

Hellmann, T., & Puri, M. (2000). The interaction between product market and financing strategy: The role of venture capital. *The Review of Financial Studies, 13* (4), 959-984.

This paper uses a unique data set of Silicon Valley start-up companies to explore the role of venture capital financing. The authors state that they were the first to empirically examine and document the interrelationship between the type of investor and aspects of the product market behavior of start-up firms. The article found that firms pursuing an innovator rather than an imitator strategy were more likely to obtain venture capital financing. Obtaining venture capital was also associated with faster time to market. From a finance perspective, the results indicated that the appropriateness of choosing an involved investor depended on the strategic objectives of the company. From an industrial organization perspective, the results showed that a firm's choice of financing seemed to affect its ability to secure first-mover advantages. The results also suggested that venture capital financing had an impact on the development path of a start-up company, and in particular on its product market position.

Nature of the study: Empirical
Nature of the data: Mail survey, interviews
Nature of the sample: 173 start-up companies in Silicon Valley
Variables: Amount of financing, venture capital financing, innovation objective of firm, firm age, time to first obtaining venture capital, time to first product sale, industry sector, presence of a business plan, patent existence, number of patents

Hills, G. E. (1984). Market analysis and marketing in new ventures: Venture capitalists' perceptions. In J. A. Hornaday, F. Tarpley, Jr., J. A. Timmons, & K. H. Vesper (Eds.), *Frontier of Entrepreneurship Research* (pp. 43-54). Boston, MA: Babson College.

The purpose of this study is to determine the propensity of the entrepreneur to seek out and utilize market information prior to start up, to determine the usefulness and predictive validity of demand forecasts included within new business plans, and to identify uniqueness concerning the marketing task during the start-up and early growth stages. The study found that venture capitalists' perceptions generally supported the following: 1) entrepreneurs tended to avoid obtaining in-depth market information prior to start-up; 2) the actual value of in-depth market analysis was high; 3) the predictive validity of demand forecasts contained within business plans was low; and 4) there were unique barriers to distribution and promotional effectiveness in new ventures and early growth firms. These were critical issues directly pertaining to the success and failure rates of new ventures.

Nature of the study: Empirical
Nature of the data: Interviews, survey
Nature of the sample: 14 members of Chicago's venture capital community
Variables: Perceptions of venture capitalists, entrepreneurs' propensity
                       toward use of in-depth market information, entrepreneurs'
                       bias toward venture idea, predictive validity of demand
                       forecasts in business plans, barriers to marketing
                       effectiveness in start-up and early growth stage

Hisrich, R. D., & Jancowicz, A. D. (1990). Intuition in venture capital decisions: An exploratory study using a new technique. *Journal of Business Venturing, 5*(1), 49-62.

This is an exploratory study that uses the repertory grid technique, drawn from personal construct psychology, to develop an understanding of intuition in the decision-making of venture capitalists. In-depth interviews were conducted to obtain information about the particular constructs venture capitalists use in thinking about investment proposals. The goal was to obtain systematic data on the content and structure of intuitions prior to the development of a questionnaire to be issued to a larger sample. The results indicated that investment constructs could be grouped into three areas: management, unique opportunity, and appropriate return. A cluster analysis showed that each venture capitalist had a unique way of structuring the intuitions involved in the investment decision. The results suggest that individuals seeking venture capital need to adjust their approach to different venture capitalists.

Nature of the study: Empirical
Nature of the data: Interviews
Nature of the sample: 5 venture capitalists
Variables: Management criteria, opportunity, appropriate return

Hughes, A. (1997). Finance for SMEs: A U.K. Perspective. *Small Business Economics, 9,* 151-166.

This paper presents findings and policy implications of the Small Business Research Programme of the Economic and Social Research Council (ESRC) of the U.K. In particular, the author explores whether a capital gap does indeed exist for small businesses in the U.K. Findings support the idea that there is a high degree of reliance by small firms upon short term finance provided by banks. However, little support is found for the gap, with some exceptions predicated upon membership in certain racial or ethnic groups. In addition, the provision of equity capital is found to be problematic for smaller firms. Venture capital investment was found to be generally insignificant, with its greatest impact on medium size firms.

Nature of the study: Empirical
Nature of the data: National SME surveys plus a meta-analysis of findings from papers drawn from the ESRC program team
Nature of the sample: 2,000 small and medium size firms
Variables: Balance sheet items, sources of financing, size of firm, industrial sector

Hustedde, R. J., & Pulver, G. C. (1992). Factors affecting equity capital acquisition: The demand side. *Journal of Business Venturing, 7* (5), 363.

This study of entrepreneurs seeking equity capital in amounts of $100,000 or more reveals that success in acquiring funding was related to four general variables: 1) the entrepreneur's education, experience, and age; 2) the enterprise's development stage, industry type, and location; 3) the request amount, the business plan, and the prospective capital source; and 4) sources of advice. Overall, it was found that the quality of advice provided to entrepreneurs needs to be improved. Entrepreneurs who fail to seek assistance are less successful in acquiring equity capital. A number of specific public policy recommendations for governments interested in improving equity capital market efficiency are presented.

Nature of the study: Empirical
Nature of the data: Mail survey
Nature of the sample: 318 entrepreneurs seeking funding
Variables: Age, experience, education, family business experience, willingness to surrender equity, aggressiveness in seeking capital, venture stage of development, product offering, metro location, communication, amount of financing sought, written business plan, location of venture capital sought, sources of advice

Jennings, D. F., & Sexton, D. L. (1985). A contextual analysis of venture activities: Implications for new research directions in venture capital. In J. A. Hornaday, E. B. Shils, J. A. Timmons, & K. H. Vesper (Eds.), *Frontiers of entrepreneurial research* (pp. 170-186). Boston, MA: Babson College.

This paper argues that an analysis of the contextual factors affecting venture activities represents an area of research that may provide answers to questions raised by the process factors research approach to venture capital. Specifically, the authors postulate that this research approach may be developed to address issues related to the "conspicuous oases" of highly innovative technological ventures.

The first part of the paper describes a model of technological progress as a three-stage phenomenon: invention, innovation, and diffusion. The second part reviews the impact of firm size, market structure, and organizational elements on the technological progress model. The third part introduces venture capital activities into the technological progress model, and the fourth part posits contextual factors that affect venturing activities: 1) market structures, 2) basic government policies concerning markets, 3) availability of tax incentives, 4) technological opportunity, and 5) organizational structure and congruence.

Nature of the study:	Conceptual
Nature of the data:	NA
Nature of the sample:	NA
Variables:	Implementation of venture projects, market structures, basic government policies concerning markets, availability of tax incentives, technological opportunity, organizational structure and congruence

Khan, A. M. (1987). Assessing venture capital investments with non-compensatory behavioral decision models. *Journal of Business Venturing, 2* (3), 193-205.

Since venture capital investments are made in new businesses, they are handicapped by limited historical data that prevent meaningful probabilistic analysis. This study presents an alternative framework modeling the decision process of venture capitalists. Specifically, two types of non-compensatory actuarial models, conjunctive and disjunctive, were used to model both venture capitalists' judgments and the environment. Results indicate that conjunctive models are superior predictors to disjunctive models. In addition, the judgments of venture capitalists appear to be poor predictors of actual investments. However, the environment-based conjunctive and disjunctive models were much more successful predictors. All of the models were found to perform better than venture capitalists' judgments, which were surprisingly poor predictors of actual outcomes. The study reveals that venture capitalists use the entrepreneur's desire for success and the nature of the product in making a decision. In the environmental model, the most important variable was the creativity and ingenuity of the entrepreneur.

Nature of the study:	Empirical
Nature of the data:	Mail survey
Nature of the sample:	36 venture capitalists with 104 investments
Variables:	Entrepreneur's desire for success, creativity, tenacity, enthusiasm, competence; uniqueness of product or service relative to competition

Knight, R. M. (1994). Criteria used by venture capitalists: A cross cultural analysis. *International Small Business Journal, 13* (1), 26-37.

An analysis is presented of a cross-cultural survey of criteria used by international venture capitalists to evaluate venture proposals. Responses were compared for differences and similarities among the regions. The primary criteria used in the study were the entrepreneur's personality and experience, characteristics of the product/service, characteristics of the market, and financial considerations. Some similarities were apparent, for example the entrepreneur's personality, but for the most part there were differences by region. One of the most interesting was the difference in emphasis on high-tech. High technology investments are not nearly as popular with venture capitalists in other parts of the world as in the U.S., and high-tech is even viewed as a negative criterion in many countries.

Nature of the study:	Empirical
Nature of the data:	Mail survey
Nature of the sample:	Venture capitalists in the U.S., Canada, Europe and the Asia-Pacific region
Variables:	Entrepreneur's personality and experience, characteristics of the product/service, characteristics of the market, financial considerations

Landström, H., Manigart, S., Mason, C. M., & Sapienza, H. J.(1998). Contracts between entrepreneurs and investors: Terms and negotiation processes. In P. D. Reynolds, W. D. Bygrave, N. M. Carter, S. Manigart, C. M. Mason, G. D. Meyer, H. J. Sapienza, & K. G. Shaver (Eds.), *Frontiers of entrepreneurial research* (pp. 571-585). Boston, MA: Babson College.

In this paper, the written contract and the negotiation process in the venture capitalist-entrepreneur relationship are discussed using two theoretical perspectives: agency and social exchange theories. This exploratory study is based on semi-structured interviews with venture capitalists and entrepreneurs in four countries (Belgium, Sweden, U.K., U.S.A.). The findings indicate that both formal and informal investor-entrepreneur investment agreements are important in shaping investment relationships. The nature and elaborateness of written contracts and the willingness of both parties to negotiate on key points is influenced by prior experience of contractors, number of investors involved, involvement preferences of both VCs and entrepreneurs, and venture stage.

Nature of the study:	Empirical
Nature of the data:	Interviews
Nature of the sample:	16 venture capitalist investors and entrepreneurs of the investee companies in the U.S., Belgium, Sweden, and the U.K.
Variables:	Prior experience of contractors, number of investors involved, type of investor, involvement preferences of VCs and entrepreneurs, venture stage, elaborateness of the written contract

Lockett, A., & Wright, M. (1999). The syndication of venture capital investment. In P. D. Reynolds, W. D. Bygrave, S. Manigart, C. M. Mason, G. D. Meyer, H. J. Sapienza, & K. G. Shaver (Eds.), *Frontiers of entrepreneurial research* (pp. 306-320). Boston, MA: Babson College.

This paper examines the question why do venture capital firms syndicate private equity? There are two dominant competing views. The traditional approach, developed from finance theory, has been to view syndication as a means of risk sharing via portfolio diversification. In contrast, the resource-based perspective views syndication as a response to the need to share and/or access information in the selection and management of investments. Overall the finance perspective provided a strong explanation of motives for syndication, but the resource-based view was found to be much more important for those firms involved in both early stage and late stage transactions. The implications for researchers are that venture capital firms should not be treated as a homogeneous group and that the investment stages in which they operate may strongly influence attitudes towards syndication. In addition, there are implications for practitioners as venture capital firms may not be attributing sufficient attention to the need to augment their own resource base in order to enable them to make superior decisions when selecting deals and managing investments.

Nature of the study:	Empirical
Nature of the data:	Mail survey
Nature of the sample:	62 venture capital firms
Variables:	VC firm characteristics, motives for syndicating deals, motives for not syndicating deals

MacMillan, I. C., Kulow, D. M., & Khoylian, R. (1989). Venture capitalists' involvement in their investments: Extent and performance. *Journal of Business Venturing, 4* (1), 27-47.

In this study, venture capitalists' involvement in a number of activities for a funded venture was evaluated, as well as the performance and other characteristics of the venture. Results showed that, compared to the entrepreneur, venture capitalists were involved most in the financial parts of the venture. The activity with the highest level of involvement was acting as a sounding board to the entrepreneur; the lowest level of involvement was with ongoing operations. Factor analysis of involvement patterns identified four distinct areas of involvement: 1) development and operations, 2) management selection, 3) personnel management, and 4) financial participation. Three distinct levels of involvement by venture capitalists were identified: 1) laissez faire, limited involvement, 2) moderate involvement, and 3) close tracker, in which the venture capitalists were more involved than the entrepreneur in a majority of the identified activities.

Nature of the study:	Empirical
Nature of the data:	Mail survey
Nature of the sample:	62 venture capitalists in the databases of Sol C. Snider Entrepreneurial Center o the Wharton School and Venture Economics, Inc
Variables:	Involvement in development and operations, management selection, personnel management and financial participation

MacMillan, I. C., Siegel, R., & Subba Narasimha, P. N. (1985). Criteria used by venture capitalists to evaluate new venture proposals. *Journal of Business Venturing, 1*(1), 119-128.

The study's most important finding is direct confirmation of the frequently iterated position taken by the venture capital community that above all it is the quality of the entrepreneur that ultimately determines the funding decision. Five of the top 10 most important criteria had to do with the entrepreneur's experience and personality.

The question the authors posed is, "If this is the case, then why is so much emphasis placed on the business plan?" In a business plan there is generally little to indicate the characteristics of the entrepreneur. The business plan should indicate by whatever feasible and credible means possible that the entrepreneur has staying power, has a track record, can react well to risk, and has familiarity with the target market. Failing this, the entrepreneur needs to be able to form a team that has such characteristics and show that he or she is capable of leading that team. The results showed that venture capitalists appeared to systematically evaluate ventures in terms of six categories of risk to be managed, namely 1) risk of losing the entire investment; 2) risk of being unable to bail out if necessary; 3) risk of failure to implement the venture idea; 4) competitive risk; 5) risk of management failure; and 6) risk of leadership failure. Three clusters of venture capitalists were also identified: 1) those who carefully assess the competitive and implementation risks; 2) those who seek easy bail out; and 3) those who deliberately keep as many options open as possible.

Nature of the study:	Empirical
Nature of the data:	Interviews, survey
Nature of the sample:	14 venture capitalists in New York Metro and 102 members of the National Venture Capital Association
Variables:	Entrepreneurs' personality and experience, characteristics of the product or service, characteristics of the market, financial considerations, characteristics of the venture team, ratings of importance for the criteria

MacMillan, I. C., & Subba Narasimha, P. N. (1986). Characteristics distinguishing funded from unfunded business plans evaluated by venture capitalists. In R. Ronstadt, J. A. Hornaday, R. Peterson, & K.H. Vesper (Eds.), *Frontiers of entrepreneurial research* (pp. 404-413). Boston, MA: Babson College.

This paper argues that if the business plan was a key factor in determining whether or not an entrepreneur got funding from a venture capitalist, then it was worthwhile to ascertain empirically whether there were inherent characteristics of a business plan that increased or decreased its chances of being funded. For the purpose of this research, three sets of characteristics were identified: 1) financial projections; 2) plan structure and the organization of the plan; and 3) the writing style of the entrepreneur. The findings indicate that for most of the variables there was a window of values that venture capitalists found acceptable. There was apparently a window of credibility as far as the conventional financial ratios were concerned. Further, the results indicate that plans in which the initial functions of marketing, finance, production, and management were over- or under-reported tended not to get funding. The results also suggest that it was important to strike a balance in the financial statements between the significance to the business of a particular line in the statement and the level of detail at which it was reported. Lastly, there was a range of adjective/noun ratios that were implicitly acceptable to venture capitalist. Plans should not contain much more than one adjective per noun, nor should they have less than about one for every two nouns.

Too low a value generally indicated that the predicted performance was unacceptably low. Too high a value appeared to signal that the persons proposing the venture were too naive about their potential business to justify support.

Nature of the study: Empirical
Nature of the data: Case study
Nature of the sample: 55 unfunded and 27 funded business plans supplied by 5
                         New York City venture capital firms
Variables: Ratios of nouns to verbs, relative sizes of entries in the
                         forecasts of income statements, financial ratios used in
                         evaluating companies, percentage of plan devoted to core
                         functional areas, decision to fund or not

MacMillan, I. C., Zeman, L., & Subba Narasimha, P. N. (1987). Criteria
        distinguishing successful from unsuccessful ventures in the venture
        screening process. *Journal of Business Venturing, 2* (2), 123-137.

This study was conducted to determine which criteria are used by venture
capitalists to evaluate venture proposals. Using 25 screening criteria and
several performance criteria, 67 venture capital firms rated a total of 150
ventures. The groups of criteria included: 1) the venture team, 2) market
characteristics, and 3) the product or service. Cluster analysis identified three
classes of unsuccessful ventures, including a venture where the venture team
is strong but the market is lost to competition because of a lack of protection
for the product. Cluster analysis also identified four classes of successful
ventures, such as the high-technology venture with a skilled venture team
that has the staying power needed to face competitive attack. Regression
analysis revealed two criteria as consistent predictors of venture success:
degree of competitive threat and degree of market acceptance of the product.

Nature of the study: Empirical
Nature of the data: Mail survey
Nature of the sample: 67 VC firms from the directories of National VC
                         Association and of *Venture Magazine*, VC Funds list in
                         Who's Who in Venture Capital
Variables: Characteristics of the venture team, of the proposed product
                         or service, of the target market, forecast financial
                         characteristics, performance

Maier, II, J. B., & Walker, D. A.(1987). The role of venture capital in financing small
        business. *Journal of Business Venturing, 2* (3), 207-214.

This study was conducted to examine the supply of venture capital to small
firms and to determine whether venture capital is a financing substitute
source, a complementary source, or an independent source from bank credit
and trade credit for small firms. Results indicate that venture capital was
available to small businesses in a variety of forms, including: 1) funds from
private investors, 2) investment and pension funds, 3) state governments, 4)
small business investment companies, and 5) joint ventures. The study also
finds that most of the venture capital investments were in small firms and

most venture capitalists received fewer than 700 requests each year. Venture capitalists, however, funded only 2% of these requests. Sixty-three of the respondents had more than 70% of their assets invested in small firms.

Nature of the study: Empirical
Nature of the data: Mail survey
Nature of the sample: 92 members of National VC Association
Variables: Size of VC firm, percentage of assets invested in small firms, investment change expected, number of requests and number of commitments

Manigart, S., Joos, P., & De Vos, D. (1992). The performance of publicly traded European venture capital companies. In N. C. Churchill, S. Birley, W. D. Bygrave, D. F. Muzyka, C. Wahlbin, & W. E. Wetzel, Jr. (Eds.), *Frontiers of entrepreneurial research* (pp. 331-344). Boston, MA: Babson College.

This paper studies the stock market return and the risk of European venture capital companies over the period 1977-1991. The average yearly stock return was negative. Less than 25% of the companies had a return that was higher than the market return. In general, U.K. companies had a significantly higher return than continental companies. This is in contrast to comparable studies in the U.S., which have shown returns higher than the market return. This might be explained by the fact that most of the stock returns in this study were taken during the period 1986-1991. This research finds that the average systematic risk (beta) was lower than the market risk. When taking risk into account, no company had a return measure that was significantly higher than zero, but four companies had a return measure that was significantly lower than zero. The authors note that most shares of venture capital firms trade at a significant discount relative to their net asset value, indicating that the long term return investors can expect in the future may be higher than in the past. Venture capital companies that were specialized in a specific investment stage had a higher return, while regional companies had a lower return than in general. The systematic risk of specialized companies was higher than that of general companies.

Nature of the study: Empirical
Nature of the data: Database
Nature of the sample: 33 European venture capital companies (18 in France, 11 in U.K. and Ireland, 2 in the Netherlands, 1 in Belgium and 1 in Spain)
Variables: Stock and market returns, systematic risk of venture capital firms (geographic specialization, sector specialization, stage specialization)

Manigart, S., & Struyf, C. (1997). Financing high technology start-ups in Belgium: An explorative study. *Small Business Economics 9(2)*, 125-135.

To date most of the studies on the financing of technology-based companies are based in the U.S. This study expands this approach to explore both start-up and growth financing of high-tech independent start-ups in Belgium. Research questions include financing patterns and entrepreneurial motives underlying financial choices. The study revealed the primary source of capital to be the entrepreneur's funds, followed by almost half of the companies reporting bank financing for the start-up venture. The use of venture capital finance was extremely limited, as it was reported by only two companies. Overall, findings were largely consistent with studies conducted with U.S. and British samples. Issues with planning the capital search and actually finding the capital sources remain important.

Nature of the study:	Empirical
Nature of the data:	Structured, non-standardized interviews
Nature of the sample:	18 high-tech manufacturing companies all less than 10 years old
Variables:	Industrial sector, start-up year, size of start-up team, sales first year, earnings first year, and long-term financial sources (entrepreneur, bank, private individual, other company, university, venture capitalist, friends and family)

Manigart, S., & Van Hyfte, W. (1999). Post-investment evolution of Belgian venture-capital-backed companies: An empirical study. In P. D. Reynolds, W. D. Bygrave, S. Manigart, C. M. Mason, G. D. Meyer, H. J. Sapienza, & K. G. Shaver (Eds.), *Frontiers of entrepreneurial research* (pp. 419-432). Boston, MA: Babson College.

This study investigates the post-investment evolution of venture capitalist portfolio companies that received funding between 1988 and 1995. Venture-funded companies were compared to non venture-funded companies on survival rate, growth, profitability, and cash flow generation.

The results show that VC-backed companies did not have a higher survival rate but reported a higher growth in total assets and cash flow than non-venture-capital-backed companies up to five years after investment by a venture capital company. In general, venture-backed companies were more risky than non-venture-backed companies, as the evolution of their sales, profit, and cash flow was more volatile. Some venture-backed companies became star companies, outperforming their peers, but losses and cash drains were also larger for some venture-backed companies than non-venture-backed companies. The research findings have implications for cash-restrained entrepreneurs. Although venture capital was a very costly source of financing, getting venture capital financing had positive effects on the evolution of a star company. Further, even though entrepreneurs often had to give up a considerable part of their equity, the increase in value of the company made the deal worthwhile.

Nature of the study: Empirical
Nature of the data: National Bank Database
Nature of the sample: 187 Belgian portfolio companies
Variables: Nature of venture funding, venture survival rate, growth, profitability, cash flow generation, venture size, activity, founding year

Mason, C. M., & Harrison, R. T. (1995). Developing the informal venture capital market in the U.K.: Is there still a role for public sector business angel networks? In W. D. Bygrave, B. J. Bird, S. Birley, N. C. Churchill, M. Hay, R. H. Keeley, & W. E. Wetzel, Jr. (Eds.), *Frontiers of entrepreneurial research* (pp. 479-493). Boston, MA: Babson College.

Business angel networks (BANs) in the U.K. provide a channel of communication between private investors (business angels) and entrepreneurs seeking risk capital. The evidence showed that BANs had a significant impact in mobilizing and channeling informal venture capital to entrepreneurial businesses. Most BANs operated locally on a not-for-profit basis, with their cost underwritten by the public sector. The authors proposed that the recent establishment of BANs by private sector organizations brings to question the government's continuing role in the financing of BANs. This study found significant differences among public sector, not-for-profit and private for-profit BANs in terms of the investments they facilitated. Private sector BANs were primarily involved with larger, later-stage deals, whereas investments made through public sector and other not-for-profit BANs were generally smaller, involved start-ups and other early stage businesses, and were local (usually raising equity capital from business angels who typically wish to play an hands on role). It appeared that local, public sector, not-for-profit BANs were filling a different market niche than were private for-profit BANs. Hence the emergence of private BANs did not eliminate the need for public sector support for locally oriented networks.

Nature of the study: Empirical
Nature of the data: Survey
Nature of the sample: 17 business angel networks in British Venture Capital Association 1994
Variables: Type of BAN, size of total and individual investment, stage of investment, sector, location of investment

Mason, C. M., & Harrison, R. T. (1995). Closing the regional equity capital gap: The role of informal venture capital. *Small Business Economics, 7,* 153-172.

This paper examines the gaps in the financing market for new ventures. It argues that most small firms encounter a shortage of long-term investment capital, particularly at start-up and initial growth. The institutional venture capital industry has not been able to fill this equity gap because of its preference for large investments in more established companies. Government sponsored programs to increase the availability of risk capital in economically lagging regions have provided a partial and costly solution. The authors argue for the public sector to support the flow of informal venture capital through organized business introduction services.

Nature of the study: Conceptual
Nature of the data: NA
Nature of the sample: NA
Variables: Venture capital, informal venture capital, entrepreneurial
                         start-ups, government organizations

Mason, C. M., & Harrison, R. T. (1993). Strategies for expanding the informal venture capital market. *International Small Business Journal, 11* (4), 23-38.

The importance of the informal venture capital market stems from the nature of angel investments (investing where formal venture capitalists rarely go) and the size of the market. This study builds on the limited existing knowledge of business angels to advance the understanding of who potential angels are and what might get them to begin to invest. "Virgin angels" were found to be similar to active angels in personal characteristics. However, they were less likely to have personally started a business and their annual household income and net worth is lower than that of active angels. The primary reason reported for not having yet made an investment was the difficulty in finding appropriate investment opportunities. Other concerns included high risk factors, concerns about exit strategies, and a lack of expertise in evaluating opportunities. The authors conclude by suggesting three relevant factors for encouraging increased angel investors 1) Virgin angels would invest if they knew the management team personally, 2) if the investment information came from a trusted source, and 3) if they could partner with more experience investors.

Nature of the study: Empirical
Nature of the data: Mail survey
Nature of the sample: Mailing lists of high net work individuals resulting in 21
                         responses
Variables: Reasons for not investing to date, factors that would
                         encourage investing, investor demographics

Mason, C. M., & Harrison, R. T. (1996). Why 'Business Angels' say no: A case study of opportunities rejected by an informal investor syndicate. *International Small Business Journal, 14* (2), 35-51.

The informal venture capital market is increasingly seen as an important source of entrepreneurial finance. This paper examines the reasons opportunities are rejected by a specific private investor syndicate in the U.K. Rejection factors included characteristics of the management team, financing, marketing, product, and a miscellaneous category. The dominant "deal-killers" were found to be 1) characteristics of the entrepreneur or management team, 2) market related factors, and 3) financial issues. Implications include the importance of a well-developed business plan and the necessity of realizing the likelihood of a protracted and sequential negotiation process.

Nature of the study:	Empirical
Nature of the data:	Interview, plus archival research of descriptive materials related to the opportunities
Nature of the sample:	Case study of the lead investor and 35 identified opportunities
Variables:	Origins of the opportunities, characteristics of the opportunities, stage of development, industrial sector, geographic location, rejection factors

Mason, C. M., & Harrison, R. T. (1997). Business angels in the U.K.: A response to Stevenson and Coveney. *International Small Business Journal, 15* (2), 83-90.

The note rebuts criticism raised by Stevenson and Coveney (1994, 1996) about the authors' earlier estimations of the size and impact of the informal venture capital market in the U.K. Mason and Harrison attribute discrepancies between their findings and those of Stevenson and Covey to differences in the samples selected. Namely, the authors argue that their sample of business angels is more representative of the population because it includes: (1) names from 10 different mailing list sources (no single source represents more than 20%); (2) corporate rate angels--companies which make minority equity stakes in unquoted companies; and (3) active investors. By not using similar criteria, the authors argue that Stevenson and Covey inflate estimates of the U.K. informal venture capital market upwards by a factor of three. Additionally, the authors justify their policy recommendations that government assist in establishing local/regional business angel networks, rather than having such networks run by a single national angel network managed by a private sector organization. The authors argue that their recommendations are justified because half of the business angels ' investments in their representative sample were made in businesses located within 100 miles of the investor's home.

Nature of the study: Rebuttal
Nature of the data: NA
Nature of the sample: NA
Variables: NA

Mason, C. M., & Harrison, R. T. (1997). Business angel networks and the
    development of the informal venture capital market in the U.K.: Is there still
    a role for the public sector? *Small Business Economics 9(2),* 111-123.

> This study explores the role of the public sector in the informal venture
> capital market in the U.K. and focuses upon business angel networks as a
> common channel of communication between private venture capital
> investors and entrepreneurs seeking risk capital. An increase in private sector
> angel network activity has raised the question of the appropriateness or need
> for continued public sector involvement. The authors develop a typology of
> Business Angel Networks (BAN) in order to analyze types of angels and the
> subsequent deals. The authors find significant differences between the public
> and private sectors. Publicly supported networks are found to be more
> involved with smaller, more local, and earlier stage businesses. The resulting
> conclusion is that there is a role to be played by both public and private
> sector angel networks.

Nature of the study: Empirical
Nature of the data: Mail survey
Nature of the sample: 1994 BVCA Guide to Sources of Business Angel Capital, p.
                        17, and 1995 Guide to Sources of Business Angel Capital, p.
                        30, representing 580 angels and 273 investments
Variables: Number of investments, size of investments (individual and
                        total), stage of investment, industrial sector, geographic
                        location, size of business, type of network

Mason, C. M., & Harrison, R. T. (1999). The rates of return from informal venture
    capital investments: Some U.K. evidence. In P. D. Reynolds, W. D. Bygrave,
    S. Manigart, C. M. Mason, G. D. Meyer, H. J. Sapienza, & K. G. Shaver
    (Eds.), *Frontiers of entrepreneurial research* (pp. 461-475). Boston, MA:
    Babson College.

According to the authors, there has been a paucity of reliable information on
the returns from venture capital investing. The investment returns to business
angels have been virtually ignored. The available information largely reflects
expected returns as venture capital funds did not generally make public any
information on their actual returns. This paper attempts to analyze the returns
to informal venture capital investment on a sample drawn from 128 exited
investments from a survey of 127 business angel investors in the U.K. The
findings suggest three important points about the performance of informal

venture capital investments: 1) the returns from such investments were negatively skewed, with 34% of exits at a total loss, 13% at a partial loss or break-even, but with 23% showing an IRR of 50% or above; 2) trade sales were the main way in which business angels harvested their investments; IPOs were a much less common means of exit; and 3) most angels held their investments for a short time period, with a median holding length of just four years.

Nature of the study:	Empirical
Nature of the data:	Mail survey
Nature of the sample:	128 exited investments of 127 business angels in the U.K.
Variables:	Number of investments made, number of exits, year of investment, company characteristics (sector, stage, and location), due diligence activity, return on investment, method of exit, length of holding period

Mason, C. M., & Harrison, R. T. (2000). Influences on the supply of informal venture capital in the U.K.: An exploratory study of investor attitudes. *International Small Business Journal, 18* (4), 11-28.

The study examines the extent to which the tax regime, economic conditions, and stock market trends influence the willingness of business angels to invest in unquoted businesses in the U.K. The results indicate that the availability of tax relief and the rate of capital gains tax had the strongest influence on investing. Apparently, angels see the front-end tax relief as reducing the risk of their investment. Economic conditions were less influential, but not insignificant. An expanding economy, stable and falling interest rates, and a low rate of inflation all influenced angels' willingness to invest. Stock market trends had the least influence on investment willingness. Overall, the economic environment had only a moderate influence on the willingness of individuals to make angel-type investments. The authors offer reducing rates of capital gains tax and tax on dividends, coupled with front-end tax incentives and equity guarantee schemes, as key policy implications of the study.

Nature of the study:	Empirical
Nature of the data:	Close ended survey of four samples of business angels.
Nature of the sample:	Questionnaires distributed at the 4th LINC Scotland conference in 1998 (business angel network) yielded 25 completed (52% response rate). Subsequent mailing to 90 members not participating in the conference yielded an additional 31 useable questionnaires. Responses to two previous surveys were also analyzed. Questionnaires sent to a convenience sample of business angels during late 1996/early 1997 yielded responses from 127 active business angels (most members of business angel networks).

	Additionally, questionnaires administered to 34 angels attending an Investors Forum in London were included.
Variables:	Investment activity in unquoted companies, tax, economic conditions, stock market conditions

Mason, C. M., & Harrison, R. T.(2000). The size of the informal venture capital market in the United Kingdom. *Small Business Economics, 15,* 137-148.

This paper reviews three methods used to generate estimates of the informal venture capital market in the United Kingdom: market-based ⌐pproaches, firm-based approaches, and capture-recapture methods. It develops an alternative approach based on scaling up from the visible segment of the market represented by business angel networks. Informal venture capital investment is shown to equate to the amount of institutional venture capital provided to start-up and early stage ventures. Because of the smaller average size of investments in the informal sector, eight times as many businesses raise financing from business angels as from institutional venture capital funds.

Nature of the study:	Conceptual
Nature of the data:	NA
Nature of the sample:	NA
Variables:	Historical information about institutional venture capital investments, number and activities of business angel networks

Milton-Smith, J. (2001). The role of SMEs in commercialising university research & development: The Asia-Pacific experience. *Small Business Economics, 16(2),* 141-148.

This conceptual discussion of "technopreneurship" in Australia develops a model based on successful facilitation of research commercialization by Yissum, the research development company of Hebrew University in Jerusalem, and Zernike, a venture capital company in the Netherlands.

Nature of the study:	Empirical
Nature of the data:	Case study
Nature of the sample:	Selected successful commercialization partnerships.
Variables:	NA

Moesel, D. D., Fiet, J., Busenitz, L., & Barney, J. (1996). Factors underlying changes in risk perceptions of new ventures by venture capitalists. In P. D. Reynolds, S. Birley, J. E. Butler, W. D. Bygrave, P. Davidsson, W. B. Gartner, & P. P. McDougall (Eds.), *Frontiers of entrepreneurial research* (pp. 377-391). Boston, MA: Babson College.

The authors propose that new venture team managers (NVT) need to discern the risk perceptions of their VCs as part of their strategy for obtaining future financing. Correct interpretations by the NVT of early signals of increased venture risk perception by the VCs is vital to promote both earlier communication and more open bargaining regarding the nature of the next reinvestment decision. To measure changes in risk perception, this study investigated average change in funding per investing firm in the VC syndicate in moving from first to second funding rounds. The paper argues that changes in perceived risk of investments in early stage ventures were more than just a function of performance results of a firm. It hypothesizes that risk perception changes were influenced by NVT reactions to VC's involvement pattern, NVT procedural justice reactions, and firm performance level, considered simultaneously, not independently. The research finds initial support for this approach.

Nature of the study:	Empirical
Nature of the data:	Mail survey
Nature of the sample:	206 firms listed in the Venture Capital Journal receiving first round funding during the period 1985-1990 (144 of which get a second round funding)
Variables:	Reactions of the NVT to strategic, operational, or conflict recognition assistance from VCs, VC risk perception of the NVT, dollar change in investment level per VC firm, average venture sales and income performance, global and mutuality-based justice, dollar change in investment level per firm, amount of total VC funding in the first round, two-year employee-count mean, change in the proportion of VC funding provided by the largest investor

Murray, G.C. (1994). The s*econd* 'equity gap': Exit problems for seed and early stage venture capitalists and their investee companies. *International Small Business Journal, 12* (4), 59-76.

The existence of an equity gap for new and small business has been posited for years. This study explores the existence of that gap from the perspective of funds working in the early stage investment arena and as related to the exit of the fund's investment. The focus is upon the relationship between the early stage investor and any potential follow-on funding. The authors propose a model of early stage venture capital investment, noting key decision points. Findings suggest that venture capitalists investing in early stage ventures are significantly different from large development capital investors. In addition, the authors suggest that the term "seed capital" should be replaced with the term "early stage venture capital."

Nature of the study:	Empirical
Nature of the data:	Semi-structured interview
Nature of the sample:	British Venture Capital Association, 1991 Directory, and KPMG's 1992 list of source of U.K. Venture Capital funds
Variables:	Size and purpose of fund, sources of follow-on capital, problems in raising follow-on capital, perceptions of fairness of resulting refinancing arrangements, exit strategies

Neiswander, D. K. (1985). Informal seed stage investors. In J. A. Hornaday, E. B. Shils, J. A. Timmons, & K. H. Vesper (Eds.), *Frontiers of entrepreneurial research* (pp. 142-154). Boston, MA: Babson College.

The purpose of this paper is to locate informal investors and identify their backgrounds, investment interests and capabilities, and how their needs could be better served in the identification of investment opportunities. Investment interests and information needs of the informal investors were analyzed by age, investment capability, and profession.

The results indicate that a substantial amount of early stage capital was available in the region; the 43 respondents represent a potential of over $8 million dollars in high-risk early stage investments per year. The implications for entrepreneurs and informal investors are as follows: An entrepreneur with a sound idea and a good management team would probably benefit from approaching an informal investor in his/her early 50s who had already started and/or bought and successfully developed a business, and therefore would be more capable of opening customer doors and giving prudent management advice. On the other hand, an entrepreneur at an early idea stage with an incomplete management team might be advised to seek an informal investor in a service-related business, since the individual's network of contacts could be a source for key management team members, and this sort of informal investor has deeper pockets for earlier stage deals.

Nature of the study:	Empirical
Nature of the data:	Interviews, survey
Nature of the sample:	51 informal investors in Northeast, Ohio with the
Variables:	Number of informal investors, potential amount of investment money, needs, interests, attitudes and feelings of informal investors, and their age, investment capability, work experience

Norton, E. (1995). Venture capital as an alternative means to allocate capital: An agency-theoretic view. *Entrepreneurship Theory and Practice, 20* (2), 19-30.

The venture capital process is one of many methods of capital allocation. In a capital allocation process, investors acquire funds, potential investments are identified and reviewed, investment terms are negotiated, and the investment must be monitored and ultimately harvested. The capital allocation process is full of potential agency problems. The venture capital process in particular provides a rich setting for the analysis of agency cost issues. This paper reviews the capital allocation process that occurs in venture capital investments.

Venture capital involves a five-step process: 1) obtaining funds from limited partners; 2) identifying, analyzing, and selecting appropriate entities in which to invest; 3) structuring the terms of the investment; 4) implementing the deal and monitoring the portfolio firms; and 5) achieving returns and ultimately exiting from the investment. The article concludes that agency theory may provide the most valuable insights into venture capital practice.

Nature of the study: Conceptual
Nature of the data: NA
Nature of the sample: NA
Variables: Identification and selection criteria and process, deal structure, monitoring, realizing returns, exit

Norton, E., & Tenenbaum, B.H. (1993). Specialization versus diversification as a venture capital investment strategy. *Journal of Business Venturing, 8* (5), 431-442.

This study examines venture capitalists' risk management strategies at the overall portfolio level. Financial theory generally assumes that risk is best controlled through diversification. Findings showed that venture capitalists who were heavily involved in seed round financing were diversified across fewer numbers of firms and industries. The results of the study indicate that venture capitalists seek to control portfolio risk by specialization rather than through financial diversification. This was especially true if the venture capitalists had information or cost advantage over other investors. The results provide empirical evidence in favor of the perspective that venture capitalists control portfolio risk through their efforts to specialize, to build reputation capital, and to become important members of information and deal networks.

Nature of the study: Empirical
Nature of the data: Mail survey
Nature of the sample: 98 members of National VC Association

Variables: Investment diversification strategy, various stages of
                              financing, ability to time cold and hot IPO markets, VC's
                              specialization and information sharing

Norton, E., & Tenenbaum, B. H. (1993). The effects of venture capitalists'
    characteristics on the structure of the venture capital deal. *Journal of Small
    Business Management,* 31(4), 32-41.

These authors propose that venture capital investors, rather than firms, play a
major role in determining the pricing and type of security to be purchased by
investors. This research focused on three basic investment vehicles that
venture capitalists use: common equity, preferred equity, and debt. The
research attempted to determine whether financing strategies differ across
deals in different financing stages and with venture capitalists of different
characteristics. The research also examined how strategies to manage risk
can affect the choice of the above investment vehicles. The results indicate
that the most frequently used financing choice was preferred stock. However,
contrary to expectations, the use of preferred equity as an investment tool did
not increase perceived high risk situations, such as early stage investments;
neither did investors who were subject to greater amounts of unsystematic
risk use relatively larger amounts of preferred equity. The evidence
supported the hypothesis that smaller, less diversified investors in the sample
made greater use of common equity investments.

Nature of the study: Empirical
Nature of the data: Previous study, mail survey
Nature of the sample: 98 venture capitalists
Variables: Choice of investment vehicle and frequency of use; type of
                         VC firm and size; investment stage and sector; factors
                         favoring/opposing the use of common stock, debt and
                         preferred equity investment

Ray, D.M., & Turpin, D.V. (1993). Venture capital in Japan. *International Small
    Business Journal, 11* (4), 39-56.

This study builds upon earlier work by MacMillan and Associates that
identified, collated, and assembled 27 criteria for the evaluation of venture
capital investment proposals. The authors collected data from the Japanese
venture capital industry and compared it to the previously collected U.S.
data. Data was organized into categories representing the entrepreneurial
personality, entrepreneurial experiences, characteristics of the product,
characteristics of the market, and financial considerations. A review of
similarities and differences between those in the U.S. and the Japanese
industries is presented. U.S venture capitalists are described as having more
stringent and more extensive evaluative criteria. Japanese venture capitalists
are reported as applying ample amounts of intuition.

Nature of the study: Empirical
Nature of the data: Mail survey
Nature of the sample: Directory of Japanese venture capitalists (15) plus three from a convenience sample
Variables: 27 criteria for investing, plus 14 additional criteria on the development of the venture capital firm and its portfolio

Reid, G.C. (1996). Fast growing small entrepreneurial firms and their venture capital backers: An applied principal-agent analysis. *Small Business Economics, 8,* 235-248.

This paper first provides a description of the venture capital industry in the United Kingdom and then examines the applicability of the principal-agent analysis to the relationship between the venture capitalist and the entrepreneur. A stylization of a typical VC is created from average values for a panel of U.K. funds, and a case study focused upon this relationship (venture capitalist/principal and entrepreneur/agent) is developed, assessing issues of risk management, information handling, and the trading of risk and information. The findings support the fit between investor-investee relations and the concepts underlying the principal-agent analysis, thereby providing confirmatory evidence for the suitability of this type of approach to economic theorizing.

Nature of the study: Empirical
Nature of the data: Archival
Nature of the sample: Panel of U.K. funds from 1988, 1990, and 1992
Variables: Principal-agent relationship, business demographics

Reitan, B., & Sorheim, R. (1999). The informal venture capital market in Norway - Investor characteristics, behavior and preferences. In P. D. Reynolds, W. D. Bygrave, S. Manigart, C. M. Mason, G. D. Meyer, H. J. Sapienza, & K. G. Shaver (Eds.), *Frontiers of entrepreneurial research* (pp. 321-332). Boston, MA: Babson College.

A number of recent studies in various countries have stated that a well developed informal venture capital market played a major role in meeting the financing needs of smaller companies. This study is the first major attempt to catalog the informal venture capital market in Norway. The purpose of this study was to describe the Norwegian business angels in terms of demographic characteristics, investment activities, investment preferences, and involvement in the projects they invest in. A comparison was made between the results from Norwegian survey and findings from the U.K. and Sweden.

Norwegian business angels had considerable investment activity, making on average 3.7 investments in three years. The average investment per investor was almost $300,000 and the average amount per investment was $76,300. Sixty percent were serial investors with a preference to invest in new ventures and young businesses in close geographic proximity. Their personal and business networks largely determined their behaviors. They were relatively passive in their personal involvement with the businesses. Compared to those of the U.K. and Sweden, Norwegian business angels were quite similar in their characteristics, preferences, and behavior. However, they had lower average income and net worth and fewer had new venture experience. They were more exposed to investments at the seed and start-up stage as well as investments in technology-based businesses than business angels in the U.K. and Sweden. And they were much less involved in the businesses than their foreign counterparts. The research shows that the informal venture capital market in Norway was an important source of equity finance for new ventures and growing small businesses. However, it was evident that the market was largely ineffective, and that the potential for investments in unlisted companies was several times greater than the actual investment activity. Although government focused attention on the market, for instance by building up five regional seed funds, there was still a need to consider various mechanisms to make the market more effective.

Nature of the study: Empirical
Nature of the data: Mail survey
Nature of the sample: 425 business angels in Norway
Variables: Investor characteristics, investment activity, investment
                         process, project characteristics

Robinson, Jr., R. B., (1987). Emerging strategies in the venture capital industry. *Journal of Business Venturing, 2* (1), 53-77.

This study was conducted to examine the future direction of the venture capital industry. Results indicate that the venture capital industry can be divided into several different "strategic groups" around four basic dimensions: 1) financial resources, 2) staff resources, 3) venture stages, and 4) use of financial resources. In addition, three priorities of venture capital firms were established: 1) annualized return on investments of 25% to 40%, 2) a 5- to 6-year investment time horizon, and 3) emphasis on the quality of the management team in evaluating new deals. Finally, it was shown that venture capital firms professed greater "certainty" about the future direction of the venture capital industry than about the direction of their firms.

Nature of the study: Empirical
Nature of the data: Mail survey
Nature of the sample: 53 members of National VC Association and National
                         Association of Small Business Investment Companies

Variables:
Type of VC firm, location, industry trend assumptions, stage of development of investees, portfolio objectives, proposals considered and accepted, financial strategies of VC firms, management assistance strategies, criteria used in evaluation

Rosenstein, J., Bruno, A. V., Bygrave, W. D., & Taylor, N. T. (1990). How much do CEOs value the advice of venture capitalists on their boards? In N. C. Churchill, W. D. Bygrave, J. A. Hornaday, D. F. Muzyka, K. H. Vesper, & W. E. Wetzel, Jr. (Eds.), *Frontiers of entrepreneurial research* (pp. 238-250). Boston, MA: Babson College.

This study reports on a second phase of research on boards of high tech firms financed by venture capital. The CEOs of high tech companies were asked to evaluate contributions of board members from their lead investor firms as compared with other venture capitalist board members and with "other" (i.e., non-management, non-venture-capitalist) board members. They were also asked whether the top 20 venture capital firms specializing in high tech investment were on the board either as lead investor or otherwise. The results indicate that the CEOs rated the contribution of the lead investor board members higher than that of other outsider board members, but barely so when the top 20 venture capital firms were represented. Furthermore, many of the CEOs stated that the contributions of their venture capitalist board members had not met their expectations, sometimes because of limitations of time or expertise, or because of concentration on short-range results. Their open-ended comments on "other" (i.e., non-management, non-venture capitalist) board members were extremely varied, but several of the CEOs placed a high value on the contributions these board members made in areas where the venture capitalists were lacking.

Nature of the study: Empirical
Nature of the data: Telephone interviews
Nature of the sample: CEOs of 98 high technology companies in Northern California and Boston and environs and in northern and central Texas
Variables: Current board composition; board member activities; ratings of usefulness of board member activities; stage of the venture; comparison of the value of VC lead investor from top 20 tech VCs, other board members, and non-management, non-venture capital board members

Rosman, A. J., & O Neill, H. M. (1993). Comparing the information acquisition strategies of venture capital and commercial lenders: A computer-based experiment. *Journal of Business Venturing, 8* (5), 443-461.

This study investigates the differences in the decision behavior of venture capitalists, using bankers as a benchmark for comparison in cases in which debt and debt-related financing were sought. Using a computer software package to trace information acquisition processes, it was revealed that venture capitalists acquired less information and followed a pattern of acquisition that was deeper within categories of information than bankers. Additionally, venture capitalists showed a stronger preference for strategic data and less interest in historical financial data. Both groups minimized the use of financial forecasts and followed decision processes persistently across different types of companies (start-up and well-established). If owners or financial planners of a new or relatively new venture are seeking external financing, they should package the business plan and request in a manner that is consistent with the source of financing.

Nature of the study:	Empirical
Nature of the data:	Computer simulation
Nature of the sample:	19 venture capitalists and 23 commercial lenders
Variables:	Amount and category of information sought, amount of money requested, general time frame for financing, stage of development, industry, financing decision

Roure, J. B., & Maidique, M. (1986). Linking pre-funding factors and high-technology venture success: An exploratory study. *Journal of Business Venturing, 1* (3), 295-306.

This study was conducted to determine the key pre-funding factors that influence the success of high-technology companies funded by venture capital. The information was analyzed and the factors that differentiate successful ventures from non-successful ones were identified. Results indicate that the founders of successful ventures had more prior experience working together, tended to form larger and more complete teams, and had more extensive experience in the function they performed in the new venture. In addition, successful founders had experience in rapid-growth firms that competed in the same industry as the start-up. Successful ventures also targeted product-market segments with a high buyer concentration in which their products could attain and sustain a competitive edge.

Nature of the study:	Empirical
Nature of the data:	Interviews and case study
Nature of the sample:	8 venture capital-financed start-ups from 2 West Coast venture capital firms
Variables:	Founders' track records, characteristics of founding team, target market, technology strategy, deal structure, performance

Ruhnka, J. C., & Young, J. (1987). A venture capital model of the development process for new ventures. *Journal of Business Venturing, 2* (2), 167-184.

This study gathered the perceptions of the chief executive officers (CEO) or managing partners of U.S. venture capital firms to determine whether firms identified the same stages in the development for new ventures. Responses to the questionnaire revealed that there was enough consensus on several aspects of the development process to construct a venture capital model of the process. The resulting model consists of five sequential stages: 1) seed, 2) start-up, 3) second stage, 4) third stage, and 5) exit. Strong consensus was found on distinguishing:1) characteristics of ventures in early stages of development, 2) key developmental goals in certain stages, and 3) major risks associated with each stage. The venture capital developmental model is 1) primarily strategic and market-oriented in focus, 2) non-venture-specific, and 3) shaped by the naturally occurring functional development of investees.

Nature of the study:	Empirical
Nature of the data:	Mail survey
Nature of the sample:	CEOs or Managing Partners of 73 VC firms
Variables:	Venture characteristics, major goals or benchmarks, major risks, stage of development

Ruhnka, J. C., & Young, J. E. (1991). Some hypotheses about risk in venture capital investing. *Journal of Business Venturing, 6* (2), 115-133.

In this article, the authors draw upon psychological risk theory of decision-making under uncertainty to identify various elements of a behavioral framework that can predict venture capitalists reactions to risk. These expected behaviors to risk are used to propose nine hypotheses about how venture capital managers behave in making investment decisions. These hypotheses involve 1) differences in variation and magnitude of returns for early-stage versus later-stage ventures, 2) explanations of how risk distributions change over the stage-wise development of new ventures, 3) differences in the behavior of "aggressive" versus "conservative" investors in screening investment prospects, and 4) strategies utilizing a lower "ideal level of risk" to reduce the chances of achieving negative or subnormal final portfolio returns.

Nature of the study:	Conceptual
Nature of the data:	NA
Nature of the sample:	NA
Variables:	Venture risks, stage of development, required rate of return, risk of loss expectations

Sandberg, W. R., Schweiger, D. M., & Hofer, C. W. (1988). The use of verbal protocols in determining venture capitalists decision making process. *Entrepreneurship Theory and Practice, 13* (2), 8-20.

This study uses verbal protocols to investigate the decision processes of one venture capitalist evaluating three venture proposals. The sequence of thoughts in the decision process showed conscious choices at an early stage to examine the product before "the numbers." The next consideration was the venture's competitive position. The process at this stage involved the capitalist's own experience-based theories about the marketing and operational advantages and disadvantages of small firms. Before examining the financial projections, the capitalist returned to specific consideration of the product. This deliberate sequence suggests a desire to establish a context for assessing financial projections and possibly management capabilities, although the latter were not articulated. Of 44 thought units in the process, 11 were related to strategy and 10 to financial performance or use of funds.

Nature of the study:	Empirical
Nature of the data:	Case study
Nature of the sample:	A venture capitalist
Variables:	Actions, product characteristics, competitive position, market demand, management capabilities, financial performance, adequacy of the plan

Sapienza, H. J. (1992). When do venture capitalists add value? *Journal of Business Venturing, 7* (1), 9-27.

Venture capitalists functioning as lead investors and the entrepreneur-chief executive officers (CEO) of their portfolio companies responded to surveys concerning the rate of the venture capitalists' involvement in the ventures. The findings indicate that the greater the level of innovation pursued by the venture, the more frequent the contact between lead investor and the CEO, the more open the communication, and the less conflict of perspective in the venture capitalist-CEO pair, the greater was value of the involvement. Neither the stage of the venture nor the CEO's experience had a significant impact on value-add. The value of venture capitalists' involvement strongly correlated with venture performance.

Nature of the study:	Empirical
Nature of the data:	Mail survey, interviews
Nature of the sample:	51 matched pairs of lead investor-CEO
Variables:	Stage of the venture, level of innovation, competitive strategy, environmental uncertainty, frequency of interaction, openness in interaction, value of VC involvement, venture performance, CEO experience, divergence of perspective

Sapienza, H. J., & Korsgaard, M. A. (1995). Performance feedback, decision making processes and venture capitalists' support of new ventures. In W. D. Bygrave, B. J, Bird, S. Birley, N. C. Churchill, M. Hay, R. H. Keeley, & W. E. Wetzel, Jr. (Eds.), *Frontiers of entrepreneurial research* (pp. 452-464). Boston, MA: Babson College.

This study examines whether the way entrepreneurs share information with their venture capitalists impacts investors' propensity to 1) trust the entrepreneur, 2) support strategic decisions, 3) closely monitor the venture, and 4) provide additional funds to the venture. The study further examines whether the amount of influence that the venture capitalist has in the venture's decision-making and strategy affects the strength of these relationships. The fundamental dilemma for entrepreneur-venture capitalist pairs is how to satisfy both the investor's need for timely information upon which future commitments of resources can be based and the entrepreneur's need for autonomy and operating control. Consistent with their predictions, the authors found that timely feedback was related to greater trust in the entrepreneur, greater commitment to his/her decisions, and less monitoring by the venture capitalist. Contrary to expectations, the timeliness of feedback had no significant impact on intention to re-invest.

Nature of the study:	Empirical
Nature of the data:	Mail survey
Nature of the sample:	118 venture capitalists
Variables:	Feedback assessment, influence, perceived fairness, commitment to decisions, frequency of monitoring, decision to invest, years since initial investment

Sapienza, H. J., & Clercq, D. D. (2000). Venture capitalist-entrepreneur relationships in technology-based ventures. *Enterprise and Innovation Management Studies, 1* (1), 57-71.

This paper presents a brief synopsis of literature focusing on venture-capital-backed high technology ventures. This literature highlights characteristics of and the rationale for venture capitalist-entrepreneur pairings as well as differences in the way venture capitalists approach high tech ventures in comparison to other ventures. Some of the implications for practice are discussed as well as future research at the intersection of technology-based new firms and venture capital.

Nature of the study:	Conceptual
Nature of the data:	NA
Nature of the sample:	NA
Variables:	Information asymmetry and investment risk, venture capitalists' networks, venture capitalist role and interactions, VCs and high-tech entrepreneurs

Sargent, M., & Young, J. E. (1991). The entrepreneurial search for capital: A behavioral science perspective. *Entrepreneurship & Regional Development, 3*, 237-252.

The purpose of this paper is to show that social processes have important effects on securing venture financing. This paper argues that the psychosocial context influences entrepreneurial funding through several interlocking affects. The study shows that basic values and definitions of an enterprise and its funding were shaped by family, education, and work experiences of an entrepreneur. The entrepreneur developed social and business relationships that provided resources and information that would shape the entrepreneur's and the investor's definitions and expectations of the new venture and funding. The finds also stress the role of learning. Entrepreneurs expanded their inventory of procurement activities by continuous application and redefinition of their view of funding possibilities. What entrepreneurs learned was in part a product of their readiness to receive knowledge. Learning can be used to break previous social and economic patterns as well as enhance prospects for securing funds. This perspective is contrasted with traditional economic and financial assumptions that emphasize rationality and profit maximization as the primary basis for funding new ventures.

Nature of the study:	Conceptual
Nature of the data:	NA
Nature of the sample:	NA
Variables:	Basic values and funding of an enterprise, entrepreneur's background (family, education, and work experiences), social and business relationships, entrepreneur's and investor's expectations of the new venture and funding

Schell, D. W. (1982). Entrepreneurial implications of the Small Business Investment Incentives Act. In K.H. Vesper (Ed.), *Frontiers of entrepreneurial research* (pp. 270-287). Boston, MA: Babson College.

In 1980, the Small Business Investment Incentives Act (SBIIA) was passed to allow venture capitalists to more easily go public to get additional capital. This act reduced many of the previous restrictions under the 1940 Investment Company Act, as amended, and allowed for the establishment of Business Development Corporations (BDCs). Acquiring risk capital from the general investing public was viewed as important for increasing the pool of venture capital available to both start-up and growing ventures. The impact of SBIIA as a vehicle for public venture capital and the need for special new-issue investment company funds was explored in this research. The objective was to determine how successful SBIIA had been in tapping the resources of the general investing public. This research was also designed to identify 1) methods for improving the flow of "public" capital and 2) institutional methods that link "public" capital to entrepreneurial opportunities within the larger economic development challenge. Preliminary findings indicate lack of knowledge about and strong resistance to utilizing the provisions of SBIIA. Suggestions for future research include analysis of the causes of this resistance and study of new institutional forms (i.e., New Issue Funds and Franchised Community Corporations), as well as changes in the tax laws.

Nature of the study: Empirical
Nature of the data: Case study
Nature of the sample: BDCs and SBIIA
Variables: Venture capital available to start-up and growing ventures, role of SBIIA in closing the capital gap, evaluation of performance of SBIIA

Shefczyk, M., & Gerpott, T. J. (2001). Qualifications and turnover of managers and venture capital-financed firm performance: An empirical study of German venture capital investments. *Journal of Business Venturing, 16*(2), 145-163.

This study investigates the relationships between manager qualifications (experience and education) and the performance of venture-backed firms. The study also addresses whether lower firm performance induced higher manager turnover and whether the venture capital firms actively influenced the manager turnover. The results show that manager qualifications of the portfolio correlated significantly with performance. Specifically, manager experience in marketing/sales, planning/strategy functional areas, and the industry were identified as critical success factors. Therefore, the findings suggest that venture capital firms should put more emphasis on 1) managers' business functional experience and, unless the firm is active in an entirely new market, 2) a high proportion of managers with experience in the relevant industry. It was also shown that venture capital firms realigned or replaced top managers in cases where success was substantially below expectations.

Nature of the study: Empirical
Nature of the data: Mail survey
Nature of the sample: 103 portfolio companies of German Venture Capital firms.
Variables: Functional, industry, management/directorship, educational experience, portfolio company and venture capital firm performance, manager turnover rate, venture capital influence on manager turnover

Shepherd, D. A. (1999). Venture capitalists' assessment of new venture survival. *Management Science, 45* (5), 621-632.

This study investigates whether venture capitalists' assessment policies of new venture survival are consistent with those arising from the strategy literature. Strategy scholars suggest that the nature of the markets, competition, and decisions made by the management team affect a new venture's survival chances. The findings demonstrate that VCs' assessment policies are predominantly consistent with those proposed by strategy scholars. VCs consider the level of uncertainty and the ability of the management team to deal with the changes in the environment when evaluating a new venture. The study provides insight into why VCs consider certain criteria in their assessment of new venture survival as well as why some criteria are more important in their assessment than others.

Nature of the study: Empirical
Nature of the data: Mail survey
Nature of the sample: 66 Australian venture capitalists
Variables: Stability of key success factors, timing of entry, lead time, competitive rivalry, industry related competence, educational capabilities, mimicry, scope

Shepherd, D. A. (1999). Venture capitalists' introspection: A comparison of "in use" and "espoused" decision policies. *Journal of Small Business Management, 37* (2), 76-87.

This paper focuses on a study that analyzed the actual decision-making of venture capitalists to determine the accuracy of their introspection. Researchers studying the decision-making behaviors of venture capitalists should be aware of potential biases and errors associated with self-reported data. Venture capital firms were asked to evaluate a series of conjoint profiles that described new ventures in terms of eight attributes: 1) timing of entry; 2) stability of key success factors; 3) educational capability; 4) lead time; 5) competitive rivalry; 6) mimicry; 7) scope; and 8) industry-related competence. The results provide evidence that venture capitalists had a tendency to overstate the least important criteria and understate the most important criteria when compared to models derived from conjoint analysis. Moreover, the findings also show that venture capitalists had only limited introspection into their decision-making when assessing the likely profitability of a new venture proposal.

Nature of the study: Empirical
Nature of the data: Mail survey
Nature of the sample: 66 individual venture capitalists from 47 Australian venture capital firms
Variables: New venture profitability, timing of entry, key success factor stability, educational capability, lead time, competitive rivalry, entry wedge mimicry, scope, and industry related competence

Shepherd, D.A., & Zacharakis, A. L. (2001) Speed to Initial Public Offering of VC-backed Companies. *Entrepreneurship Theory & Practice, 25* (3), 59-69.

This paper delves into an important determinant of VC returns. It seeks to examine the macro-level factors that affect speed to market and poses the question, what explains a portfolio company's speed to IPO? It utilizes an ecosystem perspective to investigate the effects of geography, industry, and time to gain a deeper understanding of a company's speed to IPO.

The results showed that speed to IPO was associated with a venture's ecosystem, namely its geographic location and macroeconomic trends. The venture's industry was only marginally significant. Ventures located in the West (Colorado, Arizona and California) were faster to IPO than those from the Northeast. Surprisingly, the Midwest was also faster to IPO than the Northeast. Also surprising was the fact that non-high-technology companies were faster to IPO than computer and semiconductor companies. Lastly, portfolio companies that had gone public more recently had greater speed to IPO.

Nature of the study:	Empirical
Nature of the data:	Database
Nature of the sample:	Deals recorded by National Venture Capital Association and Venture Economics
Variables:	Geography, industry, macro-economic trend, speed to IPO

Shepherd, D. A., Zacharakis, A. L., & Baron, R. A. (1998). Venture capitalists' expertise: Real or fallacious. In P. D. Reynolds, W. D. Bygrave, N. M. Carter, S. Manigart, C. M. Mason, G. D. Meyer, H. J. Sapienza, & K. G. Shaver (Eds.), *Frontiers of entrepreneurial research* (pp. 586-599). Boston, MA: Babson College.

This study was designed to provide evidence relevant to the following important question: Does increasing experience improve VC's decision-making process? Findings show that expertise does improve venture capitalists' decision-making process. Experts, as compared to novices, showed greater reliability and consensus in their decisions, and greater predictive ability in their decision models. Growing expertise also increases the use of unequal weighting of decision criteria. It appears that as expertise increases, venture capitalists use a better decision process; they tend to use richer and more stable decision models. This better decision process likely leads to more accurate decisions and stronger portfolio performance.

Nature of the study:	Empirical
Nature of the data:	Mail survey
Nature of the sample:	22 novice venture capitalists, 23 expert venture capitalists, 47 undergraduate management students and three MBAs

Variables:	Stability of key success factors, timing of entry, lead time, competitive rivalry, industry related competence, educational capabilities, mimicry, scope, likely profitability

Siegel, R., Siegel, E., & MacMillan, I. C. (1988). Corporate venture capitalists: Autonomy, obstacles, and performance. *Journal of Business Venturing, 3* (3), 233-247.

This study of the corporate venture capital community in the U.S. divides corporate entities into either independent "pilots" or "copilots," depending on corporate management independence. Pilots were marked by higher levels of organizational independence and performance, with fewer obstacles than copilots. The findings suggest that a corporate venture fund should 1) organize an independent entity with separate committed funding, 2) have the fund managed by skilled venture professionals, 3) offer commensurately high levels of compensation and authority to attract top managers, 4) focus on investment return, 5) refer proposals not meeting financial criteria to other parts of the corporation, 6) make a complete commitment of talent and capital.

Nature of the study:	Empirical
Nature of the data:	Mail survey
Nature of the sample:	52 corporate venture capitalists
Variables:	Objectives of the corporate venture entity, investment criteria, obstacles to executing the venture activity, approval process, compensation, source and structure of deals, performance of the corporate venture entity

Smart, G. H. (1998). Management assessment methods in venture capital: Towards a theory of human capital valuation. In P. D. Reynolds, W. D. Bygrave, N. M. Carter, S. Manigart, C. M. Mason, G. D. Meyer, H. J. Sapienza, & K. G. Shaver (Eds.), *Frontiers of entrepreneurial research* (pp. 600-612). Boston, MA: Babson College.

Many venture capitalists experience frustration when their investments achieve disappointing results due to weaknesses in the human capital that were not detected during due diligence. This study examines the methods that venture capitalists use to assess the senior managers of new ventures prior to making an investment decision. This study combines field research with theory from psychology and economics to attempt to generate new theoretical and empirical insights. "Human capital valuation" is introduced as a term to describe the process of appraising the human capital (people) in a venture. An a priori conceptual model was tested that accounted for more than 70% of the variance in the accuracy of human capital valuations. In addition, inductive analysis yielded several distinct typologies of venture capital approaches to the process of human capital valuation. This study identifies the constructs of this process: the range of human capital valuation methods, including job analysis, documentation analysis, past-oriented interviews, psychological testing, assessment centers, reference interviews, and work samples, as well as control variables such as VC years of experience, interviewing skill, the broader context of venture capital, stage of development, etc. What this study also suggests is that human capital is far from the "intangible" factor that it is portrayed to be by accountants and economists. Venture capitalists who were less thorough and rigorous made many mistakes in their human capital valuations, which suggests that perhaps human capital is an intangible only when ineffective methods are used to assess it

Nature of the study: Empirical
Nature of the data: Telephone interviews, in-person interviews
Nature of the sample: 51 venture capitalists with 86 cases
Variables: Types of human capital assessments used, hours spent, accuracy of assessment, VC experience in years, interviewing skill, size of VC fund

Smith, D.G. (1999). How early stage entrepreneurs evaluate venture capitalists. In P. D. Reynolds, W. D. Bygrave, S. Manigart, C. M. Mason, G. D. Meyer, H. J. Sapienza, & K. G. Shaver (Eds.), *Frontiers of entrepreneurial research* (pp. 289-303). Boston, MA: Babson College.

This study investigates the process and criteria used by entrepreneurs in evaluating venture capitalists. Of the 136 firms that responded to a question regarding the number of offers to invest that were received from venture capitalists, 97 (71.32%) said they had received more than one offer to invest. Moreover, 73 firms (53.68%) received three or more offers. The mean number of offers was 3.18. The selection process involved issues such as the time invested in gathering information, the sources of information, and the number of venture capitalists considered. Selection criteria were divided into four groups: 1) valuation, 2) value-added services, 3) reputation factors, and 4) venture capitalist attributes. The paper also examined satisfaction, sorting respondents by geographic region, industry, experience, age, time devoted to the search, and criteria ranking. Findings indicate that entrepreneurs who had previous experience selecting a venture capitalist were significantly more satisfied with their choice of venture capitalist than were entrepreneurs who had no prior venture capital experience. Satisfaction was inversely proportional to time invested in the selection process, with entrepreneurs spending 0 to 39 hours significantly more satisfied with their selection than entrepreneurs spending over 80 hours. Significant difference was found between entrepreneurs who favored valuation and entrepreneurs who relied on reputation factors, with the latter achieving higher levels of satisfaction than the former.

Nature of the study:	Empirical
Nature of the data:	Mail survey
Nature of the sample:	136 entrepreneurs
Variables:	Selection criteria, geographic region, industry, experience, age, time devoted to the search, source of information, satisfaction

Stevenson, H. H., Muzyka, D. F., & Timmons, J. A. (1986). Venture capital in a new era: A simulation of the impact of changes in investment patterns. In R. Ronstadt, J. A. Hornaday, R. Peterson, & K.H. Vesper (Eds.), *Frontiers of entrepreneurial research* (pp. 380-403). Boston, MA: Babson College.

Using a simulation model, this paper attempts to examine some of the critical patterns that have existed in investment returns and to examine how managerial decisions have aided portfolio investment performance. Traditional portfolios of venture capital investments showed consistent high rates of return. The conditions necessary for such high rates of return are: 1) that managers, after the first round of investment, can distinguish winners from losers; 2) that managers parlay their initial investment with another round of investment; 3) that returns have reasonably high persistence so the first round investment has information value; and 4) that investment portfolios be held intact sufficiently long so that geometric averaging of compound returns causes the winners to take on average portfolio results. This study also investigated the consequences of industry trends: shorter-term holdings, increased competition both for the investment position and later in the product market arena, and the lack of loyalty between investor and investee.

Nature of the study:	Empirical
Nature of the data:	Computer simulation
Nature of the sample:	Venture Economics database
Variables:	Investment rate of return, investment characteristics, managerial actions, relationship between general and limited partners

Stuart, T. E., Hoang, H., & Hybels, R. (1999). Interorganizational endorsements and the performance of entrepreneurial ventures. *Administrative Science Quarterly, 44* (2), 315-349.

This paper investigates how the inter-organizational networks of young companies affect their ability to acquire the resources necessary for survival and growth. It proposes that, faced with great uncertainty about the quality of young companies, third parties rely on the prominence of the affiliates of those companies to make judgments about their quality. Young companies "endorsed" by prominent exchange partners will perform better than otherwise comparable ventures that lack prominent associates. Results of an empirical examination of the rate of initial public offering (IPO) and the market capitalization at IPO of the members of a sample of venture-capital-backed biotechnology firms showed that privately held biotech firms with prominent strategic alliance partners and organizational equity investors went to IPO faster and earned greater valuations at IPO than did firms that lacked such connections. The study also empirically demonstrated that much of the benefit of having prominent affiliates stems from the transfer of status that is an inherent byproduct of inter-organizational associations.

Nature of the study: Empirical
Nature of the data: Recombinant Capital (biotechnology consulting firm) database and Security and Exchange Commission filings, Bioscan Directory and other databases, patent filings
Nature of the sample: 301 biotechnology firms
Variables: Time to IPO, market capitalization, environmental conditions, characteristics of the venture, prominence of exchange partners, relationship counts between biotech firms and their business associates

Swartz, J. (1991). The future of the venture capital industry. *Journal of Business Venturing, 6* (2), 89-92.

This article discusses the future of the venture capital industry. The author contends that there are enormous opportunities in all segments of the venture capital industry. The 1990s will see the development and maturing of the industry as a whole. The challenge is to manage this change and achieve a strong set of healthy, dynamic companies. Recent trends indicate that the longer-term factors for success are still in abundance in the U.S. In the short term, however, there are problems that need to be identified and solved. These problems include 1) disappointing aggregate returns, 2) unrealistic set of expectations developed for returns, 3) significant reduction in the number of firms, 4) "me, too" financing, and 5) concentration of funds suppliers.

Nature of the study: Conceptual
Nature of the data: NA
Nature of the sample: NA
Variables: Amount of funds, size of VC firms, investment opportunities, returns, standards, number of firms

Timmons, J. A. (1982). Venture capital in Sweden: A comparative study. In K. H. Vesper (Ed.), *Frontiers of entrepreneurial research* (pp. 294-312). Boston, MA: Babson College

U.S. style venture capital companies have emerged in Sweden. The first company, Svetab, was launched by the state. This paper was intended to address the following questions: 1) How has Svetab functioned and performed?; 2) What comparisons are possible with similar institutions in the U.S., and more recently those emerging in the U.K.?; and 3) What are some of the principal differences between the U.S. and Sweden in factors influencing high potential ventures? It also examines the appearance of a "risk capital gap" in Sweden and how Svetab's mission had responded to this need, and the constraints it had faced. Its activity was compared with the "top 25 independent SBICs" and the "51 most active" venture capital firms in the U.S., as well as with two recently launched venture capital funds in the U.K. The paper concludes with the entrepreneurial outlook for the 1980s in Sweden, which was judged optimistic.

Nature of the study: Empirical
Nature of the data: Case study
Nature of the sample: Svetab
Variables: Svetab's role and performance, investment activity (rate, quality, and size of investment)

Timmons, J. A., Fast, N. D., & Bygrave, W. D. (1983). The flow of venture capital to highly innovative technological ventures. In J. A. Hornaday, J. A. Timmons, & K. H. Vesper (Eds.), *Frontiers of entrepreneurial research* (pp. 316-334). Boston, MA: Babson College.

This study reports on the first phase of a National Science Foundation funded research project to examine technologically innovative firms, their founders, and their venture capital backers. Specifically, this research was aimed to answer the following questions: 1) What are the characteristics of firms, founders, and venture capital backers? 2) What factors influence the flow of venture capital to emerging highly innovative technology ventures (HITVs)? 3) What patterns and trends exist in the first round of funding to these HITVs? 4) What is the role and "value-add" of venture capital firms in developing new technologically innovative ventures? 5) What public policy instruments might be used in this process? and 6) What future research needs exist?

In addressing these questions, a database of venture-capital-backed firms was developed and classified into three groups according to their "technological innovativeness." Major findings of the research are: 1) there had been a dramatic increase in the flow of first round venture capital financing to HITVs, both in real dollars and the number of investments made; 2) developing technologically innovative ventures appeared to be a unique and specialized form of venture capital investing, creating substantial "value-add"; 3) since 1976, there had been a surge and concentration of seed capital and start-up investments in HITVs; 4) computers and computer related innovations had attracted 53.2% of all investments in HITVs; and 5) a serious seed capital gap existed for HITVs: only 1.8% of capital funding in HITVs between 1967 and 1982 was for seed stage financing.

Nature of the study:	Empirical
Nature of the data:	Venture Economics database
Nature of the sample:	1501 venture-capital-backed firms between 1967 and 1982
Variables:	Flow of venture capital to the three groups of firms 1967-1982, percentage of total investments, average size of investment, average and number of investment by stages, investment by technology and by industry, amount invested in highly innovative firms

Timmons, J. A., & Sapienza, H. J. (1992). Venture capital: The decade ahead. In D. L. Sexton & J. D. Kasarda (Eds.), The *State of the Art of Entrepreneurship* (pp. 402-437). Boston, MA: PWS Kent.

This chapter examined the evolution of the venture capital industry over the decade of the 1980s, identified key issues facing the industry in the 1990s, reviewed recent streams of research on the venture capital industry, and identified research opportunities for the decade ahead.

Nature of the study:	Conceptual
Nature of the data:	NA
Nature of the sample:	NA
Variables:	Number of venture capital firms, amount of funds under management, commitments and disbursements of funds, source of funds, worldwide geographic location, type of venture capital firm, concentration and control in the industry, industry sectors of investment, competition, stage of investment, sophistication of suppliers and users of funds, performance

Tyebjee, T. T., & Bruno, A. V. (1984). A model of venture capitalist investment activity. *Management Science, 30* (9), 1051-1065.

This study finds that venture capital deals are orderly processes of five sequential steps: 1) deal origination, 2) deal screening, 3) deal evaluation, 4) deal structuring, and 5) post-investment activities. Factor analysis of survey data determined five categories of activity: 1) market attractiveness, 2) product differentiation, 3) managerial capabilities, 4) environmental threat resistance, and 5) cash-out potential. Expected return was determined by market attractiveness and product differentiation. Perceived risk was determined by managerial capabilities and environmental threat resistance. The model, while simplistic, suggested that professional relationships with influential people help in locating capital, that the venture capital community is often smaller than it seems, and that venture capitalists differ in their choices of screening criteria.

Nature of the study:	Empirical
Nature of the data:	Mail survey, telephone survey
Nature of the sample:	41 venture capitalists with data on 90 deals
Variables:	Sources of deals, deal screening criteria, deal evaluation criteria, deal structuring, post investment activities

Upton, N., & Petty, W. (2000). Venture capital investment and U.S. family business. *Venture Capital: An International Journal of Entrepreneurial Finance, 2* (1), 27-39.

A critical aspect of succession in family-controlled businesses is finding capital to finance ownership and management transition. This research addresses the issue of transition financing by reporting the combined results of two surveys, one to venture capitalists and the second to owners of family businesses. The findings suggest that the financing of intergenerational transfers was a significant issue to owners of family-owned firms. In addition, venture capitalists were interested in participating in transition financing, usually in the form of debt or preferred stock combined with sweeteners (warrants or conversion rights). When evaluating transition investments, venture capitalists are particularly interested in the qualifications of the successor, along with the firm's strategic plans.

Nature of the study:	Empirical
Nature of the data:	Mail survey
Nature of the sample:	53 venture capitalists and 85 family businesses
Variables:	Venture capital firm size; number of requests received and funded; stage of funding; structuring of funding; investors required rate of return; perceived risk of funding family firms; screening criteria; timing of ownership transition in family firm; age, size, industry and number of active family members of family firm, amount of ownership transfer, reason for ownership transfer, means of transferring ownership, required investment return

Wetzel, Jr., W. E. (1981). Informal risk capital in New England. In K. H. Vesper (Ed.), *Frontiers of entrepreneurial research* (pp. 217-245). Boston, MA: Babson College.

Despite the contribution of young, small technology-based firms to the pace of technological innovation and new job formation, they have faced difficulty raising relatively small amounts of high-risk, seed capital. Risk capital problems have been particularly acute for new and existing firms requiring funds in excess of those available from founders and other friendly sources but without access to professional venture capital organizations or to public equity markets. This research focuses on the role of informal investors as a source of funds for three types of investment situations: 1) financing technology-based inventors, 2) start-up and early stage financing for emerging firms, and 3) equity financing for small established firms growing faster than retained earnings can support.

The results indicate that informal investors were a significant and appropriate source of risk capital for technology-based inventors and for both emerging and established firms without access to traditional venture capital sources or public equity markets. Informal investors were difficult to reach-- geographically dispersed, very diverse, and tough to identify. The sample represented approximately 10 investors per million population. Respondents reported risk capital investments of more than $16 million in 320 ventures during the five years from 1976 to 1980, with about $3 million per year in 64 ventures with average size per investment around $50,000.

Nature of the study: Empirical
Nature of the data: Mail survey
Nature of the sample: Informal investors in New England
Variables: Investment rate expectations, investment size preferences, implied capital available by size, venture life-cycle preferences, industry preferences, geographic distribution of investment, participation interest, voting control objective, rejection rate, diversification and tax-sheltered income objective, liquidation expectations, risk perceptions, rate of return expectations, non-financial rewards, satisfaction with referral sources

Wetzel, Jr., W. E. (1982). Project I-C-E: An experiment in capital formation. In K. H. Vesper (Ed.), *Frontiers of entrepreneurial research* (pp. 335-357). Boston, MA: Babson College.

This paper describes Project I-C-E (Innovation-Capital-Entrepreneurs), a joint venture developed by the Whittemore School of Business and Economics (WSBE) at the University of New Hampshire and Massachusetts Technology Development Corporation (MTDC), Boston. Project I-C-E was founded as an experimental program to test methods for expediting the commercialization of new technology by assisting promising technology-based ventures in the search for risk capital, and risk capital investors in the search for bona fide investment opportunities.

Project I-C-E was started in 1982 to serve entrepreneurs and investors located in a six-state New England region

Nature of the study: Empirical
Nature of the data: Case study
Nature of the sample: Project ICE
Variables: Performance of project ICE, identification of investment
                                   criteria of investors and investment characteristics of
                                   opportunities, provision of referral mechanism serving both
                                   investors and entrepreneurs

Wetzel, Jr., W. E. (1983). Taplin & Montle Development Fund: A case study in finance. In J. A. Hornaday, J. A. Timmons, & K. H. Vesper (Eds.), *Frontiers of entrepreneurial research* (pp. 335-346). Boston, MA: Babson College.

This paper describes The Taplin & Montle Development Fund (TMDF), an experiment in capital formation created by John Taplin, a successful entrepreneur/investor. The objective of this fund is to fill a gap in the institutional capital markets for smaller firms by drawing upon resources of private individuals for small amounts of "R&D" financing (in the $50,000 to $500,000 range). Its low risk/low return investment strategy made TMDF unique in its approach to product development financing using tax-sheltered R&D partnerships. The experience of TMDF revealed the inefficiency of the informal risk capital market. The author proposes that because of its organizational structure and promotional efforts, TMDF was successful in improving the efficiency of the informal risk capital market.

Nature of the study: Empirical
Nature of the data: Case study
Nature of the sample: Taplin & Montle Development Fund (TMDF)
Variables: Function and role of TMDF, amounts from private
                                   individuals that are available for R&D financing

Wetzel, Jr., W. E. (1987). The informal venture capital market: Aspects of scale and market efficiency. *Journal of Business Venturing, 2* (4), 299-313.

This article describes the informal venture capital market, the market in which entrepreneurs raise equity-type financing from private investors (business angels). Private venture investors are described as usually self-made persons with substantial business and financial experience and a net worth of $1 million or more. These private investors managed a $50 billion aggregate portfolio of venture investments. By participating in smaller transactions, they financed more than five times as many entrepreneurs as professional venture investors. In spite of the apparent scale of the informal venture capital market, evidence indicates that the market was relatively inefficient. The market was characterized by a shortage of information about investors and investment opportunities. In addition, a number of entrepreneurs and private investors were unfamiliar with the techniques of successful venture financing.

Nature of the study: Empirical
Nature of the data: Various published sources
Nature of the sample: NA
Variables: Wealth, income and asset distribution of U.S. households; attitudes toward financial risk and liquidity; regional risk capital; capital market efficiency

Wetzel, Jr., W. E., & Wilson, I. G. (1985). Seed capital gaps: Evidence from high-growth ventures. In J. A. Hornaday, E. B. Shils, J. A. Timmons, & K. H. Vesper (Eds.), *Frontiers of entrepreneurial research* (pp. 221-240). Boston, MA: Babson College.

Through the New Hampshire Department of Resources and Economics Development (DRED), the State of New Hampshire began to address issues regarding capital availability in the state, in order to preserve the state's competitive economic advantages for the long run. Of interest was whether the institutional risk capital markets contained "gaps" that precluded the financing of one or more classes of entrepreneurs with otherwise viable proposals. If institutional gaps existed, the authors sought to determine where successful entrepreneurs had found alternative sources of funds.

The authors conclude that analysis of data suggested that institutional "gaps" did exist. Forty percent of the companies reported that growth in sales and employment had been inhibited because of problems raising capital to finance expansion. The equity and long-term requirements of the smaller, more rapidly expanding companies were the most difficult to fulfill. These companies were also experiencing cash flow problems as a result of relying upon short-term debt to finance expansion. With respect to equity investment in high-growth firms and types of equity investors, the survey findings suggest that 1) a strong relationship existed between a company's growth rate and the probability of its seeking venture capital and its relative attractiveness to venture investors; 2) professional venture capital firms and independent individuals were the most active types of equity investors in New Hampshire, but served distinctly different categories of growth companies; 3) small, rapidly expanding companies appeared to benefit from a more efficient means of accessing individual equity investors, and 4) merging as a means of raising expansion capital appeared to be a more desirable strategy for rapidly expanding companies than offering stock publicly.

Nature of the study: Empirical
Nature of the data: Mail survey
Nature of the sample: 83 independent, New Hampshire firms with at least 50 employees and growing at rates of 15% or more per year
Variables: Growth rate, probability of seeking venture capital, attractiveness to venture investors, growth problems attributed to limited access to expansion capital, reliance on short-term debt, shortage of expansion capital, number of companies solicited by equity investors, type of equity investor, company characteristics, access to individual investors, alternative means of raising expansion capital

Wright, M., & Robbie, K. (1998). Venture capital and private equity: A review and synthesis. *Journal of Business Finance & Accounting, 25* (5/6), 521-570.

This paper reviews and synthesizes research relating to venture capital and highlights the future of venture capital. Importantly, it analyzes the issues relating to the demand side of the industry. The paper addresses the definition of venture capital, differences between venture capital and mainstream corporate finance, a Porter model of the industry, issues related to the governance and investment processes of venture capital firms, and venture capital firm performance.

Nature of the study: Literature review
Nature of the data: NA
Nature of the sample: NA
Variables: Attributes of traditional corporate finance and venture capital, rivalry among firms, power of suppliers and customers, threat of new entrants and substitutes, governance and the venture capital process, venture capital firm performance

Wright, M., Robbie, K., & Ennew, C. (1997). Venture capitalists and serial entrepreneurs. *Journal of Business Venturing, 12* (3), 227-249.

This paper examines the importance of serial entrepreneurs to the venture capital industry. The results showed that despite a stated preference for using experienced entrepreneurs in their portfolio again, the major role the serial entrepreneur played for the venture capitalists was as a consultant. Previous ownership and management experience were not the only elements considered by venture capitalists for assessing serial entrepreneurs. Also important was personal attributes such as age, knowledge, family background, links to the venture funding institution, and financial commitment. The study also predicted differences between venture capital firms that preferred serial entrepreneurs and those that didn't, but did not find strong evidence of that. Assets of previous experience generally exceeded liabilities for serial entrepreneurs, that the negative aspect of serial entrepreneurs was their inability to recognize personal limitations, and that serial entrepreneurs did not appear to perform better than novice entrepreneurs in whom venture capital firms invested during the same period.

Nature of the study: Empirical
Nature of the data: Mail survey
Nature of the sample: 55 venture capitalists
Variables: Venture capital preference for investing in serial entrepreneurs, criteria for assessing entrepreneurs, previous relationship to the venture capitalist, performance of serial entrepreneurs

Zacharakis, A. L., & Meyer, G. D. (1998). A lack of insight: Do venture capitalists really understand their own decision process? *Journal of Business Venturing, 13*(1), 57-76.

The majority of venture capital studies have relied on post hoc methodologies to capture the VC decision process. Post hoc methods assume that VCs can accurately relate their own decision processes but studies from cognitive psychology suggest that people in general, and experts in particular, are poor at introspecting. Introspection is subject to rationalization and post hoc recall biases. As such, past research may be biased. Using Social Judgment Theory and the associated lens model as a framework, this study investigates how well VCs introspect about their own decision process. In general, it appeared that VCs did not have a strong understanding of their investment decision process, especially when confronted with information-rich decisions such as they face in making an investment decision; as the amount of information available for decision-making increased, insight actually decreased. However, despite the fact that venture capitalists did not necessarily understand the process they used, they were very consistent in their decision-making process.

Nature of the study: Empirical
Nature of the data: Mail survey
Nature of the sample: 51 VCs from the Colorado Front Range (primarily the Denver/Boulder metro area) and the Silicon Valley, California
Variables: Venture capital firm characteristics: investment stage, size, age, investment industry, geographic focus, funding amount, VC firm type, number of co-investors; venture capitalist characteristics: age, gender, educational level, education type, tenure, other experience; experimental characteristics

of venture: market familiarity, leadership ability; proprietary protection, market size and growth, track record, competitors, competitor strength, completeness of team, product superiority, development time, buyer concentration

Zacharakis, A.L., & Shepherd, D.A. (2001). The nature of information and overconfidence on venture capitalists' decision making. *Journal of Business Venturing, 16* (4), 311-332.

Venture capitalists are considered experts at identifying start-up companies with high growth potential. Although numerous studies examine the decision-making criteria VCs use to identify top investment candidates, not enough attention has been paid to cognitive differences in how VCs make decisions. This study investigates whether VCs are overconfident (defined as having the tendency to overestimate the likely occurrence of a set of events) and the factors surrounding the decision that led to overconfidence.

The results of the study indicate that VCs are indeed overconfident and that overconfidence negatively affects VC decision accuracy. The level of overconfidence depended on the amount of information, type of information, and VCs' belief in whether the venture would succeed or fail. The study also reveals that VCs were intuitive decision makers and in addition to having overconfidence bias they also had "availability bias" in their decision-making. Overconfidence bias did not necessarily lead to wrong decisions but could inhibit learning and search for relevant information. The authors suggest that VCs can reduce the effect of overconfidence by using techniques like counterfactual thinking, actuarial aids to decompose decisions, and "humbling effect."

Nature of the study:	Empirical
Nature of the data:	Experiment
Nature of the sample:	53 venture capitalists from the Denver/Boulder & Silicon Valley area
Variables:	Market familiarity, leadership ability, proprietary protection, market size and market growth, track record, competitors, competitor strength, completeness of team, product superiority, time to development and buyers concentration

PART 4

OVERVIEW THE DIANA PROJECT

Diana was a heroic woman, a huntress. Women seeking capital are hunters rather than gatherers. They are hunting for capital in a traditionally male-dominated arena.

The *Diana Project* was established in 1999 to raise the awareness of investors and the expectations of women business owners regarding the growth of their firms. The growth of women's businesses is central to wealth creation, innovation, and economic development in all countries. The creation of the five-member *Diana* research consortium coincided with efforts of other groups around the world to support and advance the growth and development of women-owned businesses.

A core belief of *Diana* researchers is that rigorous research provides a powerful base for influencing systems. Information and knowledge that come from solid data can have irrefutable effects on changing attitudes, opinions, and practices.

The *Diana Project* research investigates the apparent disconnect between opportunities and resources in equity funding for high growth women-owned businesses. Funded by the Entrepreneurship and Small Business Research Institute (ESBRI), the Kauffman Center for Entrepreneurial Leadership, the U.S. Small Business Administration, and the National Women's Business Council, the project has two primary objectives:

> *Supply Side.* To educate equity capital providers about opportunities for enhanced portfolio diversification and new investment possibilities through investment in women-owned businesses.

> *Demand Side.* To raise awareness and expectations of women business owners for the growth of their firms, to educate women business owners about the characteristics of equity-funded businesses, and to provide detailed information about how the equity funding process works.

The research has been organized into four phases: Background Research; Demand Side--Women Seeking Financing; Supply-Side--The Venture Capital Industry; and *Diana International.*

RESEARCH PHASES

1. Background Research:

    a. This annotated bibliography reviews nearly 300 academic articles on venture capital and women's entrepreneurship, as well as related articles on women's self-employment, careers, motivations, networking, and social structures. The review provides an overview of theories and findings that guided the development of a theoretical model of women's access to equity capital.

    b. The baseline status of equity investments in U.S. women-led companies was established by drawing on data from the National Venture Capital Association (NVCA) between 1957 and 1998. The NVCA data were collected by Venture Economics and include information on companies funded by venture capital since 1957. Because the original data was not coded by gender, each listing required coding to designate which ventures involved women-led initiatives. The data set includes information on 20,000 portfolio companies, 34,000 executives, and 120,000 company investments and is provided by 4,500 private equity firms administering a total of 7,000 private equity funds.

2. Demand Side--Women Seeking Financing

To better understand the growth strategies, funding expectations, experiences, and characteristics of women entrepreneurs and their teams, *Diana* assembled and analyzed data sets that focus on this population of business owners. Previous studies have relied on data in which male-led businesses predominated, which may provide questionable insights into the experiences of women-led ventures.

    a) In January 2000, the National Women's Business Council and a consortium of partners launched Springboard 2000 Venture Forums, a path-breaking initiative intended to enhance the proportion of investments in women-led businesses by putting the spotlight on worthy ventures. The catalyst for the initiative was the disparity between the number of women-owned businesses and the small share of equity capital they received. This is a disadvantage not only to women-owned businesses, but also to investors who may be unaware of attractive investment opportunities. In 2000, forums were held in Silicon Valley (San Francisco), the Mid-Atlantic (Washington, D.C.), and New England (Boston). Subsequent forums have been held in the Midwest (Chicago), the Southwest (Dallas), and New York City. The forums have attracted over 2,500 applicants and featured more than 230 women-led ventures. A total of $1.02 billion was sought by the companies, for an average of $10 million per firm; by fall 2002, the firms had raised $750 million and counting. To better understand characteristics of women entrepreneurs seeking equity investments and aspects of their companies, we analyzed data from all applicants for the Springboard 2000 Venture Forums.

b) With funding from the Kauffman Center for Entrepreneurial Leadership, a follow-up survey of the initial 2000 Springboard applicants was conducted to establish the first wave of a panel study of more than 100 high-tech women entrepreneurs. The research tracks the growth strategies and funding experiences of applicants, and explores particularly the effect of human capital (management team experience and composition) and social capital (contacts, network, and advisors).

3. Supply Side--The Venture Capital Industry
   The venture capital industry consists of both the venture capital firms and the investors who fund them. Venture capital firms are the dealmakers who bring together capital suppliers and capital users with an objective of achieving high returns on the funds invested through a liquidation event. To better understand the nature of the venture capital industry in the U.S., *Diana* researchers analyzed the employment strategies and characteristics of venture capital firms and career paths of women investors. Information was obtained from *Pratt's Guide* and recoded so that all women in the industry could be tracked by position and compared to men in similar firms. Firm level data supplements this information, as do in- depth interviews with women investors.

4. *Diana International* - Entrepreneurship is central to economic growth around the world. Equity investments fuel the growth and development of new ventures, yielding innovative solutions for consumers and businesses. *Diana* researchers have established that women-led ventures in the U.S. are underrepresented in the distribution of equity capital and in decision-making positions in the venture capital industry. To what extent do U.S. conditions generalize to other parts of the world? *Diana International* seeks to answer this question. The *Diana Project* has documented that many explanations for women's lack of capital to grow their ventures in the U.S. are myths. *Diana International* expands the *Diana Project* to the international arena to put the spotlight on high growth women-led ventures around the world. Cross-country comparisons of women's experiences in attempting to access growth capital are examined and documented by research partners in host countries to explore whether the myths documented by *Diana* apply to women-led ventures globally. Researchers in other countries interested in partnering with *Diana* are encouraged to contact us.

OUTCOMES

The project has a number of outcomes such as journal articles, working papers and presentations. Updated information is accessible at the DIANA-website: http://www.esbri.se/diana.asp

DR. CANDIDA BRUSH

Dr. Brush is Associate Professor of Strategy, Policy Director of the Council for Women's Entrepreneurship and Leadership (CWEL), and Research Director for the Entrepreneurial Management Institute at Boston University. She was a Research Affiliate to Jönköping International Business School, Jönköping, Sweden. She received her DBA from Boston University, MBA from Boston College and BA from the University of Colorado. She is the author of two books; *International Entrepreneurship: The Effect of Age on Motives for Internationalization*, and *The Woman Entrepreneur: Starting, Financing and Managing a Successful New Business* (Lexington Books, 1986), and has written eleven book chapters and more than 45 articles published in scholarly journals such as *Journal of Business Venturing, Strategic Management Journal, Entrepreneurship Theory and Practice, Academy of Management Executive, Journal of Small Business Management, Journal of Venture Capital,* and *Journal of Business Research.* She has authored papers for the Organization for Economic Cooperation and Development (OECD) and International Labour Organization (ILO). She is the 2001 recipient of the Entrepreneurship Mentor Award, given by the National Academy of Management's Entrepreneurship Division, and co-authored a paper recognized by the Small Business Institute Directors Association (SBIDA) as best conceptual paper for 2002. Dr. Brush was one of 18 researchers selected to participate in the 1995 *White House Conference Research Project: The Future of Small Business and Entrepreneurship into the Year 2010*, and was recognized by *INC Magazine* in 1995 as one of the top 16 researchers in entrepreneurship in the U.S. She served on the Research Advisory Committee for the National Foundation of Women Business Owners and the Defense Advisory Committee on Women in the Services (DACOWITS), an advisory committee to the Department of Defense. She is a member of Fleet-Boston's Advisory Board and The Women Entrepreneur's Connection.

DR. NANCY M. CARTER

Dr. Carter holds the Richard M. Schulze Endowed Chair in Entrepreneurship and directed the John M. Morrison Center at the University of St. Thomas, Minneapolis, Minnesota. She is Scholar-in-Residence at the Entrepreneurship and Small Business Research Center (ESBRI), in Stockholm, Sweden, and prior to joining the faculty at St. Thomas in 1997 was the Coleman Foundation Chair in Entrepreneurial Studies at Marquette University. Professor Carter directs the MBA entrepreneurship program at St. Thomas and served on the teaching team for the Kauffman Center for Entrepreneurial Leadership's Dynamic Classroom (LEEP), a training program for new entrepreneurship faculty from around the world. She has worked professionally in advertising and marketing research and works closely with government and private sector initiatives promoting women entrepreneurs. Dr. Carter serves on the International Board of Advisors, Jönköping International Business School, Sweden, and the Board of Directors of the Women's Business Research Center, Washington, D.C. Her research interests include the emergence of organizations, with a special emphasis on women- and minority-owned initiatives, and the founding strategies of new businesses. She has published extensively, including articles in *Journal of Business Venturing, Academy of Management Journal, Strategic Management Journal, Entrepreneurship and Regional Development, Management International Review, Organization Studies, Journal of Management Studies, Journal of Management, Human Relations,* and *Journal of Managerial Issues.* She serves on the editorial review boards of *Entrepreneurship Theory and Practice, Journal of Small Business Management, Journal of Development Entrepreneurship,* and the editorial team of the *17th and 18th* editions of *Frontiers of Entrepreneurship Research.* Her research on women and minority entrepreneurs is funded by awards from the National Science Foundation, the U.S. Small Business Administration, the National Business Women's Council, and the Kauffman Center for Entrepreneurial Leadership. She co-founded the Entrepreneurial Research Consortium, the organizing group for the Panel Study of Entrepreneurial Dynamics (PSED). She received her PhD in Business Administration from the University of Nebraska, MA in Mass Communications from California State University, and BA in Journalism from the University of Nebraska.

DR. ELIZABETH J. GATEWOOD

Dr. Gatewood is the Jack M. Gill Chair of Entrepreneurship and Director of The Johnson Center for Entrepreneurship & Innovation at Indiana University. She directs Center activities, teaches MBA Students, and conducts research on entrepreneurial topics. Her research has appeared in the *Journal of Business Venturing*, the *Journal of Venture Capital, Entrepreneurship Theory and Practice*, the *Journal of Small Business Management, Frontiers of Entrepreneurship Research*, and *Entrepreneurship and Regional Development*. She is a member of the editorial review boards of *Entrepreneurship Theory and Practice* and the *Journal of Small Business Management.* She is a member of the National Advisory Board for Entrepreneurship Education of the Kauffman Center for Entrepreneurial Leadership. She also serves on the Advisory Board for Spring Mill Ventures, a venture capital firm of the Village Ventures network. She is a past chair of the Entrepreneurship Division of the Academy of Management. She received the 1996 Advocate Award for outstanding contributions to the field of entrepreneurship from the Academy of Management. Dr. Gatewood was named the Texas Women in Business Advocate of the Year by the U.S. Small Business Administration. Her work in entrepreneurial cognition received the National Foundation of Independent Business Award for best paper at the 2001 Babson-Kauffman Foundation Entrepreneurship Research Conference. Prior to her August 1998 arrival at Indiana University, Dr. Gatewood was Executive Director of the University of Houston Small Business Development Center, an organization that provides training and consulting services to small businesses in the greater Houston region. In addition to her responsibilities as UH SBDC executive director, Gatewood was a Research Professor in the Department of Management at the University of Houston's College of Business Administration. Dr. Gatewood served as the Director of the Center for Business and Economic Studies at the University of Georgia from 1983 to 1989. She holds a BS in Psychology from Purdue University and an MBA in Finance and Ph.D. in Business

Administration with a specialty in strategy from the University of Georgia. She taught at the Nijenrode Institute of Business in the Netherlands.

DR. PATRICIA G. GREENE

Dr. Greene is an Associate Professor at the University of Missouri--Kansas City (UMKC), where she holds the Ewing Marion Kauffman Chair in Entrepreneurial Leadership. She completed her PhD at the University of Texas at Austin in 1993. Her research focus is on the interaction between characteristics of the business creator and the creation process, analyzing the subsequent structure and operations of the organization. She is particularly interested in that analysis in the context of minority- and women-owned businesses. Her work has been published in *Academy of Management Executive, Journal of Business Venturing, Journal of Small Business Management, Journal of Small Business Strategy, Journal of Business Research, Frontiers of Entrepreneurship Research, Small Business Economics, Venture Capital, National Journal of Sociology,* and En*trepreneurship: Theory and Practice.* Together with Bruce Kirchhoff, she was awarded the Coleman Foundation Best Paper Award for the 1995 Babson College- Kauffman Foundation Entrepreneurship Research Conference. She serves on the Editorial Review Board of the *National Journal of Sociology* and the *Academy of Management Learning and Education*, as well as ad hoc reviewer for numerous management and entrepreneurship journals. She is active in presenting her research at the national and international levels and has been quoted in popular periodicals including *Business Week, USA Today, Inc., Fortune,* and the *Christian Science Monitor.* She currently serves on the Advisory Boards of the Small Business Council of the Greater Kansas City Chamber of Commerce, the Helzberg Entrepreneurial Mentoring Program, the Growth Opportunity Connection, the Kansas Women's Business Center, and the State of Missouri Small Business Development Centers. She is the area coordinator for the entrepreneurship emphasis of the graduate curriculum at UMKC and serves as the Director of the Entrepreneurial Growth Resource Center and the Business Research and Information Development Group of the University of Missouri Outreach and Extension. She previously taught at Rutgers University where she held the State of New Jersey Small Business and Entrepreneurship Chair and was responsible for the development of the entrepreneurship curriculum, led the founding team of the Rutgers Center for Entrepreneurial Management, and served as entrepreneurship curriculum coordinator.

DR. MYRA M. HART

Dr. Hart holds the Class of 1961 Chair in Entrepreneurship at Harvard Business School (HBS) and has served as co-chair of the Entrepreneurship faculty for the past five years. Hart and co-chair William Sahlman were recognized for their leadership of the faculty with the Greenhill Award in 2000. Hart has introduced several new courses in entrepreneurship since joining the faculty in 1995. Working collaboratively, Professors Marco Iansiti and. Hart created "Starting New Ventures", a course for which they won the Apgar Award for Innovation in Teaching in 1998. In 1999, she and Professor Lynda Applegate introduced "Women Building Businesses," a field-based seminar for aspiring female entrepreneurs. Dr. Hart is also responsible for the creation and direction of several entrepreneurial executive programs: The Entrepreneur's Tool Kit, Women Leading Business, and Charting Your Course: Working Options. Dr. Hart's research interests include high growth ventures, and women entrepreneurs. Her work with women entrepreneurs includes chairing the Marjorie Alfus/Committee of 200 case writing initiative at HBS and serving as chair of Springboard New England in 2000 and 2001. She is chair of the Center for Women's Business Research, a member of the Committee of 200, and a trustee of Cornell University. She serves as a director or advisor to several start-up enterprises, including Texada Software, Ortega, Versura, eLane, and Pasha's.

CONTACT INFORMATION

Elizabeth J. Gatewood
Jack M. Gill Chair of Entrepreneurship
Kelly School of Business
Indiana University
1275 East Tenth Street
Bloomington, IN 47405
ph: (812) 855-4248; 812-855-2751; email: gatewood@indiana.edu

Nancy M. Carter
Richard M. Schulze Endowed Chair in Entrepreneurship
University of St. Thomas
MPL 470, 1000 LaSalle Avenue
Minneapolis, Minnesota 55403-2005
ph: (651) 962-4407; fax: (651) 962-4410; email: nmcarter@stthomas.edu

Candida G. Brush
Associate Professor of Strategy and Policy
and Research Director, Entrepreneurial Management Institute
Boston University
595 Commonwealth Ave.
Boston, MA 02215
ph: (617) 353-3146; fax: (617) 353-5244; email: cgbrush@bu.edu

Patricia G. Greene
Ewing Marion Kauffman/Missouri Chair in Entrepreneurial Leadership
Henry W. Bloch School of Business and Public Administration
University of Missouri - Kansas City
5100 Rockhill Road
Kansas City, MO 64110-2499
ph: (816) 235-5841; fax: (816) 235-6529; email: greenep@umkc.edu

Myra M. Hart
Class of 1961 Professor of Management Practice
Harvard Business School
Harvard University
114 South Hall
Boston, MA 02163
ph: (617) 495-6904; fax: (617) 496-5305; email: mhart@hbs.edu